How Nkrumah Fell

OPERATION COLD CHOP

the inside story

Peter Barker

PETER BARKER

with love

Foreword by Sam Okudzeto

First published 1969 by the Publishing Division of the Ghana
Publishing Corporation, Private Post Bag, Tema, Ghana

Second Edition with corrections 1979

Third edition with additions 2010
Published by Digibooks Ghana Ltd
P. O. Box BT 1 Tema.
Tel No: +233 (0) 303 414720 / 0246493842
E-mail:admin@digibookspublishing.com

ISBN 978-9988-1-4506-4

Original drawings and maps of 1969 edition
Drawings by Prosper Tawiah
Maps by Kweinortey

Other books by Peter Barker

Peter Dagadu, Man of God 1983
Peoples, languages, and religion in Northern Ghana 1986
Changed by the Word – The Story of Scripture Union, Ghana 2003

OPERATION COLD CHOP

"Chop" is West African pidgin English for "food", and "cold chop" is a meal that can be served instantly, without heating or cooking. "Cold Chop" has thus become a slang expression for anything that can be got easily or without much effort.

Reference to the biographical notes and index will make it easier to identify personalities and the posts they occupied.

* * * * * *

(Based on interviews with the main characters given in March and April 1966)

GHANA IN 1966

Roads
Route of Kotoka's troops
from Tamale to Accra

DEDICATION

Dedicated to the memory of the late Lieut-General Charles Mohamed Barwah, Army Chief of Staff, who was shot on 24 February 1966, and to all other defenders and attackers who lost their lives on that day, including six Russians who died in Flagstaff House.

Contents

Foreword

What constitutes a great political leader and why does a great leader lose greatness? In telling the story of Nkrumah's rise and fall this book answers those questions.

I lived in Accra from November 1955 to September 1956 when I left for the UK to study. Dr Kwame Nkrumah was at the zenith of his popularity. He was called "Kwame Nkrumah Showboy". Indeed he was a charismatic individual whose presence drew everyone to him. He knew how to use phrases that inspire: "The independence of Ghana is meaningless unless it is linked up with the total liberation of Africa. The new African is ready to fight his own battles and show that after all, the black man is capable of managing his own affairs. Africa must unite." His white handkerchief and horse whip, his northern fugu, were all symbols of the African Personality of which he was the embodiment. The rich women of Makola almost worshipped him as a god.

He believed passionately that Africa could unite with a continental government and continental army. Perhaps he hoped to be the leader of such a government. He lavished support on the liberation movements of Africa, and brought young men and women from Southern Africa to Ghana to be educated at the expense of the Ghanaian taxpayer; his motive was to train the manpower which would equip those countries after their independence.

But political leaders need to appreciate how fragile power is. It needs to be exercised with caution and circumspection. It is merely temporary; there is an account to give. Nkrumah did not accept that. He deprived the electorate—the shareholders in a corporate nation—of the power to withdraw the mandate at the time of election, no matter what the leader believes but based on what the electorate thinks or feels. The political barometer is difficult to predict—it swings without warning. And by 1965 to 1966 much of the aura around Nkrumah, at least in Ghana, had waned.

A political leader also needs loyal friends and workmates. But loyalty requires honesty and openness—the need to tell the leader the truth and not lies to please him.

In Matthew 11:13 Jesus asked his disciples, "Who do people say I the Son of Man am?" They replied, "Some say John the Baptist, others say Elijah; and still others, Jeremiah or one of the prophets". But Jesus asked them "But what about you? Who do you say I am?" This passage should be the prescription for leaders, but Nkrumah I believe was let down either by his own attitude that drove fear into many of his inner circle who could not tell him the truth, or by their deliberate dishonesty.

The tragedy of one of the greatest sons of Africa in the 20th century's dramatic story is told not by a Ghanaian but by Peter Barker, a British minister of the Presbyterian Church who had lived in Ghana throughout the rule of Kwame Nkrumah. I had the good fortune to meet him on board the Elder Dempster Lines *mv Aureol;* I was returning to Ghana after seven years studying in England and Belgium; he had gone back to England to marry and was returning to Ghana with his bride, whom he was diligently teaching the Twi language.

Peter's previous service in the British East African Army prepared him to understand ranks and structures of the Ghanaian units involved in the story of the coup that overthrew Nkrumah. My own interrogations of former CPP leaders and ministers, as a lawyer for Ghana's Bureau of National Investigations, revealed to me the frailty of Nkrumah's administration: how little education or work experience many of these men had before becoming Nkrumah's MPs and ministers of State.

Peter Barker provides the reader with a vivid insight into events and personalities of 1966 which otherwise would never have been known. He gives us all the chance to learn from the tragedy of the fall of Osagyefo Dr Kwame Nkrumah. This book is warmly recommended as a must read for all students of politics, for every politician and indeed for all.

Sam Okudzeto.

Accra, 8th December, 2010.

PREFACE

of NOVEMBER 2010 by Peter Barker

When Nkrumah was overthrown by the military coup of 24 February 1966, I had been in Ghana just over ten years, and was serving the Presbyterian Church of Ghana as minister of the newly-opened church in Kaneshie and at the same time editor of the monthly paper, *Christian Messenger*. Within the week or two after the coup a number of visitors, both civilian and military, called on me in my office overlooking Makola Square, Accra, and told me vivid stories of how the coup had affected them. I therefore wrote to the National Liberation Council for their permission to write and publish an account of the coup and the events that led up to it. Their response was simply to ask me for a list of the people I would like to interview. That is how *Operation Cold Chop* began.

I said in the original Preface of 24 February 1968,

"The planning which lay behind the dramatic events of 24 February, the characters of the main actors, and the hour-by-hour progress of the operation, were soon subjects for eager speculation in Ghana and abroad. It seemed that a contemporary account of these things, based on first-hand information, would be of interest and value to the public.

"Most of the research for this book was done in April 1966, when the details were fresh in everyone's memory. Some fifty people were interviewed, from Lieutenant-General Ankrah, the late Lieutenant-General Kotoka, and other members of the National Liberation Council to junior civil servants and teachers. I should like to thank all of them for their courtesy and frankness in satisfying a writer's curiosity: I wish I thought that an African writer, carrying out this sort of assignment in Britain, would have a similar reception.

"The narrative contains a good deal of direct speech quoted to me during interviews. Sometimes I have adapted other material from interviews to make dialogue, but at all important points conversation in inverted commas is based on at least one person's account of what

v

was said, and in most cases it has been read by someone else who was present.

"The manuscript was read in whole or in part by the leading figures in the story, and I am grateful to all of them for comments which have helped to make the book more accurate and more vivid."

The first edition was published in 1969 by Ghana Publishing Corporation, one of Nkrumah's many state ventures in industry and commerce. It was reprinted by GPC in 1979, during the Limann administration, with a text practically identical with the original. In this third printing, the basic narrative is identical with the second printing of 1979, but unnecessarily harsh phrases applied to Osagyefo Dr Kwame Nkrumah have been replaced by more neutral and objective language. We are now living in a different age from the 1960s, and emotional language appropriate 50 years ago needed adjustment.

However, facts, quoted speech and historical records are unchanged from the original edition; the author feels it is essential to preserve the integrity of the original story.

The narrative is based on personal interviews in March and April 1966 with the main actors in the story. Many are typed, but most are the author's original rough hand-written notes made at the time verbatim from the lips of Kotoka, Afrifa, and 40 or so others. Because of the intense historical interest of these papers they have been kept safely and are carefully indexed. The twenty-five main interviews were as follows:

EIGHT ARMY OFFICERS (ranks and locations at the time of the coup)
Major Akwasi Afrifa, Brigade Major (2 Brigade) Tamale
Major Coker-Appiah, Commander, Field Regiment of Engineers (1 Brigade) Teshie
Captain Darkoh, Reconnaissance Regiment (1 Brigade) Burma Camp
Major Dontoh, Commander, Reconnaissance Regiment (1 Brigade) Burma Camp
Colonel Emmanuel Kwasi Kotoka (Commander, 2 Brigade) Kumasi

Captain Kwashie, Secretary, 37 Military Hospital, Accra
Colonel Albert Kwasi Ocran (Commander, 1 Brigade) Accra
Capt Seshie, a company commander in 2 Battalion (2 Brigade) Tamale
TWO POLICE OFFICERS
Tony Deku, deputy head of Special Branch
J W K Harlley, head of Special Branch; from 1965 Commissioner of Police
FOUR CIVILIANS
B A Bentum, chairman of Trades Union Congress executive board
Michael Dei-Anang, senior civil servant
T K Impraim, deputy secretary to the cabinet
Eric Otoo, secretary on security matters
FIVE DETAINEES four detained by Nkrumah
Reggie R Amponsah, former United Party Member
M K Apaloo, former United Party MP
Lawrence Otu Cantey, law student
William Ofori-Atta, lawyer and United Party member
ONE detained by the National Liberation Council
Alex Quaison-Sackey, Ghana's representative at UN, and from 1965 minister of foreign affairs

Transcripts of these and several other interviews will be lodged with selected national libraries, for reference by future historians.

Figures in the text refer to notes which appear at the end of the book. Some of them refer to documents quoted, including "Hansard", the record of parliamentary proceedings, Ghana government official publications, and other sources.

28 October 2010
Kuku Hill, Osu
Peter Barker

A First Word

Samuel Kennedy Yeboah wrote the following vindictive words in the heat and passion of two historic weeks after the coup of 24 February 1966. A year later, or now, 54 years later, he might have written with better perspective, more balance, and greater generosity to a man to whom, despite human faults, Ghana then owed much and still owes much today. But the harsh sentiments he expressed so eloquently were shared by millions of Ghanaians.

The fact that the CPP's own *Evening News* could print such a piece barely a couple of weeks after the assault on Flagstaff House is evidence enough that "something had been rotten" in the Republic of Ghana. Samuel Kennedy Yeboah was not subsequently pilloried for his impudence. He overstated his case; but there was a case to state. This raw and abrasive diatribe is a useful reminder to those of us living in a later age that the fall of Nkrumah was not an aberration; it was a painful yet necessary step in Ghana's march to a greater future.

In 1969, this book was necessary simply to record, from the lips of those who carried it out, the somewhat haphazard chain of events which led to the successful coup of 24 February 1966. In 2010, all those concerned to understand Ghana's past and to make our nation great and strong will do well to reflect on the characters of the coup leaders and the situations that drove them to such a desperate response.

0 Nkrumah, how art thou fallen –
>> You who exalted yourself above God,
>> *How art thou fallen!*
You who hired people to worship you,
>> *How art thou fallen!*
You who falsely called yourself the Messiah of Africa,
>> *How art thou fallen!*
You who hypocritically called yourself the friend of the poor,
>> *How art thou fallen!*
You who mercilessly taxed the people to build mansions for yourself,
>> *How art thou fallen!*
You who greedily took from the poor to build mansions for yourself,
>> *How art thou fallen!*
You who craftily snatched from the poor to feed your concubines,
>> *How art thou fallen!*
You who dictatorially threw the innocent into dungeons,
>> *How art thou fallen!*
You who by threat monopolized power for yourself,
>> *How art thou fallen!*
You who guiltily tried to impose communism on Africa,
>> *How art thou fallen!*

Samuel Kennedy Yeboah
from the *Evening News*
of 7 March 1966

DID THE CIA PLAY ANY PART IN THE COUP?

Governments around the world store the documents they generate during their term of office; some are immediately accessible under freedom-of-information laws; others are "classified" for a given number of years, and the public get access only when they are declassified at the end of that period.

American government papers relating to Ghana and the coup of 1966 which overthrew Nkrumah were eventually declassified and published in 1999. These papers included diplomatic and intelligence memos, telegrams, and reports on Africa, including US Central Intelligence Agency documents which proved that Ankrah, Otu, Kotoka, and others had revealed their plans to American agents long before the coup took place. The much-reviled CIA had known from 1965 that Ghanaian soldiers and police were plotting the coup that took place the following year.

The first suspicions of foreign involvement in the 1966 coup were raised in 1978 when John Stockwell, who served in the US Côte d'Ivoire Embassy in the 1960s, published his memoirs, *In Search of Enemies: a CIA story*. Although the US government published the documents relating to the mid-1960s in 1999, in their ongoing official history of American foreign policy, *Foreign Relations of the US, Africa: Volume XXIV, 1964-68*, it was another 7 years before the facts were freely available to the Ghanaian public: in 2006 *AEON*, a monthly journal published in Accra, printed a 30-page collection of CIA and other papers which named some of the coup plotters and showed that they had communicated their intentions to American diplomats.

Immediately there were claims that the coup had not been a Ghanaian operation after all, but a CIA plot. A feature article by Michael White Kpessa published on the fortieth anniversary of the coup, 24 February 2006, claimed that the coup was "masterminded" or "engineered" by the US government, and particularly by Howard T Banes, who, while officially serving as a political officer in the US Embassy, was secretly chief of the

CIA in Accra. Michael Kpessa even claimed that president J F Kennedy "presided over" the overthrow of Kwame Nkrumah.

The fact that Major-General J A Ankrah had approached officials of the US Embassy as far back as 1964 is indisputable; documents in the USA's official history prove it. A CIA memo of 19 June 1964 said, "disaffected military/police officers could well move against the régime, possibly during Nkrumah's trip abroad (for the Commonwealth Conference) . . . the Otus have also been in close touch with pro-Western Police Commissioner Harlley, who is said to be thoroughly fed up with the régime and has aligned himself with them."

Another CIA document summarized notes of a meeting on 11 March 1965 when US ambassador to Ghana William P Mahoney met with CIA Director John A McCone in Washington: "Mahoney says that he is uncertain whether the coup, being planned by Acting Police Commissioner Harlley and Generals Otu and Ankrah, will ever come to pass".

On 22 March Nkrumah gave a major speech bitterly attacking the way America was meddling in Africa, especially their support of Moise Tshombe in the former Belgian Congo; Nkrumah blamed the USA squarely for many of Africa's other problems. A few days later Ambassador Mahoney described in a telegraph to the US Department of State his own emotional response to that speech, during a call at Flagstaff House, and the pressures that Nkrumah himself was under as he saw his old friends the United Kingdom and the USA withdrawing the support that had been keeping Ghana solvent, and his new friends the Soviet Union and China unwilling to step in and fill the gap.

Mahoney described his private interview with Ghana's President and his comments on the speech: "I said I would never have believed that a man of his sophistication and refinement would use language like that against my country, and it shocked me to hear him do so." Mahoney says that Nkrumah conceded that the rhetoric in his speech was "loaded and slanted throughout", but that "he had a special purpose in mind". As Mahoney further criticized Nkrumah's speech, defending US policy in Africa, Nkrumah had his head in his hands, and Mahoney added, "I looked up and I saw he was crying. With difficulty, he said I could not understand the ordeal he had been through during the past month. He recalled that there had been seven attempts on his life."

On 27 March that year Robert W Komer, a National Security Council staff member, wrote a memorandum to McGeorge Bundy, President Johnson's Special Assistant for National Security Affairs, that plans to overthrow the Ghana government "were looking good . . . We may have a pro-Western coup in Ghana soon . . . certain key military and police figures have been planning one for some time, and Ghana's deteriorating economic conditions may provide the spark. The plotters are keeping us briefed, and [name unclear] thinks we're more involved than the British. While we're not directly involved (I'm told) we and other Western countries (including France) have been helping to set up the situation by ignoring Nkrumah's pleas for economic aid." Mahoney said he felt "there was little chance that either the Chinese communists or the Soviets would in adequate measure come to Nkrumah's financial rescue and the British would continue to adopt a hard-nosed attitude towards providing further assistance to Ghana". His expectations proved correct.

In October 1965 Nkrumah published his seminal work *Neo-Colonialism: the last stage of Imperialism*, in which he predicted that Africa would suffer persistent meddling by the intelligence agencies of foreign governments, particularly the American CIA and the Russian KGB. Nkrumah was equally correct in this prediction.

In January 1966 the magnificent Akosombo dam was completed, 660 m (722 yards) long, 111 m (364 feet) high. At a memorable ceremony at the site of the dam, Nkrumah, Mahoney, and a host of foreign dignitaries saw the water gush through the mighty penstocks for the first time; hydro-electric power began to flow into Ghana's new electricity grid.

The following month Nkrumah was overthrown. He went into exile in Guinea, and eventually died in Romania in 1972 from skin cancer, aged 62.

This book seeks to show that although they did keep the Americans informed about their plans, Ankrah, Otu, Harlley, and Kotoka were not junior partners in a coup "masterminded" or "engineered" from Washington, as suggested by Michael White Kpessa. The planning behind the events of 24th February 1966 was done entirely by Ghanaians on the soil of Ghana. The finance, vehicles and weaponry used to carry out the attack on Flagstaff House and to detain the leading figures of Nkrumah's government were not provided by any outside agency: the most sophisticated tool used in the whole operation was the Russian recoil-less rifle used by troops of the President's Own Guard Regiment to defend Nkrumah's residence and repel the first attackers at the main gate.

The CIA did not know the attackers' detailed plans, and doubted whether they would really launch any coup at all. The forces which Kotoka deployed on the morning of 24 February 1966 were starved of proper equipment, utterly inadequate for the task, and nearly half of them failed to turn up at the right places and at the agreed times. In logistical and strategic terms the coup did not deserve to succeed.

McGeorge Bundy's talk of a "pro-Western coup" was fanciful nonsense. The coup was a thoroughly Ghanaian affair, from its humorous title to its benign and largely bloodless completion.

In the following months and years the resulting military régime, the National Liberation Council, sought and received co-operation and economic help from the West because Western countries, particularly Britain and the USA, had been Ghana's traditional supporters. But the coup was not conceived out of sympathy for Western politics, but out of the necessity to save Ghana from economic and political disaster.

It worked because the majority of Ghanaians had begun to be afraid of arbitrary arrest, tired of Marxist rhetoric, and eager for a new beginning.

In the event, the procession of military and civilian administrations which has exercised power precariously and with mixed results since 1966 has failed to deliver that new beginning. We pray today for the integrity, efficiency, and godly dedication which we long to see and achieve.

One thing we have not seen is a return to imperialism, either in the leaders of the 1966 coup or in any subsequent government. Ghana's economy is still largely dependent on the West and on the great new economies of Asia, but politically and in most other respects Ghana is, as Nkrumah himself said, "free for ever".

If God inspires the rulers of today and the future with the proud vision of true independence which Nkrumah saw as it were from a distance; if citizens of Ghana are inspired to work selflessly for the good of the nation – Ghana's destiny is safe. Let that be our prayer and our sincere commitment.

1

KWAME NKRUMAH: HIS RISE TO POWER
– TWO ASSASSINATION ATTEMPTS

KWAME NKRUMAH, Bachelor of Theology, Master of Science (Education), Master of Arts, honorary Doctor of Laws of Lincoln University, Pennsylvania, was President of the One-Party Republic of Ghana, a position he had attained by 15 years of brilliant campaigning, by creating a popular political party, and by winning free and fair democratic elections. Under Nkrumah, Ghana achieved independence from Britain on 6 March 1957, and became a Republic and One-Party State in July 1960.

Two years later, on 1 August 1962, Nkrumah was returning from talks with President Maurice Yameogo of Upper Volta. The convoy of a dozen or so cars crossed the Ghana border 500 miles from Accra, in the far north-eastern corner of the country. Soon they came to the little village of Kulungugu where they saw a huge crowd gathered to greet them. No stop was planned but Nkrumah decided on the spur of the moment to acknowledge the enthusiastic reception. The leading cars came to a halt and the others closed in gradually behind as Nkrumah got out, accompanied by his Ewe bodyguard, Superintendent Kosi.

Suddenly a little ball of steel came flying over the heads of the crowd and exploded with an earsplitting crack at Kosi's feet.

Kosi's left leg was suddenly numb and at the moment when he should have been at hand to help his master he was just sprawling on the ground. His foot was an ugly sight, oozing blood. He was writhing in pain; sixteen fragments of the grenade had hit him—he was lucky not to have died on the spot.

Where was Nkrumah? As the grenade fell he managed to turn and leap out of the way, and he had fallen to the ground a few feet away from Kosi, with a number of wounds in his back. One of the school-boys in the welcoming party died, and altogether 56 people were injured.

Nkrumah himself was not so badly hurt but the attack made an indelible impression on his mind: he determined that in future no pains should be spared, no expense would be too great, if only he could establish a security force that would make further attacks of this kind quite impossible.

Why had many Ghanaians turned so sharply against their leader? For more than a decade Nkrumah had brilliantly personified Ghana's determination to be free from imperial rule, and his name was now a household word all over the world, a name that had inspired a whole generation of African politicians to fight for freedom in their own countries. Why did he have enemies among his own people?

WE FLASH BACK 35 YEARS TO 1927, WHEN NKRUMAH WAS 18 YEARS OLD

Kwame Nkrumah was born in the humble coastal village of Nkroful, in the south-west extremity of Ghana, to Madam Nyaniba whom he faithfully cared for throughout her long life. He started school at the age of nine, and in 1927, when he was about 18 years old, he entered the Government Training College, Accra, to prepare himself to be a teacher. After the two-year course he taught at Roman Catholic schools in Elmina, Axim, and Amisano.

Nkrumah in the USA – 1936 to 1944

There was no University in the country then, and every ambitious young Gold Coaster hoped to go overseas for further education. Nkrumah's chances looked dim, for the teacher's certificate awarded after the two-year course would not qualify him for entry to any university in the world; besides, his father had died in the year he entered training college and his family was not rich. However with the help of two relatives he managed to scrape together nearly £200, and in 1936 he somehow persuaded the Dean of Lincoln University—a small Presbyterian institution in Pennsylvania, USA, with an enrolment of between 200 and 300 students—to accept him for admission. Founded in 1854, Lincoln was the first college chartered to grant academic degrees to Americans of African descent.

When the young man from the Gold Coast reached the busy campus of Lincoln he had only £40 left in his pocket. It was not enough to pay the first term's fees. But the kindly Dean decided to give Nkrumah a chance, and for the next eight years he worked his way through college, doing jobs of many different kinds to help pay his way, and successfully earning degrees both at Lincoln and at the nearby University of Pennsylvania.

Nkrumah in London – 1945-1947

There followed two hectic years in London. He had gone there to study law; but he soon found himself caught up in a busy whirl of political activity. He spent most of his first four months in England, from June to October 1945, helping two West Indians, George Padmore and T R Makonnen, organize the Fifth Pan-African Congress at Manchester. He became secretary of the West African National Secretariat, helped to launch a short-lived monthly paper called *The New African*, and was employed in the office of the Coloured Workers' Association. He laid ambitious plans for a West African National Congress to be held in Lagos in 1948, but it did not materialize. He formed what he termed a "vanguard group" of the West African National Secretariat, with the mysterious title, "The Circle", visualized as a group of politicians from various parts of West Africa who would secretly work, each in his own country, towards a "Union of African Socialist Republics".

His contacts were all with the political left wing. He had been impressed by the writings of Marx and Lenin, and felt that their teaching held the secret of banishing British imperialism from West Africa; it was said that he carried in his pocket a Communist Party membership card.

The legal studies which he had come to Britain to begin were completely neglected. Instead Kwame Nkrumah became more and more eager to throw himself into the battle for emancipation in the Gold Coast itself. The opportunity he was looking for fell into his lap; a new political party, the United Gold Coast Convention or UGCC, had been inaugurated at Saltpond on 4 August 1947. It was led by Dr J B Danquah, scholar and author, often described as "the doyen of Gold Coast politics". Its interim general secretary was Dr J W de Graft Johnson. Danquah, de Graft Johnson, and other leading members of the Committee, were nearly all practising lawyers, and they immediately realized they must appoint a general secretary who could devote his full time to the movement. They had heard reports of Nkrumah's energetic activities in London, and later that year, after a few enquiries, they invited him to return home and become the UGCC's general secretary. Nkrumah packed his bags, left for home, and landed at Takoradi on 16 December 1947. Exactly a month later, on 15 January 1948, Nkrumah was warmly welcomed back to Ghana and introduced to the UGCC leaders and members at a ceremony in the Palladium cinema, Jamestown, Accra.

He came to a country commonly regarded as a model colony. The Gold Coast had just said farewell to an energetic governor, Sir Alan Burns, whose five years of office were described by a Legon academic, Dennis Austin, as "a period of almost uninterrupted reform".

Under Alan Burns, in 1942, Africans were for the first time appointed to the administrative service as assistant district commissioners; Africans were appointed to the governor's executive council. The following year adult suffrage was introduced in municipal elections, beginning with Kumasi Town Council. In 1944 the Colony native authorities* were

4

strengthened as units of local government; in 1946, when Ashanti and the Colony were brought together under the unofficial majority constitution, a regional territorial council was inaugurated for the Northern Territories. The crowning point of these reforms was the 1946 constitution itself, with its legislative council of eight officials (British colonial servants appointed by the Governor) and 24 unofficial members, 18 elected and six nominated, which united the Colony and Ashanti in a single legislature and brought the country as a whole to the clearly defined stage of "representative government". Burns was well pleased: "the people are really happy" he told the Empire Parliamentary Association, "and really satisfied with the new Constitution they have gained".[1]

* The Gold Coast at that time consisted of three distinct parts: the coastal areas which Britain had annexed unilaterally in 1874 and subsequently described as "the colony"; Ashanti, which was annexed as a colony in 1901 after a series of nine battles and wars between 1900 and 1924; and the Northern Territories which were declared a British protectorate in 1902.

Nkrumah back home in Ghana – 1947 – 1948

Within two months of disembarking at Takoradi in this colonial paradise, Nkrumah was in prison, together with five other leaders of the United Gold Coast Convention. A boycott of foreign-owned stores, prompted by resentment at the rising prices of imported goods, and led by Nii Bonne II, a chief in Osu, had been followed by an ex-servicemen's protest march in which three men died when a frightened and impetuous British police officer took it on himself to open fire on the procession. This sparked off a wave of looting and rioting in Accra and around the country; 29 people died and some 200 were injured. The colonialists picked on six members of the UGCC leadership, including the new general secretary, as convenient scapegoats— Danquah, Obetsibi-Lamptey, Ofori-Atta, Akufo-Addo, Ako Adjei, and Nkrumah.

Though the "Big Six", as they came to be known, were detained in police cells in remote corners of Ghana, the British

5

Labour government's Colonial Secretary commissioned an English lawyer, Mr. Aiken Watson, to "enquire into and report on the recent disturbances in the Gold Coast and the underlying causes, and to make recommendations on any matter arising from their enquiries". Watson, to the horror of old Sir Alan Burns, the former governor, now in retirement and writing his memoirs, wrote off the 1946 constitution of which Burns was so proud as "outmoded at birth". In December 1948 the Colonial Office entrusted to an all-African commission, under the chairmanship of Mr. Justice Coussey, the responsibility of drawing up a new constitution for the Gold Coast.

The Coussey Commission (1948) and "Self-Government Now"

The Coussey Commission's proposals were very moderate. The British governor was to have an executive council of eight representative ministers, who would be African politicians, and three ex-officio heads of department, who would be British colonial servants. Adult suffrage was introduced for the first time in the Colony and Ashanti, but more than half the members of the Legislative Assembly were to be nominated: 18 by the houses of chiefs, 19 by a Northern electoral college, and 6 by foreign trading and mining interests. In the 81-member Legislative Assembly, only a handful, the 5 municipal members, were to be directly elected. The other 33 "elected members" were to be chosen by a system of electoral colleges covering the rest of the Colony and Ashanti. The vote was confined to those who had paid their local levy. British colonial servants were confident that popular demagogues like Nkrumah would never win political power under this constitution. Even if a number of the new type of politician succeeded at the polls, their influence would be cancelled out by the presence in the assembly of 37 members chosen by the chiefs and the Northern Electoral College, whose interest was to safeguard tradition and resist drastic change. There would be a sort of balance of power in the new assembly; neither the progressives nor the traditionalists would have it all their own way.

6

Apart from all these deliberate safeguards against a take-over by radical politicians it seemed that Nkrumah himself had overplayed his hand. In September 1948 his disagreements with the UGCC leaders had resulted in his both resigning and being dismissed from his post. He founded his own daily paper, the Accra *Evening News*, and devoted himself to a country-wide campaign of speech-making and organizing to build up the youth wing of the UGCC; it was called the Committee on Youth Organization, or CYO for short. The secretary of the CYO was Nkrumah's old friend Kojo Botsio, and the chairman was K A Gbedemah. Together they developed the CYO into a powerful organization which was strong enough to challenge the parent body. The CYO grew increasingly impatient with the moderate lawyers and traders who still controlled the UGCC, and in June 1949, before the Coussey Commission had even finished its work, the CYO voted to become a completely separate party, the Convention People's Party.

When the Coussey Commission presented its weighty report after ten months of dignified consultation, Nkrumah convened a Ghana People's Representative Assembly at a few weeks' notice, and the Assembly with breath-taking impudence rejected the Coussey Report and demanded immediate self-government. Nkrumah's Assembly had no constitutional significance, but it had one advantage over the Coussey Commission. It perfectly expressed the impatient nationalism of a great many citizens of the Gold Coast. Encouraged by the reaction, the fiery orator Nkrumah, now in his fortieth year and at the height of his powers, began to preach a new doctrine: Positive Action.

Early in January 1950 the Meteorological Employees' Union was engaged in a dispute with the government. The TUC supported them in their stand, and called for a strike. Nkrumah saw his opportunity to make this into a nation-wide general strike, and declared Positive Action on 8 January. The strike dislocated national life. Three weeks later Nkrumah and other CPP leaders were arrested and charged with inciting workers to engage in an illegal strike, and with sedition. Nkrumah was given three sentences of one year, to be served consecutively.

Under Gold Coast law a term of imprisonment not exceeding one year did not disqualify Nkrumah from being on the electoral roll or from standing for election himself.

The Gold Coast's first general election was to be held in February 1951; the British colonial government, with magnificent devotion to the rule of law, allowed the prisoner who was so safely locked away inside the 300-years-old walls of James Fort, Accra, to stand for election in the two-member constituency of Accra.

Nkrumah's CPP swept to victory in the 1951 election

Nkrumah and Thomas Hutton-Mills, the CPP candidates for Accra's two municipal constituencies, got 20,780 and 19,812 votes respectively; the four other candidates together polled less than 4,500. Not only did Nkrumah himself defy all predictions: the Convention People's Party, pitted against all the obstacles and constitutional checks which had seemingly been designed to keep them out, confounded the experts' calculations and swept to a landslide victory. They won all five directly elected seats and 29 of the 33 seats contested through the electoral colleges. In addition, five of the nominees of the southern houses of chiefs sided with the CPP. Nkrumah had a party 39 strong in an assembly of 80 voting members.

The Governor, Sir Charles Arden-Clarke, took an epoch-making decision: he concluded that he had no choice but to cede victory to the man who was nearing the end of the first of his three one-year sentences in James Fort Prison. Many who became rulers of independent Commonwealth countries had suffered imprisonment on their way to power, but never before had a man been released from one of Her Majesty's dark, evil-smelling cells, and the very next day been ushered into the presence of the Queen's representative to be entrusted with the duty of forming a government.

Nkrumah was a national hero. Every title of praise was heaped on him by an admiring country. He even allowed them to call him Saviour, Messiah. When "Lead, kindly Light" was sung at a Party meeting, many of the singers were privately invoking Kwame Nkrumah.

He still had enemies, of course. Dr Danquah and other leaders of the UGCC were desperately afraid of this impulsive young student, scarcely out of his thirties, only just back from studies overseas, and completely without experience of politics in Ghana. His sense of balance was untested; his integrity was untried. Yet Nkrumah suddenly held the power that the veterans of the struggle for independence had been working and campaigning for during the past ten years. His arrival at the centre of the political stage, as Leader of Government Business, might spell disaster for the country. They resisted Nkrumah's headlong rush towards independence on his own terms with what little influence they could command.

The UGCC was defeated in 1952 and 1954 by Nkrumah and his CPP

The UGCC contested Ghana's first local council elections early in 1952, but the CPP captured nearly all the seats. The UGCC were defeated again at the general election of 1954, held under Nkrumah's new constitution which abolished electoral colleges and created an assembly of 104 members, all directly elected. The CPP, with 55 per cent of the total poll, got 72 seats in the assembly. When it became clear that Nkrumah intended to lead Ghana to independence within the next few years the opposition campaigned for a federal form of government—they were sure of controlling Ashanti and the North even if the CPP held on to power in the Colony.

Nkrumah would not compromise for a moment with such a plan, and the UGCC leaders could see no hope of influencing the decision. The only way in which they could publicize their policy was to boycott the constitutional conference, where they would have been a helpless minority, and to absent themselves when independence was discussed in the National Assembly. Their repeated warnings that Nkrumah would turn out to be a dictator and that the CPP itself would ultimately be a slave of its idol fell on deaf ears.

The obstinacy of the opposition leaders had one result: it forced the British Colonial Office to recognize that the country was not really united on the constitutional issue; Britain had to give the people of Ghana a further opportunity to declare their views in a second pre-independence general election in 1956. Yet what alternative programme could the opposition put forward? "Until Independence," Nkrumah told a visiting journalist, "there is only one political platform—that is, independence—and I happen to be occupying it.."

From the 1956 General Election to Independence and legislation limiting human rights
The 1956 election was hugely important, because the CPP-dominated parliament was to be in power not just for five years as provided in the Constitution, but for ten, as we shall see below. The CPP used every one of its many advantages as the government of the day—access to funds, campaign vehicles provided (free and illegally) by the government's Cocoa Purchasing Company, promises of local development, and not least Nkrumah's personal reputation as the architect of independence—to influence the results: yet, significantly, the oppositon held on to the position it gained in the 1951 election, with 43 per cent of the poll and 33 seats in the assembly.

Despite the opposition's remarkable survival the election was a clear mandate to the CPP to carry Ghana on to Independence. The great day came with the glitter of fireworks and visiting celebrities, and left behind it the glow of victory and the exhilarating expectation of greater achievements to come.

Within a year of Independence Nkrumah had used his majority in parliament to launch a series of Acts limiting civic liberties. First was the Deportation Act of 1957, under which the government deported two Muslim leaders who claimed Ghana citizenship and had spent all their lives in Kumasi, but who had family links with Nigeria. They seemed to have committed no crime other than being active members of the opposition party.

Next came the Emergency Powers Act of 1957, and "PDA", the Preventive Detention Act of July 1958, under which a person could be detained for five years without trial or any right of appeal to the courts. It seemed to confirm what Nkrumah said in the preface to his autobiography, that from such men as Lenin, Mussolini, and Hitler he had learned "much of value . . . and many ideas that were useful".

Corruption increased. Ministers and Party members in the assembly who had been supposed to surrender their salaries to the CPP and "live simply and modestly and so maintain contact with the common people" began to build mansions far beyond their means. There were repeated warnings from the dwindling opposition, but it was gradually being worn down by a mixture of threats, inducements, and imprisonment under "PDA".

But by 1960 the parliament elected just before independence was nearing its end and the opposition was preparing for a general election. There seemed to be a very good chance of defeating the CPP at the polls.

In 1951 there had been only a few elected seats in the assembly, and only four non-CPP candidates won seats contested indirectly through "electoral colleges". Three years later, in the 1954 and 1956 elections, the opposition vote had increased significantly to around 44 per cent, and there were 32 or 33 opposition men in the 104-member assembly. Since then public opinion had begun to see dictatorial dangers in Nkrumah's behaviour. Nkrumah himself was well aware that in a free election the CPP might be defeated; but he was not prepared to risk going into opposition. He looked for a way out—and found one.

The 1960 referendum approved a Republic and a ten-year Parliament

Early in 1960 Nkrumah announced that the government would hold a referendum to seek approval for a republican constitution, and then hold an election for the office of president. But a further issue was tacked on to the voters' decision: a vote in favour of the republic would also be a vote to prolong the life of the 1956 parliament for another five years, until 1966. He explained this as a device to save money, in view of the extra expense if there were a general election as well as a referendum.

It was natural for Ghana to become a republic and for Nkrumah to become its first president, but the voters failed to see the danger of giving the 1956 parliament ten years in power without a general election. If before 1966 he were to fall out of favour and the people had no democratic means of removing him, there could easily be a violent outcome.

There were complaints about intimidation among the voters and sharp practice at the polling stations, but Nkrumah got a positive vote and the republic was initiated on 1 July 1960 amid adaptations of ancient Ghana customs, along with the now familiar diet of flags, flood-lighting, and firework displays.

It was soon clear that the people had made a dangerous decision. From this time onwards, by-elections ceased to be contested, and the CPP candidate for any vacant seat was always declared elected unopposed. Just three years after independence, Nkrumah had made it virtually impossible for an opposition candidate to win a seat in Parliament.

As if to underline the fact that Ghana was moving faster and faster in the direction of totalitarian rule, Nkrumah went off on a two-month visit to the communist states of the Soviet Union (Russia) and eastern Europe from July to September 1961. Two days before he left, F K D Goka, Minister of Finance, introduced an unpopular budget. While Krobo Edusei, Tawiah Adamafio (recently released from custody) and Kwaku Boateng set off with Nkrumah to tour the communist world, it was left to Gbedemah, Botsio, and Goka to lead the government in the face of growing public resentment.

The additional five per cent tax—a scheme for so-called compulsory savings which many suspected would never be repaid (they never were)—brought resentment to boiling point. In September the workers of Takoradi went on strike. Despite the efforts of press and radio to minimize the importance of the protest, the strike spread to Accra and Kumasi, and threatened

12

to bring the nation to a standstill. On his return to Ghana, Nkrumah attempted to appease public opinion by sacrificing his closest colleagues—Gbedemah and Botsio, the men who had adopted him as their co-worker in the old CYO when he had ceased to be secretary of the UGCC back in 1948. Four other cabinet ministers and Geoffrey Bing, the attorney-general, were made to resign. J B Danquah and fifty other opposition leaders were arrested under PDA; and unknown to the public in other parts of the country, hundreds of strikers in Sekondi and Takoradi were thrown into prison.

The very next month the Queen of England paid a state visit to Ghana and drove with Kwame Nkrumah through cheering crowds in many parts of the country. Duncan Sandys, Britain's Commonwealth Relations Secretary, had visited Ghana a few weeks earlier to try to assess the likelihood of an attack on Nkrumah during one of their public appearances. He judged that it would be safe for the Queen to come, and so it proved. But public resentment was not quenched: it was smouldering, waiting for another breeze to fan it into a blaze. Nkrumah, the hero of Ghana and of Africa, was losing his hold on the affections of his people. He had effectively destroyed every means by which he could be voted out of power constitutionally: violence had become the only way he could be removed.

Grenade attack at Kulungugu

That is what the grenade seemed to say as it exploded at Nkrumah's feet at Kulungugu in 1962. Nkrumah was quick to get the message. If they meant to use violence, he could find a way of blocking that method as effectively as he had blocked the constitutional one.

From that time onwards Nkrumah developed a lively interest in security in all its aspects, which soon became an obsession. Within a week or so he had obtained an expert in security matters straight from the Kremlin in Moscow—a mild-looking Russian by the name of Sweskov, who was courteous and small of stature but as hard as nails and extremely knowledgeable

13

when it came to protecting unpopular rulers from their opponents. He did not speak English, but with the help of a Russian interpreter, plenty of imagination, and Ghanaian good humour, Sweskov set to work to give the President of Ghana a first-rate force for personal defence. He politely brushed aside the two-man security committee headed by John Harlley of the Special Branch, which was in any case discredited in Nkrumah's eyes since the attempt at Kulungugu, and began to recruit a para-military force to be trained as soldiers but not to form part of the army. It would be known as the Presidential Guard Department. Nkrumah, who disliked the implication that he was always under guard, came across an alternative phrase, "Detail Department", in a book written by one of the late President Kennedy's security officers: so Presidential Detail Department it became.

Sweskov proposed a security force comprising six different units (1) Bodyguard Unit, to guard Nkrumah's own person: (2) Protection Unit, to guard buildings and routes used at any time by the President: (3) Functions Unit, responsible for functions attended by Nkrumah: the arrangements and programme, the people involved, the route and the venue: (4) Comptroller's Unit, comprising Nkrumah's own domestic staff: (5) Counter-intelligence Unit, to keep an eye on all other personnel of the Presidential Detail Department and on anyone else likely to come into contact with them: (6) President's Own Guard Battalion, for ceremonial and military defence purposes (there was already a President's Own Guard Company; this was to be raised to battalion strength and separated rigidly from the rest of the Ghana Army, so that the posting of officers and men should be controlled exclusively from within the security organization).

The Russian security expert intended that the whole department should be controlled by a single commander, responsible to Nkrumah, and Ambrose Yankey, a member of Nkrumah's existing bodyguard and an increasingly influential adviser, had his eye on the appointment. Ambrose Yankey was tall, brawny, and boastful, but he was a man of little education

14

and had first entered Nkrumah's household as a steward soon after independence. He had the advantage of coming from Western Nzema, Nkrumah's own home district, and was reputed to have played the trumpet in his village brass band, but the President had the good sense to see that he would have been quite unable to control the Detail Department. Nkrumah had a genius for the policy of "divide and rule"; he knew how to play off one personality against another and to keep them all vying for his own favour. He gave the command of the President's Own Guard Battalion to Captain Zanlerigu, already commanding officer of the President's Own Guard Company: he put Salifu Dagarti, a police officer of irreproachable record, and a crack marksman into the bargain, in charge of the other units. Ambrose Yankey was given a role as controller of the counter-intelligence unit.

In Russia a security officer had to be a party member and a convinced Marxist. Here in Ghana party membership was no guarantee of anything, and as for ideology, it was less than twelve months since Nkrumah had revoked the regulation banning the import of communist literature. In any case Sweskov and his friends from Russia had little opportunity of pressing their point of view since Salifu Dagarti and David Zanlerigu were both nurtured entirely in British police and army traditions, and what little knowledge Ambrose Yankey had of administration derived from his work, as a small scale capitalist, selling "nkonto" fish in Sekondi market.

All hope that the security force would be either ideologically pure or even professionally efficient were soon dispelled by Ambrose Yankey's interference. He recognized in Nkrumah's increasing distrust of everybody else a golden opportunity to advance his own power; he tried to fill the ranks of the security force with his own friends and with fellow-countrymen from Western Nzema. The army and police, instead of being asked to post a given number of men to the Presidential Detail Department, began to get lists of individuals who were to be transferred; not a few bribed Ambrose Yankey to nominate them, as joining the security force would involve a rise in pay.

Many of these new recruits subverted the confidentiality that should surround a secret service by boasting to their friends that they were members of it.

The Russian President's own safety reclaimed Sweskov's attention after a few months, but he left behind him a permanent security adviser, Nikolay Ivanovich Gladkiy; and he returned in mid-1963 with a fresh colleague, Robert Issakovich Akhmerov, bringing proposals for an even larger security service.

The Russians now suggested uniting every organization connected with either security or intelligence under a single authority. The Special Branch was to be separated from the police. The customs and preventive service which operated on Ghana's frontiers was to be the nucleus of a "border guard", still responsible to the Comptroller of Customs and Excise for customs purposes, but now reorganized on a para-military basis as a first line of defence against any attack. Military intelligence, while not being cut off altogether from the army, was also to be an integral part of the security service.

*   *   *

"10 per cent" financing the Party

It was during the period when Sweskov was perfecting these new arrangements that Tony Deku of the Special Branch made a puzzling and disturbing discovery. He came into Harlley's office and told him about it quietly and deliberately, using their common language, Ewe:

"I've just found that CPP officials are getting their pay by cheques drawn on a private company, sir."

"Which one—N A D E C O (National Development Company)?"

"That's it! How did you guess?"

"I began to be suspicious about that company because I couldn't make out where they got their profits from. I discovered they were spending more than they could possibly earn from legitimate business. You know it was founded by Nkrumah himself?"

16

"Yes, in 1958.

"And they control the State Insurance Corporation."

"That's right, sir. Besides, it is the chief agent for British Fire Insurance Company. Our masters have a funny way of turning Ghana into a socialist country—capitalism financing the people's party."

"They have no alternative, Tony. You don't suppose that million-pound, four-storey CPP headquarters was paid for out of a hundred thousand membership fees, do you?"

"Are you going to bring a charge against them?"

"Oh, the N A D E C O affair is nothing; the real trouble is all this corruption in high places—and in Flagstaff House itself."

"You don't mean Nkrumah is implicated?"

"That's just what I do mean. I've got proof of it too. This 10 per cent on all government contracts is not just private bribery by ministers: it's a systematic plan to finance the Party. All the companies know they're expected to pay 10 per cent in order to get contracts, so they just add that to their estimates and pay it out cheerfully. The money, or most of it, is paid into N A D E C O, and Nkrumah uses it just as he pleases".

"Then why did he bring in the Public Property and Corrupt Practices Act?"

---

* NADECO, despite the uplifting name, was a receptacle for slush funds and existed in the shadows to grease the party machine and also service Nkrumah's foreign outposts.[12] (Baffour Agyeman-Duah in *Ghana: Governance in the Fourth Republic*) Digibooks, 2008

"Just a pretence, Tony, just a pretence. How many charges have been brought under that Act since it was passed last year? No, I'm afraid we're fighting a losing battle. We're working loyally for the Old Man, trying to stamp out bribery and corruption, but the Old Man himself is financing his Party illegally."

Deku could hardly believe his ears. It was extremely dangerous for anyone to talk in this way: it meant that Harlley trusted him.

"As far as I can see," Harlley went on, lapsing into English: "we have every constitutional right to apprehend him. The Ghana Police, being in possession of information that the President is involved in criminal transactions, can prepare charges against him. A copy of the charges will be handed to the Chief Justice, the original will be delivered to Nkrumah, and we shall give him an ultimatum—a date and time at which he must either abdicate or face the consequences."

"And if he refuses to abdicate?"

"A military task force would be ready in positions surrounding Flagstaff House to effect his arrest. The Commissioner of Police would drive into Flagstaff House in an armoured car, together with the Chief of Defence Staff, declare Nkrumah destooled[4], and take him away."

"It all sounds very easy. Have you discussed it with Commissioner of Police Madjitey, or with General Otu?" It was as though Deku had pricked a balloon. Harlley's tone of quiet determination gave way to despair.

"No. I dare not discuss it with a soul. I didn't trust you till you saw the situation for yourself. And now, with this new security service, we haven't got a chance. Oh, why should one man sit on our necks like this? Why does God allow it?"

Deku, like Harlley, was a Catholic, but he had no answer. He looked away at the flagged charts on the walls and the secret files awaiting attention, half fearing his chief would weep with the tension of it.

Harlley was not a theologian either, but he had received part of his education in that stronghold of Presbyterianism,

18

Akropong, and in this time of crisis he was looking to God for the solution. "I've been praying about it, Deku, but the more I pray the more I am convinced that God is not going to step in himself and deliver the people from this situation. He must do it through a man, through some citizen of Ghana. And I think to myself, 'Harlley, you're an adult: perhaps you can do something'. Then I see the security forces getting stronger every day, and I wonder how much time we have left, or whether it's too late already. Do you realize we've only got another month or so here? The Special Branch is going to form part of the new security service and it will be detached from the police and come directly under Nkrumah himself."

"What will happen to us?" asked Deku.

"I've heard the heads of the security service are going to be called to a meeting at Flagstaff House next month; after that we may know the details. But one thing is certain: with the security boys and the President's Own Guard defending Flagstaff House, the police can't overthrow Nkrumah without the co-operation of the army."

Deku commented, "I know one or two army officers, but I dare not say a word to them about overthrowing Nkrumah!"

"You leave the army to me. Do you know Captain Kwashie? He's a countryman of ours and I know he's fed up. Let me sound him out."

"How many troops has he got under him? Could he get us tanks, or artillery?"

"He's the secretary of the Military Hospital!"

They had to laugh at that. Then Harlley gave Deku his assignment: to find out what the security service was doing; to keep in touch with their colleagues at the Special Branch, in case they were both moved to another unit; above all, to anticipate Nkrumah's intentions towards the police and the army, which were the only powers in the country still capable of unseating him.

The meeting of heads of the security service took place in the President's office one afternoon late in 1963. Kwaku Boateng, Minister of the Interior, and Kofi Baako, Minister of Defence, were there: so were Madjitey, the Commissioner of Police, and Major-General Otu, Chief of Defence Staff. Enoch Okoh, secretary to the cabinet (an able civil servant who had been secretary to the university Socialist Club in his Cambridge days) and Eric Otoo, Nkrumah's newly appointed "secretary on security matters", made up the party. They all shook hands, then sat around Nkrumah's desk and got down to business. All except Madjitey, who was a Krobo, understood Fante or some other Twi dialect thoroughly, but the meeting was conducted in English.

"I have called you together this afternoon to explain the new Security Forces Act," the President began, looking quickly round the group. "You each have before you a copy of the Act, a memorandum which I have prepared, and other documents relevant to your own departments. The plans which we have adopted will stop enemies of the state and accomplices of the imperialists, colonialists, and neo-colonialists from penetrating our defences." The two civil servants glanced anxiously across the desk. This language didn't go down well with policemen and soldiers: even Boateng and Kofi Baako, must find it a trifle hackneyed. When would the President learn to treat a meeting of this kind like a small, intimate group, not like a mass rally? Probably the trouble was that Nkrumah got no chances these days to address mass rallies; since the bomb-throwing incidents at Kulungugu and in the following few weeks public appearances had become too dangerous both for the masses and for himself—yet it was still only six years since Nkrumah had triumphantly led Ghana into independence　.

General Otu was asking awkward questions: the two civil servants were quickly on the alert.

"I just want to know whether my Director of Military Intelligence will still work at Burma Camp, and whether we shall have any access to the information he collects."

20

"Yes, of course you will," said the President curtly, "only in future, as Supreme Commander of the Armed Services, I will be directly in charge of his department."

"And his place of work?"

This one caught Nkrumah on the wrong foot. He leaned over to the secretary on security matters, who opened the memorandum at the appropriate place; he read out the reference. "The Director of Military Intelligence will still work at Burma Camp. Is that perfectly clear?"

A few more questions were asked. The President told Madjitey to be ready to withdraw his police from Flagstaff House and hand over to the security force early in January 1964. Then the politicians, officials, and service heads withdrew, and as the door closed Erica Powell, Nkrumah's British secretary, rang through with a list of people who wanted interviews.

Nkrumah sometimes kept important people waiting. When they had built up enough impatience and frustration he would receive them with much warmth and affection and blame the delay on his secretary. It was his own private brand of gamesmanship and gave him a tactical advantage in awkward interviews; from Nkrumah's point of view that more than outweighed the embarrassment it caused Erica Powell and her colleague Mr Badoe. But there was no need to try this on today; he was tired and wanted to finish early. Besides, something was beginning to worry him: Arku Korsah, the Chief Justice, had still not given judgement in the treason trial arising out of the Kulungugu bomb attempt.

*　　　　　*　　　　　*

The man accused of arranging the 1962 bomb attempts was Obetsebi Lamptey, a Ga lawyer, an Accra man. Nkrumah had seized on the Kulungugu incident as an excuse to get rid of three Ga people who had too much influence in the Party to be safe: Ako Adjei, the foreign minister: Tawia Adamafio, the virulently anti-Western minister of information and broadcasting: and Cofie Crabbe, executive secretary of the CPP. Nkrumah particularly suspected Tawia Adamafio of ambitions

21

to supplant him as President. The case was tried in the newly-formed special court for treason offences, from whose decisions there was no appeal, and it dragged on from August to October 1963. Kwaw Swanzy, Attorney-General, made out the best case he could against them, on the flimsiest of hunches and suspicions. Judgement was reserved and the public awaited the verdict with apathy, suspecting that whatever happened the three men would not get off. However the President did not like having to wait for independent decisions of the judiciary; Korsah was old enough to be his father, having studied at the Middle Temple during World War 1 and been called to the Bar in 1919; could he be trusted to declare the three Gas guilty?

It happened that Nkrumah did not have much longer to wait. Sir Arku Korsah read his judgement quietly but defiantly to a packed court on the morning of 9 December 1963. He found that Robert Otchere and Yaw Manu were implicated in the conspiracy, but that Ako Adjei, Tawia Adamafio, and Cofie Crabbe, despite all the attorney-general's allegations, were not involved. He acquitted them and it seemed they would be free to walk out of the court and go home.

The whole paraphernalia of justice was powerless to save the three Ga politicians; indeed, Nkrumah regarded it as an anachronism, like the lawyers' ill-fitting wigs and the chief justice's magnificent gown—a quaint survival from colonial days. Ako Adjei, Adamafio, and Cofie Crabbe were taken straight back to prison and the news of the judgement was carried to the President.

At first he did not seem at all perturbed. Perhaps he had not really expected Swanzy's legal arguments to succeed. Perhaps he was too busy planning the new security force. Perhaps it did not matter to him whether he kept his former colleagues locked up with or without legal justification. Later in the day, however, he began to take a more serious view of the matter.

Suddenly Flagstaff House was thrown into one of its periodical crises. The police tightened their grip on the buildings and those who entered them. The President's Own Guard, resplendent in their scarlet uniforms, stamped about at the main gate with even greater show of martial zeal. Erica Powell was deluged with notes to type, appointments to arrange, and phone calls from all and sundry. And Geoffrey Bing, whose normal routine was boring after his previous job as Ghana's attorney-general, strode importantly along the passages, puffing a cigar and riding on the wavecrest of the nation's troubles. The crisis would not last long—trust Bing to see to that—but while it lasted he would return briefly to the limelight.

Whether by chance or by design, Sir Arku had timed his verdict to coincide with the celebration of Human Rights Day. Next morning the same papers which reported his reserved judgement were full of comments on the universal declaration of human rights. A leader-page article in the *Daily Graphic* quoted from the declaration and mentioned "freedom from arbitrary arrest, detention, or exile, slavery, and servitude". The leading article itself innocently commented, "It is significant that this year's anniversary of the historic proclamation is being celebrated at a stage in history when many people and countries in many parts of the world have won political freedom, and, with it, human rights which had long been denied them".

The public read on another page that the three men acquitted by the chief justice had been rearrested and taken back to their cells.

The President first of all acted quickly against Korsah himself. On the very next day Swanzy summoned a press conference and declared that the Chief Justice's verdict was a mockery of justice. The Party organized compulsory demonstrations of puzzled junior civil servants, who were made to march through the streets with placards denouncing Korsah's wickedness; newspaper photographers took pictures to prove that the nation was solidly united behind their Leader. Then on 11 December, by virtue of his powers under the 1960 republican constitution, Nkrumah revoked the appointment of Sir Arku Korsah as chief justice of Ghana, and the following day Sir Arku announced his retirement from the judicial service.

23

Then there was a lull. If Sir Arku Korsah knew the value of clever timing, so did the President. He would use this judgement as an excuse to tighten his grip on the life of the nation, but he would forestall the first spontaneous public reaction by delaying his announcement till the Christmas and New Year holidays. At that time the whole nation would be relaxed: offices would be deserted, the shops would be glittering with materialistic diversions, most of the leaders of national life would be away in their home towns and villages celebrating the festive season. That was the time to act. Later, in the first week of January, the nation would wake up to find the crucial moment for united protest already gone.

An emergency session of the National Assembly was called for Monday 23 December, and an amendment to the Criminal Procedure (Amendment) Act of 1961 was introduced under certificate of urgency, which meant that the measure would pass through all three readings and consideration stage too during one morning. The amendment was to enable the President to declare any decision of the special treason court to be of no effect. The assembled MPs were told that this point had somehow been overlooked in the drafting of the 1961 Act, and it would be made retrospective to that year. Next evening Nkrumah broadcast to the nation. In addition to giving Christmas greetings, he said, "In exercise of the powers conferred on me by the National Assembly I have today declared the recent treason trial as of no effect whatsoever. In other words the judgement is declared null and void".

Ghanaians celebrated a Christmas of record-breaking affluence with hundreds of thousands of crates of beer, made-in-Ghana Gem biscuits for the children, and an unprecedented slaughter of turkeys, goats, and chickens. Many people, as they worshipped in their churches or sat round in their halls and back-yards to discuss family affairs, had an uncomfortable feeling that arbitrary imprisonment in defiance of judicial decisions was no part of African tradition or of modern democracy; but with all these security men and Young Pioneer school children about it was becoming dangerous to express

24

such feelings openly. Besides, after a century of autocratic rule by superior white-faced foreigners it was possible to forgive Nkrumah many things. The British had found legal pretexts for imprisoning opponents of colonialism: if Nkrumah did the same to his enemies it was not worth protesting about, and risking detention oneself.

The nearest thing to a protest was a resolution denouncing Korsah's dismissal, passed at the annual congress of the Ghana Union of Students. It was drafted by Lawrence Otu Cantey, a wiry, stern-looking young law student, and a native of Apirede, Akwapim. Cantey, who had just started studying for his LL B, was one of the representatives of Commonwealth Hall, Legon, at the congress. Fortunately for him he was not a member of the executive committee, all five of whom were arrested a month later. Neither the resolution nor the arrest was reported in the Ghana press.

1964: a One-party State

Satisfied with the quiet acceptance of his second step, Nkrumah proceeded to the third and most extreme measure: the formal inauguration of a one-party state, conferring power on the President to dismiss high court and Supreme Court judges at any time without giving reasons. To this was linked a change in the Ghana flag, making it identical with that of the CPP except for the central five-pointed black star. He argued the necessity for these changes in a New Year message to the nation on 31 December 1963:

In the performance of their duties judges are not interfered with by the chief executive, and to this extent they exercise the judicial powers of the State independently of the executive. But under our constitution the office of the Chief Justice is not solely judicial. It is also quasi-political. It involves active co-operation and understanding with the President in securing justice, law and order, peace and stability. In other words, the position of the Chief Justice of Ghana is such that the holder of the post must be conscious of his political responsibility.

25

A treason trial, by its very nature, is political and can lead to unrest, disturbances, and even violence. For this reason, our Government was bound to be interested in the treason trial by virtue of the fact that it is the responsibility of the Government to maintain law and order and to ensure the security of the state. The failure of the Chief Justice to take the President into his confidence in regard to the judgement of the special court showed a serious disregard for the office of the President. His failure also to recognize the effect that the judgement, whatever it was, would have on peace, stability, and order throughout the country, for which the Government would be responsible, was a clear indication of his lack of political responsibility.

The Judges of the special court, by their failure to take me into their confidence, meant to create discontent and terror throughout the country. You, the people of Ghana, have made me the conscience of the nation. My duty is not only to govern but to ease the conscience of the people by giving them peace of mind and tranquillity. The nation cannot tolerate a dishonest and corrupt judiciary. . . In the circumstances, the Government, in the interests of the people, wishes to take advantage of the situation created by the judgement in the treason trial to make certain amendments to our constitution. I and the Government have therefore decided that a referendum should be held between the 24th of January and the 31st of January next year (1964) to seek the approval of the people for the amendment of the constitution in the following respects:

(1) to invest the President with power in his discretion to remove a judge of the supreme court or a judge of the high court at any time for reasons which appear to him sufficient:
(2) to provide that in conformity with the interests, welfare and aspirations of the people, and in order to develop the organizational initiative and political activity of the people, there should be one national party in Ghana, which shall be the vanguard of our people in their struggle to build a

socialist society, and which shall be the leading core of all organizations of the people.

*　　　　　*　　　　　*

The broadcast came to an end and the nation gave no reply. For nearly forty-eight hours there was no reply, and by the afternoon of 2 January 1964 Dr Kwame Nkrumah felt he had successfully taken one more crucial step towards his goal of a secure and unassailable one-Party Republic. He reflected on it with satisfaction: instead of delaying the advance towards Nkrumaist socialism, Arku Korsah had actually speeded it up. Without the Chief Justice's verdict, he could hardly have announced the referendum on the one-party state in his New Year's Eve broadcast; but now he would change the constitution, and the one-party state would be a reality by the end of the month.

The presidential stomach gave a reminder that it was lunch time; Nkrumah glanced at his watch and remembered that he had a visit to make by car and that he would not get his lunch for a while longer. He called his secretary, Badoe: "Tell Salifu Dagarti I'm leaving the office. Let him come at once." Salifu Dagarti, as his surname implied, came from Dagao, in the dry, infertile north-west corner of the country. In the tradition common to many of their colonies, the British had chosen to recruit many of their police and soldiers from these remote and less developed regions; their heads were not so full of political ideas as the southerners'.

In 1901 - 02 the British had annexed Ashanti and declared the northern territories a protectorate. A few years later Salifu Dagarti's father left the round mud huts and conical grass roofs of his native village and enlisted in the Gold Coast Regiment. Little Salifu first saw the light of day in July 1913, in the severe and disciplined atmosphere of the barracks at Kumasi. By the time he was 17 his father was a sergeant-major, and Salifu decided to enlist in the police as a band learner. In 1946, at the early age of 33, Salifu himself reached the exalted rank of sergeant-major, and before independence in 1957 he was an Assistant Superintendent of Police.

Just over a year earlier he had become Nkrumah's personal ADC, replacing the man who was so badly cut up in the attempt on the President's life at Kulungugu in August 1962. Recently he had been appointed head of Nkrumah's security force. Salifu Dagarti stood sharply to attention in the President's office. His head was high, his shoulders braced back, and with the knuckles of his thumbs he could feel the seams of his trousers. He would never forget that six-month drill course in England with the Brigade of Guards, and that monster of an RSM barking at them, "Thumbs on the seams of your trousers—what in heaven's name do you think your trousers have got seams in them for, except to show you blasted dim-wits where to put your little thumbs when you stand to attention?"

Nkrumah got up quickly and together they walked out into the sunlight. Coming out of the airconditioned office was like walking into an oven. There was a path across the grass from the office to the residence and a car was waiting outside the main entrance. Overhead the neem trees waved gently in a breeze that came hot and dry from the direction of the Sahara desert. Four policemen, each armed with a rifle and five rounds of .303 ammunition were on duty as usual in the area between the office and the residence. They snapped to attention and presented arms with their rifles pointing vertically upwards (the rifleman's traditional salute to senior officers) as the President came out: but the corporal in charge was not there. His men had been at Flagstaff House since six am and would go off duty in three-quarters of an hour; Corporal Sissala happened, just at that moment, to be in the toilet.

The peaceful atmosphere was shattered by the crack of a rifle shot. The President and his ADC turned round to see something that neither of them could believe for a moment. One of the policemen was standing there, not presenting arms, but with his rifle pointing straight at them, and a wisp of smoke was gliding from the barrel.

28

From the other end of the sights Seth Nicholas Kwami Ametewee blinked back at his target. Like the President he was born on a Saturday, and shared the same name, Kwame. Today was a Thursday and it must be Nkrumah's last one. Kwami Ametewee pulled back the bolt to eject the used cartridge case and reload; a moment later another shot rang out, and he missed again.

Ametewee was a crack shot but he was firing in the difficult standing position, with no support on which to rest his elbows. He had been in the police service only just over four years, and the excitement coupled with the weight of the rifle was too much for him.

Salifu Dagarti had recovered his presence of mind and began shouting wildly at the assailant. He couldn't shield the President, who was running for cover in Flagstaff House, and anyway he wanted to keep his eyes on Ametewee. "Shoot at me," he shouted, dodging about under the neem trees and trying to keep in the line of fire so as to put him off his aim.

Ametewee obeyed too well. The third round hit Salifu Dagarti in the head and he collapsed in a pool of blood under the neem trees, mortally wounded. Corporal Sissala came up from the toilet at the double to find out what the noise was about, but no one approached Ametewee. The security men inside the offices and the residence looked out to see what had happened. A platoon of the President's Own Guard Regiment in their scarlet coats stood at the next gate ready to give Nkrumah a ceremonial salute as he drove out, but their rifles were not loaded and for the next few vital seconds no one ordered them to move.

Ametewee had two rounds left. He had been promised a reward of £2,000 and the chance of further education overseas if he succeeded in killing the other Kwame. He left his first victim sprawled on the grass, and with his rifle at the high port he ran swiftly after the President, who was making for the kitchen yard at the back of the residence. He tried to reload as he ran, but he jogged the bolt and in addition to the empty cartridge one of the

two remaining precious rounds sprang out and fell on the ground with a mocking tinkle.

He was now passing another member of the four-man guard, John Amihere. He stopped and raised the rifle to aim at Nkrumah for the last time. Suddenly John Amihere shouted at the top of his voice, "In the name of Jesus Christ I command you ..."

In a moment Ametewee had swung round and aimed at his comrade. Amihere feared that his turn had come and spoke not another word, but the distraction probably saved the President's life: by the time Ametewee had turned back towards the kitchen yard Nkrumah was out of sight and the security men were coming up behind his assailant. He started to run after the President once again, but was knocked to the ground by a blow from behind. The next day's papers carried photographs of Nkrumah crouching over the miserable policeman, and reported that the President had overpowered him single-handed. Children in the schools lost any doubts they might have had before as to the myth of Nkrumah's immortality.

John Harlley, head of the police Special Branch, heard of the incident within minutes of the shots being fired. He was sitting in his office less than half a mile from the spot, at Police Headquarters—a new five-storey building, complete with modern lifts, tiled floors, and fluorescent lighting. He called his deputy on the intercom. Tony Deku stepped out of a nearby office and walked down the gleaming passage, where constables and plain-clothes men jumped to attention as he passed.

"You called me, sir." Tony Deku stood inside his boss's office, tall and well-built, round-faced, with a kindly twinkle in his eye. He had been in the Special Branch for sixteen years, and could remember Nkrumah being imprisoned in 1948, a year before Charles Arden-Clarke replaced Gerald Creasy as governor. Harlley, like himself an Ewe, was full-cheeked and four years his senior, and looked every bit of his forty-five years as he passed on the news of the shooting. But why was he so upset? Only a month before, Deku had been sitting in this very room,

31

discussing with his chief the necessity for getting rid of the President. Now that someone had attempted to do it, Harlley was obviously annoyed.

The head of the Special Branch had not suddenly been converted to Nkrumaism: what worried him was that someone had organized a clumsy conspiracy and bungled it. Harlley was already reflecting that it would make the task of carrying out a successful coup d'état ten times more difficult—perhaps impossible.

Ametewee was speaking the wrong language and giving the wrong message. He might well have killed Nkrumah and caused a great deal of confusion, but the Party would have survived unless the army had intervened, and the army was not ready. Anyway, he missed.

*   *   *

That evening John Harlley, head of the Ghana Police Special Branch, was still meditating on the position. The broadcast on New Year's Eve had sounded quite bad enough; now everything was infinitely worse.

The shooting was done by a policeman so the police would be blamed. No doubt it was a fact that police officers were involved—it was common knowledge that the police were soon to withdraw from Flagstaff House and hand over its defence to the security force; perhaps some officer had seen this as a last opportunity to attack Nkrumah while the police were still near him.

Any moment now Nkrumah would act against them—indiscriminately, since no one knew who was really involved. Perhaps Harlley would be the scapegoat. Certainly, Nkrumah would find a way to stop the police from carrying out another attempt. What an awful mess! Why must this happen just when their plans to remove Nkrumah looked like bearing fruit? Why hadn't these crazy people consulted him before making the attempt?

Then he had a miserable feeling of utter helplessness. Nkrumah had created a situation in which nobody would trust

32

anybody else. Harlley thought the others were loyal—they thought he was loyal. But surely Nkrumah was not deceived: it seemed most likely that he, Harlley, was already under suspicion and about to go into Nsawam Prison. Was there no way to break out of this frustrating net of suspicion and counter-suspicion?

On Wednesday 8 January, six days after the shooting, Nkrumah ordered the dismissal of eight senior police officers, including E R T Madjitey, the commissioner of police, and his two deputies. The man chosen to succeed Madjitey was none other than John Harlley himself.

2

1964: THREE OF THE "BIG SIX" IN PRISON AGAIN

DURING the first few days of his new appointment as commissioner of police, Harlley had no time to think of removing Nkrumah: he was working overtime, helping the security service to throw scores and hundreds of people into prison till there were about 1,000 Ghana citizens detained without trial, including three of the original "Big Six"; Danquah, Ofori-Atta, and Ako Adjei. Out of the six who gaze calmly at us from every Ghana bank-note, only Nkrumah himself and Akufo-Addo were still at liberty; Obetsibi Lamptey, who had been imprisoned without trial two years before under the Preventive Detention Act following the Kulungugu grenade attack, had died in prison just last year.

Nkrumah even ordered Sir Arku Korsah to be arrested, but the new Commissioner of Police foresaw the uproar that would result both in Ghana and abroad if the former chief justice were put in prison, so he asked permission to hold him for questioning before formally detaining him. Nkrumah absentmindedly agreed and Korsah was quietly released after a couple of days. Months later the President was still under the impression that Sir Arku was safe under lock and key; he was at last disillusioned when he chanced to see a newspaper report of Korsah's presence at a social function.

Danquah and Ofori-Atta, however, had been arrested. Both of them had been in the fight for independence when Nkrumah was a young student in America. Both were founding members of the United Gold Coast Convention. Both, in 1947, had invited Kwame Nkrumah back home to become the first full-time secretary of the party: Danquah was fifteen years his senior. Nkrumah was abusing his elders, one of the gravest sins in the African code of morality. But the nation looked on in silence while the press poured congratulations on him, and revived the myth of his immortality.

Ofori-Atta had been summoned from his morning Bible study by an assistant superintendent and then searched by men in plain clothes. They took him to Police Headquarters, where he waited around all day and was finally questioned at five in the evening. "What were you doing on Thursday 2 January?" he was asked. "Have you any relations in the police? Have you ever sent any funds to Obetsebi Lamptey?" He answered the questions as best he could and was finally sent to Jamestown Police Station to spend the night in a dismal cell.

Like Danquah he was a declared enemy of Kwame Nkrumah's increasingly autocratic rule, and like Danquah he was prepared to use every legitimate means to unseat him; but they could not possibly connect him with the shooting of a fortnight earlier.

Why should they have arrested him? Funny, too, that it should have happened just when he had started taking an interest in Bible reading! Perhaps it would have been better to steer clear of Christianity—he'd got on all right without it all his life, and if this was the result it certainly wasn't doing him any good!

In the police cell he developed a severe cough and was taken to the military hospital for treatment; but when the doctor (who had been his pupil years before at Achimota) said that he ought to be admitted there he was sent instead to the notorious "special block" at Nsawam Medium Security Prison. It was seventeen days since his arrest. He was still not served with a warrant or detention order. Being a lawyer, Willie Ofori-Atta had no illusions about the nature of Nkrumah's prisons.

35

Preventive detention was theoretically for a maximum of five years but several detainees had already been in longer than that.

Modesto Apaloo and Reggie Amponsah, for instance, had been suspected in 1958 of trying to import military insignia which could be used to impersonate army officers. They had never brought such insignia into Ghana, and it was so difficult to find any evidence against them that they were at length lured to a meeting place by false messages purporting to come from each other; then they were arrested, accused of conspiring to overthrow the government, and held for five years under the Preventive Detention Act. In 1963, shortly before they were due to be released, the National Assembly approved an amendment to the Act:

Notwithstanding the provisions of section 2 of this Act, the President may, at any time before the expiration of an order under that section, direct that the period of the detention authorized by that order be extended for a further period not exceeding five years if in his opinion the release of the person detained would be prejudicial to the matters specified in paragraphs (a), (b) or (c) of subsection 2 of this Act.

—which is just a lawyer's obscure way of saying that the Government may lock you up permanently, perhaps until you die, as Obetsibi-Lamptey had done.

When news of the Act reached Reggie Amponsah in the prison at Cape Coast Castle his worst fears were confirmed. Nkrumah was said to have declared he would never release "R R". Reggie thought of his wife, trying to live a normal life without him. It was even harder for her than for him.

Supposing Nkrumah were still in power after the second five years, he thought to himself, was he justified in expecting his wife to go on leading a single life? He might as well be dead as far as the love or help he could give her was concerned.

He must write her a letter. He shuddered at the thought of it, but it seemed the only thing to do: he would write offering to release her from her obligation to him, if she so wished. When the Director of Prisons next visited the jail Reggie told him what he planned to do.

"Don't write that letter," said Abban. "If, you do, you will kill her!" In the past five years, unknown to Reggie, his wife had often been in Abban's office, pleading for permission to see her husband, but Abban had strict orders not to allow it. He understood the wife's feelings even better than Reggie himself. Abban knew Reggie Amponsah intimately, too. More than once when he visited his cell he had found him in prayer. "I know you are a Christian," said Abban. "You believe in God. You had better just keep on praying."

Modesto Apaloo's reaction, in Ussher Fort, Accra, was different. He had made a habit of daily prayer throughout the period of his imprisonment, but when the fifth anniversary of his detention passed and he was not released, he gave up praying to be set free. So Danquah, Ofori-Atta, and the other new detainees knew exactly what was involved when they entered the gates of Nsawam Medium Security Prison. They might be released after six months, as some had been, or they might remain in detention for the rest of their lives.

The building was clean and modern and comprised ten cells on the ground floor and ten upstairs. Danquah was installed in Cell 9 up above. Ako Adjei, Tawia Adamafio, and Cofie Crabbe were in adjacent cells. On the ground floor, anonymous behind doors of the corridor down which William Ofori-Atta was now led, were Madjitey, the former commissioner of police, Amaning, one of his two deputies, and three politicians of the former opposition party. Other cells were occupied by condemned murderers.

Ofori-Atta was admitted to No 6, down landing—or rather, he *became* No 6, for at Nsawam you are no longer William Ofori-Atta Esq, BA (Cambridge), Barrister-at-law: you are not even plain Detainee Ofori-Atta: nor can you rejoice in nicknames like "Duke of Wa", as he had when he was imprisoned at Wa by the colonial Governor in 1948 following the shootings and riots of that year: you are reduced to a mere number. You are just a bundle of flesh and bones, contained in a sack of skin. Provided

37

that the skin is kept clean and the heart continues to beat, the authorities are satisfied.

The door was locked behind him, and No 6 looked about him and took stock of his new situation. His clothes, shoes, and personal belongings, including his spectacles, had been taken away. In their place they had given him a prison cloth to wear, his sole article of clothing, by day or by night. The cell contained no furniture, indeed it was so small that there was no room for much furniture; but he had two blankets to spread on the cement floor, a small pillow, and a chamber pot in the corner, without a cover.

First thing every morning the doors were unlocked and the prisoners were one by one escorted out by a warder to empty their chamber pots. They were not allowed to speak to one another. Prisoners were forbidden to stand while another prisoner was passing down the veranda outside.

Breakfast consisted of a pot of *koko*—light corn porridge—and two cubes of sugar. Towards mid-day each prisoner was taken to the shower to have his bath; as No 6 handled the block of cheap yellow soap, and tried to make it lather, he briefly recollected the luxury of his tiled bathroom at home in Mataheko. He dried himself on one of the four or five towels provided for the ten detainees and condemned murderers, and was taken back to his cell. For the whole process he was allowed less than three minutes. Later the warder brought lunch: one could not know how much later, because watches were not allowed, and when warders mentioned the time it was always something "past"— perhaps "a quarter past"—but the hour was not mentioned. Meals consisted of stew containing one small cube of meat per man, with either rice, cassava, or a sour variety of kenkey. At every change of warder the prisoners were stripped naked—a simple enough operation as a cloth was their only dress—and the few contents of the cell were searched by the one coming on duty. Once a week each prisoner was weighed naked on a pair of scales on the veranda; warders shaved them weekly, first locking the prisoners' hands in handcuffs.

The only relaxation was reading, and Nkrumah restricted many of the 1,000 detainees to one book, the Bible, perhaps on Marx's contention that religion is the opiate of the people. Hundreds who previously had no time for this sort of thing now had months or years at their disposal and nothing else to do. Some gave up after reading a few pages. Others read on and came out of detention with their whole outlook on life changed as a result—including Willie Ofori-Atta.

As soon as the authorities consented to let him have his spectacles, No 6 resumed his interrupted programme of daily Bible study. A couple of weeks later he returned to Psalm 55 verse 22, the passage he had been studying on the morning of his arrest. This time instead of bringing comfort it brought ruthless condemnation. "Cast thy burden upon the Lord . . . he will not suffer the righteous to be moved . . ."—No 6, you cannot go on and on saying "cast thy burden upon the Lord"! You have to go further than that. The trouble with you, No 6, is that you are not righteous.

One by one, relentlessly and with awful completeness, No 6 saw the misdeeds of a lifetime pass before him; every act of selfishness, every surrender to temptation, all the occasions when his actions had done harm to another person. O my God, he whispered in his solitude, is that really what I'm like? He had expected detention to be unpleasant, but he had not prepared himself to be tortured by his own conscience. His limbs ached from the hardness of the cement floor all the time he sat or lay on his blanket. The solitude was gradually breaking down his reserves of defiance. Wasn't the physical and mental suffering enough? Why should he have to battle with a guilt complex too? He tried to comfort himself by reflecting that this was quite artificial, a mere psychological reaction to detention, perhaps a kind of religious mania. Then it gradually dawned on him that in the recollection of his sins he had seen reality—this moment of truth would have come before if he had not deliberately run away from it into a hectic round of duty and pleasure; the deeds he was recalling were not inventions, they were sober fact. If anything was artificial, it was the way he had for many years been suppressing those memories.

Now that social life and business activity, name, and reputation, had all been stripped away from him, No 6 came face to face with his God. For the next two days he was plunged into a depth of misery that transcended the austere cell and the callousness of those who had detained him.

Then he saw a vision of Jesus Christ, hanging on the cross between the two criminals. One of them was struggling to speak. In the agony of death he managed to force out the words, "Jesus, remember me when you come in your kingdom!" The Master replied, "Today you will be with me in Paradise." William Ofori-Atta had known it very well in theory, but now it made sense to him. Jesus Christ died for sinners.

Next day he seized the Bible hungrily and turned again to Psalm 32:

Blessed is he whose transgression is forgiven, whose sin is covered...
When I declared not my sin, my body wasted away
through my groaning all day long . . .
I acknowledged my sin to thee,
and I did not hide my iniquity;
I said, "I will confess my transgressions to the Lord;"
then thou didst forgive the guilt of my sin.

If he could have written a diary of the past two days, he need have said no more than that.

NOTE
When this book was first published in 1969 by Ghana Publishing Corporation the editor, Mr David Zwart, an Australian, at first refused to print the above story of William Ofori-Atta and his sins. "It is libellous," said Mr Zwart, "and Mr Ofori-Atta is now Chairman of the Cocoa Marketing Board; we cannot put that in the book." As author, I insisted that this is what William Ofori-Atta said, and it was part of the manuscript. In the end Mr Zwart said he would not print it without "Paa Willie's" personal agreement.

Together we went to Mr Ofori-Atta's office on the top floor of Cocoa House, and David told Paa Willie that he objected to revealing his misdeeds in this way.

"Read the passage," said Paa Willie, and Mr Zwart read it.

"That's what I told Mr Barker," said the Chairman of the Cocoa Marketing Board; and he added, with a smile and a gesture heavenwards, "The glory belongs to God!"

It was the first time Mr Zwart had met the kind of Christian who is prepared to admit his faults publicly.

*   *   *

The harsh life to which the detainees were subjected was one of calculated cruelty, blatantly contravening prison regulations. Conditions varied, apparently with the President's whims. It was said that when he suspected detainees were being fed too well he gave verbal orders that they were to have smaller rations than other prisoners. Once their diet was limited to garri and water for a period.

The cells were six feet by nine in size, no bigger than an average bathroom. There were no windows, apart from small openings high up in the walls. In Ghana's tropical heat, confinement in such a place with the door shut was enough to break down both the body and the spirit of any ordinary man: and Danquah was 68 years old at the time of his detention. He immediately suffered a return of his old affliction, asthma.

But Danquah's spirit was not broken. In April he began to prepare a characteristically vigorous and witty petition to Nkrumah asking to be released. He wrote it sitting on the floor, trying to keep the paper steady on his knees as the phrases came from his pen. The effort brought on an additional distress: he became lame in one leg.

"It arose", he afterwards wrote, "out of my having to sit upon the floor to read draft petitions, and to correct them, with my legs crossed or spread out or bent under my body as fakirs and others do in the East. I had to do that because there was no chair, nor, at the time, a bed in the cell, nor, of course, a table.

41

During the period of my lameness I was compelled to limp to the bathroom on my one good foot, dragging the other with me, to empty my latrine pan, which I held in one hand, and to collect water for drinking in my jug, which I held in the other hand. (There was no question of a walking stick to help.)"[5]

When at last the petition was ready, on 23 May, it started on its slow progress through the tortuous corridors of officialdom, from the prison offices at Nsawam to the Director of Prisons in Accra, and thence to the Ministry of the Interior. It did not reach Nkrumah's desk till 3 July. In a covering letter the Director of Prisons said:

2. As regards the petitioner's complaint at page 4, the Prison Medical Officer, Nsawam, comments as follows: "The above-named special prisoner has never been suffering from any serious disease for which he could be admitted to the Prison Hospital. The Medical Officer has been regularly visiting the special block and also visiting whenever he is called to see any of the prisoners kept there. The above-named prisoner has been seen almost a dozen of times for his vague signs and symptoms, and always been given proper treatment. The question of hospitalisation arises only when actually a patient needs it. In this case the above-named prisoner does not need hospitalisation."

3. Reference the post-script at page 9, the Assistant Director of Prisons, Nsawam, observes that "Regarding the petitioner's statement that he broke his two upper teeth in his attempt to chew what he termed 'tough meat' given to him, I have observed that two of the petitioner's upper teeth which supported his denture are out of the gums and petitioner is thereby unable to use his denture. The Medical Officer informs me that this was caused by nature as petitioner is old. According to the Medical Officer a dentist will soon be available in the Prison who will attend to dental cases."[6]

Despite the Director's promise, it is uncertain whether Dr Danquah was attended to by a dentist right up to the end of his detention.

Danquah's petition eventually reached the desk of the President of Ghana. To Nkrumah's astonishment the theme of the petition was neither penitence nor pleading but sheer boredom:

Dear Dr Nkrumah,

I am tired of being in prison on preventive detention with no opportunity to make original or any contribution to the progress and development of the country, and I therefore respectfully write to beg, and appeal to you, to make an order for my release and return home . . . You will recall that when in 1948 we were arrested by the British Government and sent to the North for detention they treated us as gentlemen, and not as galley slaves, and provided each of us with a furnished bungalow (two or three rooms) with a garden, together with opportunity for reading and writing. In fact I took with me my typewriter and papers for that purpose, and Ako Adjei also did the same, and there was ample opportunity for correspondence. Here, at Nsawam, for the four months of my detention up to date (8th January to 9th May 1964), I have not been allowed access to any books and papers, except the Bible . . . I am . . . required to sleep or keep lying down on the blankets and a small pillow for the whole 24 hours of the day and night except for a short period of about five minutes in the morning to empty and wash out my latrine pan, and of about ten to fifteen minutes at noon to go for a bath. I am occasionally allowed to do a short exercise in the sun say once a week for about half an hour.

That is all I have been engaged on for four months with any talents, such as I possess, going to waste and my health being undermined and my life endangered by various diseases without being allowed to be taken to the Prison Hospital for continuous observation and treatment.[7]

In conclusion Danquah named three manuscripts on which he was working and which he wished to complete for publication: *The Ghana Doctrine of Man*, research into the dual family system of the Akan people; *The Elements of Ghana Culture*, a collection of lectures and essays on national origins and links with ancient Ghana; and *Sacred Days in Ghana*, dealing in particular with the traditional Akan calendar of a seven-day week.

Just a few days before the petition reached Nkrumah Dr. Danquah was facing subtle tortures of mind and body which even Nkrumah himself had not anticipated—Danquah who had been described as long ago as 1948 as the "doyen of Gold Coast politics", Danquah the scholar, Danquah the lawyer, Danquah who had had the courage to contest the presidential election of 1960, though he knew well that all the odds were stacked against him. This Danquah had become a play-thing of illiterate prison warders.

A E Inkumsah, who was in charge of the Ministry of the Interior during part of Danquah's detention, wrote thus of his own imprisonment three years later:

. . . the prison officers have been regimented in a particular way of drastically treating prisoners so as to cow them down. The moment you enter the prison yard, you are regarded as a convict and a nonentity. Everybody is reduced to a low level and regarded as faeces . . . The administration in the prison there is also very poor indeed: every prison officer trying to demonstrate whatever authority he has, often ending in contrary orders being given here and there which result in abuses and fighting between prison officers and inmates . . . [8]

Thus it came about that on 30 June 1964 Danquah complained to a senior prison officer, Mr Agbale, that Mr Sagoe had a day or so earlier ignored his request for the usual exercise in the sun. Sagoe was near by and retorted, "He is under punishment and should not be taken out for exercises".

"Shut up!" said Danquah, forgetting for a moment where he was.

Those two simple words, perfectly understandable under the circumstances, unleashed a torrent of abuse from the junior warders, particularly one Sergeant Dogo Moshie, who had long been threatening to put Danquah in chains. "You abuse Prison Superintendent?", cried the poor fellow: "today I go chain you!" But let Danquah give his own account of the incident, as he subsequently recorded it in a written statement to the Assistant Director of Prisons:

Dogo Moshie . . . returned with the irons in the hands of one Halidu Wangara, a biggish type of man. I believe this man was that day on duty at the Down Landing and that Dogo Moshie brought him up especially to do the chaining. Dogo opened my cell and entered with Halidu, and a large number of warders followed them to my cell, and some stood at the door. I stood up when Dogo entered. He told me to sit down. I said, "Well, the big man has come to my cell, and so I must stand up". They all shouted "Sit down". I was forced down with my legs towards the entrance (east) and my head across my blankets on the floor at the west wall. Dogo said, "Why you tell Prison Superintendent 'Shut up'? I go chain you today. Go on. Put the chains on him!" . . . Thereupon Halidu took hold of my legs, assisted by other warders ready to chain me.

I struggled with Halidu Wangara. At the same time Dogo was kneeling by my side, and I asked him: "Have you the authority of the Assistant Director of Prisons or the Director to chain me?" To this he replied with an answer which seemed to me to be a display of sharp native wit. He said, "Did you get the Director's permission before you told Prison Superintendent to shut up?"

That was cleverly said, I thought, but the struggle was going on with Halidu and he was meeting great resistance from me. But, before I knew where I was, Corporal Olukuma, who was standing near Halidu, noticed that he was finding it difficult to put the leg irons on my legs, so he said to Halidu: "Oh, you don't know how to do it? This sort of thing is easy work for me. Give me the chains." Upon saying this he took over from Halidu and with great force clapped the chains on my left leg, followed soon by action on the right leg. I had not, in the meantime, given up the struggle, but I noticed that my hands were not in action. They were in the firm grip, beyond my head, of Mr Asare, who had thereby pinned my hands down. I tried to force my hands out of his grip but I felt his tight hold at my chest and could not breathe freely. I moaned, "My chest, my chest. My asthma. I am dying!" for my chest had become very tight, as in an attack of asthma.

By this time Olukuma had finished with me. Asare, seeing that it was all over, left my hands, and I stood up in leg irons, both feet. There was a sort of big noise in the entire premises. I was locked up and many of the warders stood in the corridor jeering at me.

I was so kept in chains, both feet, till I was called upon to come for my bath, at about one o'clock. Sergeant Dogo Moshie . . . with the help of Corporal Olukuma, removed the chains from my legs.[9]

During a subsequent enquiry every single man denied having done it. Only the Assistant Director of Prisons, Mr Baiden, who was in charge of Nsawam Prison at that time, believed Danquah's story and said so in his report on the case.

From August onwards Danquah began to suffer acute attacks of asthma at night. On each occasion a nurse had to be summoned from the prison hospital by telephone, often arriving after a long delay. On 8 November Danquah asked the doctor to ask the government to transfer him to the prison hospital. "Oh no," said the doctor, "I cannot write to the President." The significance of the remark was not lost on Danquah, who commented in the petition which he completed at the end of that month:

The fact that the Medical Officer in this connection mentioned "the President" and not simply "the Government" clarified the position for me, that this question of whether or not to remove a detainee from the "Special

46

Block" to the Prison Hospital is one of special concern or interest to your Excellency personally.[10]

Nkrumah's solicitude for his prisoners had in fact resulted in slight improvements in their conditions. From May onwards both Danquah and Ofori-Atta had their cell doors left open from 6.00 am to 5.30 pm daily and each was allowed to receive monthly visits from his wife. In June Danquah was granted a pair of sandals "to guard my feet, left naked for four months" as he put it in a later petition.[11] In September he was given an iron bed; Ofori-Atta got his two months later. Then both were issued with pyjamas, after eleven months without.

23 December 1964: Twelve months since the Act enabling Nkrumah to quash decisions of the special court (a power that he had never used since and was never to need again): another twelve months of government without accountability to a democratic assembly, with Nkrumah still more firmly in control and the security service beginning to function efficiently at last.

The referendum on the one-party state had been held in January, shortly after Danquah and Ofori-Atta had been detained; the apathetic electorate had looked on helplessly as the CPP hailed results that no one took seriously: the government claimed that in five of Ghana's eight regions not a single vote had been cast against their proposals.

The police had been entirely disarmed. Somehow Harlley had survived his first year as Commissioner of Police, but he felt he was clinging to his post for dear life. The Special Branch had been cut off from the police as planned, and now formed part of the security service. Deku had been pulled out of it—a waste of sixteen years' experience—and in his place Ben Fordjoe was making an attempt to master the filing system and hold together an effective staff.

23 December 1964: Ofori-Atta had asked for pencil and paper to make notes on his Bible study. At the same time he had asked his wife to bring copies of *Matthew Henry's commentary*, the *New Bible Handbook*, and *Search the Scriptures*, a guide to daily Bible study. On 23 December she brought the news that his request had been refused.

47

It was a heavy blow, and as soon as his wife left Ofori-Atta slumped down on his iron bed with his head in his hands. Outside, the world was engaged in another mad Christmas rush, forgetting the Babe of Bethlehem. In the quiet of his cell he prayed that by some miracle he might get access to those precious books after all. Next evening, 24 December, at seven o'clock, Ofori-Atta was set free. Nearly a thousand other detainees spent Christmas in jail, including Danquah, whose November petition revealed a lawyer's acute awareness of the wrong that was being done to him:

I am fully conscious, Your Excellency, that it was under a law ... called Preventive Detention Act, ... that I was committed to Cell 9 of the "'Special Block'" of the Nsawam Prison, and the several maladies I have contracted, or from which I have suffered, therefore, come wholly within Your Excellency's jurisdiction. They are sufferings which affect a far greater thing than my liberty, namely, my life, since it was in restraining my liberty that my life is endangered. Your Excellency has the power and authority to release me from the commitment, to enable me to seek cure and avert the danger to my life in the right atmosphere. What I need is really a free guarantee of my life as a citizen of Ghana, a guarantee which is already seriously endangered by my commitment to a cell of the "Special Block", condemned by the medical authorities here as prejudicing my health, and in consequence, my life.[12]

About the same time his former wife, Mabel Dove, one of the CPP's leading journalists, had written to Nkrumah begging for Danquah's release:

. . . About 30 years ago a man said to me, "You write charming letters; I am sure you could write a column". That was how I wrote the Marjorie Mensah articles, other articles in Nigeria and Sierra Leone, and short stories abroad. That man was Dr Danquah. He will be seventy this month[13] and today he is in a narrow cell in Nsawam prison . . . Though that compliment of long ago laid the foundation of my writing career, I have never been able to help Dr Danquah politically with my writing talent, and I remember attacking him once when I sat for a short time in the editorial chair of the Accra *Evening News*. Today, Mr President, I want you to help me to pay my debt to someone who gave me confidence to write ...

It is in the interests of Ghana to take consideration of Dr Danquah's age and his health. He suffers from asthma—a choking sensation when the patient finds it difficult to breathe; when I think of him having an attack in that narrow cell without the asthma powder to inhale I feel I am in a way responsible ...

Now, Mr President, I close this letter with the full hope that my appeal will not be in vain and the Christmas season will unite father, wife, and children. A happy Christmas and a prosperous new year in advance.

Yours sincerely,
Mabel Dove

Nkrumah's reply was brief and sombre:

Dear Miss Dove,

I have only today received your letter dated 6 December. The appeal you make in this letter does not move me a bit. It rather incenses me. I am glad you are not a politician—I am sorry that I am; but remember that I am a human being.

If this matter is what you want to see me about, there is no need for you to have an interview with me. I have passed on your other suggestions to the appropriate quarters.

With best wishes for a happy Christmas and a prosperous new year.

Yours sincerely,
Kwame Nkrumah [14]

3

THE CPP DECLINES;
DANQUAH DIES IN PRISON

AT THE beginning of 1965 Kwame Nkrumah was still firmly in power, but the party that had put him there so successfully was getting weary. The "dynamic CPP" depended for its dynamism firstly on the keenness of hundreds of branches up and down the country, and secondly on the fact that Nkrumah used it both as an organ of policy and as a means of intimidating his opponents. During the past few years both of these sources of energy had dried up. Intimidation was effectively carried out by the security forces with the extended Preventive Detention Act behind them; Nkrumah had swung back to the civil service rather than the Party for the execution of government policy; since Kulungugu and the bomb-throwing scare which followed it, few local branches had maintained their early zeal for rallies and public demonstrations.

Take, for example, Ward 16, Accra. Up to 1962 this branch had an attendance of over 200 at the weekly general meeting in a large classroom at New Era School. Ward 16 included both the mud-wall slums opposite Accra lorry park, and the sophisticated Ridge—comfortable bungalows built on concrete stilts in the 1920s to keep empire-builders cool and healthy, but now occupied by their Ghanaian successors.

The CPP Ward meeting was an impressive cross-section of Ghanaian life, even if the classrooms of New Era School hardly

50

made a sufficiently impressive background. It used to be held one evening every week. The members gathered at seven thirty: there was the Hausa trader who lived in a simple mud house but was richer than many civil servants, notwithstanding their smart suits and radiograms; he turned up in flowing robes dispensing waves of perfume, straight from his evening prayers to Allah: the clerks and typists, Quarshie who worked at the Ministry of Education, Risberg of the Ghana National Construction Corporation, and his sister Emily: the market women, always careful to bring their membership cards (for if you paid up two or three years in advance and showed the District Commissioner pages full of "red cockerel" stamps at three shillings each he would surely give preference to your application for a permit to sell akpeteshie, home-distilled gin): then there were the senior civil servants including some heads of departments, once even the secretary to the cabinet himself.

Ward 16 had a prize that no other branch could boast: a real live Englishman, a minister of the Anglican church too: the Rev Arthur Howarth, chaplain of the Ridge Church, who had to be pushed in by his Nigerian servant in a wheel chair because he was paralysed from the waist down. He would beam benevolently in all directions, calling everybody "My dear", and quote profoundly (to those who could understand what it was all about) from the latest number of *L'Osservatore Romano,* a Catholic periodical from Rome.

The proceedings invariably started with a prayer. Then the minutes were read in English, followed by seemingly interminable translations into Ga, Twi, and Hausa. After "matters arising", they dealt with new business—a circular letter from Party Headquarters, a picnic to be held at Tema, or plans for a big function at which all the ladies must appear in their Party uniform. Then there would be a talk on some aspect of the political struggle, or on the intentions of the imperialists, and the meeting would end with hearty handshakes and perhaps the singing of the party song, "There is victory for us".

All that changed after the bomb-throwing incidents of August and September 1962. One never knew where the next attempt would be. People felt insecure at gatherings of as many as 200 CPP supporters; attendance at branch meetings in many parts of the country dropped sharply and never recovered. In Ward 16, membership dues were no longer collected with the usual efficiency, rallies were not held, and but for a fearless nucleus of fifteen or twenty stalwarts the branch would have ceased to exist altogether.

The situation in the Party branches might have been saved if Nkrumah himself had not deserted the CPP. In the early days of independence Nkrumah had looked on the Party whose sincere political activity had put him in power as the backbone of the nation. The civil service, on the other hand, was a creation of the imperialists: it perpetuated ways of thinking that might be appropriate in the British government offices of Whitehall but not in fast-developing tropical Africa. He put professional administrators in their place with a hurtful aphorism: "We want civil servants," he had said, back in 1957, "not civil masters".

Wherever Nkrumah came across bureaucratic masters cloaking their urge to dominate with suave British civility he ignored them and set up his own organizations. "Red-tapism" became a dirty word; adherence to formalities, procedures, and committee decisions only clogged the wheels of progress. Thus when the Ministry of Education would not open new schools on a party political basis, Nkrumah put funds into an independent Party organization, the Ghana Educational Trust, and built new schools whenever and wherever he wanted. When local officials of the various ministries would not do what he wanted in the regions, he reinforced the once-hated office of district commissioner, and appointed Party men as DCs throughout the land.

The British "district commissioner" of colonial days was sometimes a boy straight from university; occasionally he made a serious attempt to understand the life and language of the people he administered; often he acted with a wise and benevolent paternalism; but he was hated by every African politician because he could not be limited by any kind of democratic control. Magistrate and town clerk, arbitrator of

52

other people's disputes, and keeper of the prison, the autocrat with the khaki shorts and the foreign culture could never become a popular figure. Yet without any attempt to disguise what he was doing, Nkrumah called the local representatives of his own administration by the same old title, District Commissioner.

Nkrumah discovered that although the wheels of bureaucracy turned slowly, in the end one was better off with a level-headed civil servant in the British tradition, who would reluctantly do three-quarters of what you wanted, than with a political enthusiast who was anxious to please but not very competent and all too often proved to be dishonest. Within a few years Nkrumah swung back in despair from the Party to the civil service.

He allowed the new secondary schools established by the Ghana Educational Trust to come under the control of the Ministry of Education once again, and left the DCs to their fate as one after another fell foul of the law and were convicted of embezzlement, blackmail, obtaining money under false pretences, and other similar offences.

After Kulungugu Nkrumah lost faith in politicians. Formerly he had been close to Cofie Crabbe, and had given him the key post of executive secretary of the Party; Adamafio had been his ideological right-hand man. Now he turned against the whole tribe of politicians, and his advisers were Oxford-trained civil servants like Alex Quaison-Sackey, Ghana's permanent representative at the United Nations, and T K Impraim, who had fought in Burma in World War 2 and was one of the first Africans to receive the King's commission as an officer in the British army.

Early in 1964 the massive Party Headquarters near the National Museum was in a state of sad confusion. Incoming mail averaged 40 or 50 letters a day; outgoing mail averaged 40 or 50 letters a month—the great majority of communications addressed to the dynamic CPP were scarcely looked at. Both of the lifts were out of order, and those who worked on the top floor had to sweat up four flights of steps. A stock of blank membership cards was lying in a store room, on the top floor; some had been spoiled by water, all were getting dusty, faded, and creased. When new cards were wanted, someone approached the pile, sorted some out at random, and retired quickly.

The CPP still had extensive powers, and the fact that one could not get the Party to reply to letters was often very inconvenient. Nkrumah was general secretary, Welbeck had succeeded Cofie Crabbe as executive secretary, and he had one deputy; but around these three men was a maze of some fifteen committees, sections, and bureaux, several with overlapping functions, none of them subject to any clearly defined chain of command. Welbeck was the only man who had authority to make policy decisions and, since there was far more business than one man could handle, in practice every man did exactly as he liked.

Appointments were made without any attempt to assess qualifications and ability, or to standardize terms and salary scales. This led to jealousy and attempts by some to boost their own importance. For instance there was a dispute between the regional party secretaries and the regional party education secretaries who were in theory subordinate to them. Some of the latter had formerly worked at Party Headquarters and still drew over C1,800 per annum, plus car and travel allowances, which was as much as the regional party secretaries themselves were paid, in some cases more. As a result they would not take orders from their regional bosses.

Then the education secretaries crossed swords with the party propaganda secretaries at headquarters and in the regions; the propaganda secretaries were always interfering in party education matters. The existence of an information and publicity bureau, with responsibilities overlapping into both of the other departments, added further to the confusion. In the end the civil servants were forced to mount a rescue operation to save the CPP from collapse. The old world of red-tapism was called in to redress the monumental incompetence of the Party.

Impraim, deputy secretary to the cabinet, one of Ghana's top civil servants, was on friendly terms with Welbeck, the executive secretary of the CPP, so he began with humorous remarks about delay in dealing with correspondence. Welbeck enjoyed a joke, even at his own expense, and Impraim was encouraged to take it a step further.

"Have you heard of the O and M people?"

"What does O and M stand for?"

"Organization and Methods—it's a department under the Office of the President: Bentil runs it. They deal in work efficiency and so on."

"Time and motion study?"

"Yes, work study as it affects administration, and all that kind of thing. You should call them in to have a look at the Party offices!"—and the two of them laughed until their sides ached at the thought of it.

A few days later, as Impraim had hoped, Welbeck returned to the subject in a more serious mood. The O and M people came in, carried out a study, and produced a confidential report. They recommended regrouping the maze of Party activities into three new bureaux with their own secretaries, each responsible to Welbeck but each competent to make policy decisions within his own field.

The report was accepted, and in June 1964 a senior civil servant, D K Ntosuoh, was appointed secretary of the general administrative bureau: S K Tandoh became secretary of the party organization bureau: and Kweku Akwei secretary of the education and information bureau. Ntosuoh was the only one of the three who really understood the meaning of administration.

So the formidable CPP, once the effective voice of the Ghanaian people, settled into honourable retirement as a kind of minor government department ruled over by a civil servant. A year later when Welbeck became Minister of Party Propaganda the post of executive secretary was abolished. The triumph of bureaucracy over political enthusiasm was complete.

Many others combined loyalty to Nkrumah with administrative efficiency. A few miles up the road, at the offices of the Special Branch, Ben Fordjoe, a keen member of the choir at Calvary Methodist Church, was struggling to maintain the traditions left by Harlley and Deku, but with this difference: Harlley and Deku knew the truth about Nkrumah; Ben Fordjoe still passionately believed that Nkrumah was incorruptible, and saw it as his mission to vindicate the President and the good name of Ghana by putting an end to the evil of bribes, "ten per cent", and favouritism in high places.

There seemed to be good reasons for believing Nkrumah was honest. When Kofi Baako's father-in-law, Yaw Boahene, had been found making arrangements to forge Ghana currency notes, had Nkrumah not allowed the case to go on, even though Kofi Baako made every effort to stop it? The recent import licence scandal was even more conclusive: had not the President appointed Mr Justice Akainyah to enquire into these irregularities, and when he reported[15] that Assistant Commissioner of Police Owusu-Sekyere had taken a bribe of £5,000 from Mr. Vashi, an Indian merchant, had not Owusu-Sekyere been removed from the service? Ben Fordjoe could not foresee that Mr Justice Ollennu, reporting a few years later on further import licence irregularities, would say: "I find that the house of Mrs Akainyah was a clearing house for illegal transactions, bribery and corruption in connection with import licences."[16]

Ben Fordjoe innocently made it his ambition to catch the really big fish, cabinet ministers, those who were closest to the President; if one or two of these people were convicted for corruption and Nkrumah did not intervene to protect them, others would also fear to practise these things.

There was that clown Ambrose Yankey, for instance; he was influential, but still he was a standing joke around Flagstaff House. He was famous for his periodical trips to Guinea to consult "Kankan Nyame", the priest of a small town in the north-east of that country. Whenever he returned he brought a list of do's and don'ts for Nkrumah's benefit: "Trust this man . . . Don't trust that man. . ." No doubt Ambrose Yankey actually visited the priest; no doubt he believed in the power of the god; but what is certain is that he always advertised these visits well ahead of his departure, so that ministers, parliamentarians, and party officials who wanted to be on the right side of Kankan Nyame's list had the opportunity to secure his favour by a generous donation.

Ambrose Yankey's antics were bringing the name of Osagyefo himself into disrepute; people said he could get away with anything because he gave part of the bribes to Nkrumah. But if Nkrumah showed that he was prepared to check bribery even if Ambrose Yankey himself were the culprit—why, that would make Ben Fordjoe's job so much easier.

Early in February 1965 two Lebanese merchants came to the Special Branch to complain that Ambrose Yankey junior, son of the President's close adviser, had for a long time been blackmailing them and demanding £2,000. At first they had put the young man off with vague promises, but now they began to fear that he would do them some harm; and Ambrose Yankey junior had said they must pay the money that very night.

The two Lebanese were welcomed into an office at the Special Branch and told their story. "But please, I beg you," said one of the Lebanese, "don't tell Mr Harlley or Mr Fordjoe. Ambrose Yankey said if they hear about the case it is all up—finish—we go back to Lebanon. So please, don't tell Mr Fordjoe. You promise me?

Ben Fordjoe smiled back across the desk. It was small wonder that they did not recognize him as the head of the Special Branch. When he had realized someone was waiting outside he had got up himself to bring them into the office: that was his usual habit—a strange one for a head of department—but for once it had gained him an important advantage. If the enquiry had gone to one of his subordinates it might never have reached him.

"I'm Mr Fordjoe," he said, "but you need not worry."

"You won't deport us?"

"We shall look into your own offence, but I have no doubt that Ambrose Yankey's blackmail is a more serious crime than anything you have done."

"Then what shall we do tonight?"

"Go to meet young Ambrose, and ask for a reduction and more time to pay. But you can promise to pay him something if he will come to your house tomorrow. We will arrest him and you will get your money back." Two Lebanese faces shone with relief on the other side of the desk. Ben Fordjoe sprang to his feet with his customary agility and had opened the door to let them out almost before they had thanked him.

They made an appointment with Ambrose Yankey junior for two o'clock next afternoon. A squad of the Special Branch were in hiding all round the house when the young man arrived with a friend. After some realistic bargaining the Lebanese parted with £500 and the two young Ghanaians walked out into the arms of the Special Branch, who arrested them and seized the notes. Back at the office they were still taking their statements when Ambrose Yankey senior drove into the yard and started shouting angrily, "Where's Ben Fordjoe? My God, the President shall hear of this. What the hell does that rat Fordjoe think he's doing?"

He got into Fordjoe's office and for once the head of the Special Branch remained seated. There were no greetings.

"Why was my son arrested?" he stormed. "I sent my son out on duty and you arrested him. What the hell do you mean by it?"

"All right," said Fordjoe, quietly. "You let me have your report on the incident and I'll take action. But you know the law is no respecter of persons."

"No!" barked Yankey. "Don't tell me that. You let him go!"

"I am not prepared to."

"Then he must be released on bail."

"That will depend on the investigation. I've had no report yet. When I get it I'll decide whether to agree to bail or not."

Ambrose Yankey swept out as unceremoniously as he had entered, and as he was leaving he caught sight of his son by the door. He seized him by the arm, dragged him into his own car, and drove off, leaving the men of the Special Branch in dumb confusion. If one had to choose between offending either Ambrose Yankey or Ben Fordjoe, Ambrose Yankey would certainly be the more dangerous and the more unscrupulous enemy.

Ben Fordjoe sent his most reliable men after the younger Ambrose, with orders to bring him back even from the inmost citadel of Flagstaff House: but to their amazement the arrest presented no problems; they met him on his way back to the Special Branch to fetch his car, which had been impounded at the Lebanese merchant's house. This time he was locked up safely and Fordjoe rang the law officers to arrange for the case to go before the court early next morning.

Next morning Ben Fordjoe had a committee meeting in town, so he took the precaution of going straight there lest he should find instructions to drop the case awaiting him at the Special Branch. Sure enough, messages and phone calls from Flagstaff House soon began to reach his desk. But by this time Ben Fordjoe was sitting at the offices of Ghana Prisons, trying to take an intelligent part in the proceedings of a routine meeting, but all the time glancing down at the minute hand of his watch, and trusting the speed of the law officers and the inertia of the telephone system to land Ambrose Yankey junior in jail. The Special Branch telephonist tracked him down at about nine o'clock: could he please come to the office—he was wanted urgently by Flagstaff House.

He took leave of the meeting and made for the Special Branch, taking care not to exceed the speed limit on the way. He found that the worst had happened: Nkrumah himself had ordered that the case should be dropped. Then the President in whom he had trusted so implicitly was protecting people like Ambrose Yankey after all; if so, his job held no more interest for him—he might as well throw it in straight away. He rang the attorney-general and asked him to drop the case. Kwaw Swanzy promised to do so, but now it was nine-thirty and the case had been heard: the magistrate had remanded Ambrose Yankey in custody, and bail had been refused.

The President appointed a committee to go into the case, and it recommended that in the interests of the service, and to prevent further scandal, the case should go on. Ben Fordjoe dared to hope that right would triumph after all. By this time Nkrumah was on holiday in his home district, Half Assini— fifteen days of fasting and meditation, the *Ghanaian Times* called it. The report of the committee went to him and back came the reply: "Don't carry on with the case till the President returns". Next day Ben Fordjoe had another message: "Set Ambrose Yankey junior free".

It was hard to believe that the messages were genuine. Ambrose Yankey senior was down at Half Assini with the President and could easily have sent them in Nkrumah's name. Ben Fordjoe had to ask for an adjournment, but he determined not to withdraw the case till he had confirmation from Nkrumah himself. Next Monday he got a copy of a letter from the President's Office to the director of public prosecutions, ordering the case to be withdrawn for security reasons.

Nkrumah returned to Accra after his fast and meditation and Ben Fordjoe used his prerogative as head of one of the branches of the security service to seek an interview with him at the Castle. "I believe it was very unwise to withdraw the case against Ambrose Yankey, sir," he began. "The Special Branch arrested him and we should have been consulted before he was released. If we don't observe that procedure we shall all be in confusion."

Nkrumah sat behind his desk gazing out of the window at the blue sea. "Your boys were mistaken," said Nkrumah briefly. "I have investigated the case myself—I investigated it personally."

"How did you do that, sir?"

Ben Fordjoe knew instinctively that he had gone too far. No one likes to justify himself in front of a subordinate. "You are wrong, Fordjoe; you are wrong. You'd better be very careful!"— and with that the interview ended.

The following Tuesday Nkrumah called the heads of the security service to make an announcement to them:

"I have decided that there must be a reorganization: at the moment it seems the various departments do not know their proper assignments; the Special Branch has been doing the work of the CID and vice versa. I want it to be clear that in future the Special Branch should concentrate on the jobs they have been given." They left Nkrumah's office and gathered to discuss the situation.

"I'm afraid you've had it," said Eric Otoo to Fordjoe. "The Old Man has instructed that you hand over to Owusu-Sekyere, and he has transferred you to the State Functions Secretariat." There was consternation all round. They all knew what that meant: the State Functions Secretariat came directly under the President's Office, and if Ben Fordjoe went there Ambrose Yankey would soon arrange his downfall. They decided on the perilous course of going back to Nkrumah and asking him to reconsider his decision.

For a moment they watched the President's reactions with bated breath. He was capable of losing his temper and dismissing them all on the spot. The attempt to thwart Nkrumah's will could end up in Fordjoe going straight to Nsawam—two blankets, prison cloth, and chamber pot in the corner. What was going on behind that familiar profile?

Nkrumah took it quietly. "All right," he said; "then let Fordjoe hand over the Special Branch to Eric Otoo. Then he can go on leave and I'll think about letting him return to the police." They heaved a sigh of relief and the meeting broke up for the second time. A few days later Owusu-Sekyere was installed as head of the Special Branch.

*　　　　*　　　　*

Nkrumah's most illustrious detainee, the lion-hearted Dr J B Danquah, was still busy penning letters and petitions from his narrow cell in Nsawam Medium Security Prison.

On 8 January 1965, the first anniversary of his detention, Danquah wrote a spirited attack on Nkrumah and his government, demanding immediate release and claiming £800,000 damages.

The situation . . . created by the President's failure or disinclination to allow me to be removed to a Hospital, together with the fact that I am not entitled to be attended by a medical man of my own choosing, tends to confirm the growing conviction that at the bottom of my imprisonment lurks an attempt or desire to damage my physical body and my mental equipment, even the salvation of my soul—or that those responsible for my imprisonment do not care if I experience such damage . . . I would say that any step taken by His Excellency the President and the Honourable Ministers and Members of the Ghana Government to make satisfactory amends in this matter will be considered an honourable act of Ghana's Government and in no sense humiliating to the nation, or to her sons and daughters wherever they may be. In my view the nation only becomes humiliated when in the face of an obvious fault her Government persists in bluffing at the facts.

I wish to assure you, Mr. President and Ministers and Members of the Government of Ghana, that I do not think that, from Ati to Nsoko, and from Half Assini to Jasikan, there is any person alive who loves Ghana more than I do. If need be I could claim a greater love for this Ghana than most Ghanaians of my acquaintance. For this and other reasons, namely that we love this land and nation of ours, I feel very strongly that we should not allow to be repeated in Ghana, in the twentieth century, the tragic misconception which led eighteenth century France into the débacle which eventually ushered in a revolution so unsparing in bloodshed as to make historians shudder even now to contemplate it. It all started with a misconception on the part of the King of France: "The State?" asked Louis XIV, King of France: "I *am* the State!"

In Ghana, of course, the position is different. No servant or officer of the State *is* the State. As we are a democracy, an "attack" or a criticism of any democratically elected or appointed person is not an attack on the state, or, to quote the words of the Grounds for Detention, it is not an "activity designed to endanger the security of the State". A false and grandiloquent enlargement of employees to be the equivalent of Mother Ghana is an illusion and should be banished from every one's imagination or thought.

But much the most serious misconception is the idea that a Preventive Detention Regulation, or Act, can be used to commit offenders or criminals to prison as if they had been convicted by a Court of Law. Unfortunately it is not alone the Executive Officers of the Government who are blameable for this widespread but wrongful idea. It is my view that the Supreme Court of Ghana, and also some of the High Courts of the land which have had to deal with *habeas corpus* applications under PDA are blameable for this abuse of preventive detention in any shape or form. This aspect of my letter can best be studied with the assistance of lawyers much practised in *habeas corpus* and detention cases, and who are prepared to study the English cases often cited by the High Courts and the Supreme Court in their interpretation of what should be done with a *habeas corpus* application.

Let this be illustrated with the judgement of the Supreme Court in Baffour Osei Akoto's appeal in his *habeas corpus* application in respect of an Order under the Preventive Detention Act . . . [17]

And then Danquah, after twelve months in a cell nine feet by six without access to any legal book, launched into a learned argument on this judgement, referring in detail to an English case cited in it and to the constitutional situation in war-time England.

This is the man—the writer of this letter—whom the Ministry of the Interior had examined by a psychiatrist on 29 January 1965. The psychiatrist wrote his report two days later: "Apart from hypertension of 220/120 there was nothing significant"— no, nothing significant from a psychiatric point of view. The mind was alert and powerful, disciplined in the school of suffering; cut off for a long, lonely year from stimulating company and intelligent conversation, yet still full of legal arguments and witty sayings. If the Ministry of the Interior had wanted to find a madman they should not have sent their psychiatrist to Cell 9.

Nothing significant—apart from dangerously high blood pressure, which when linked with chronic myocarditis, as it was in Danquah's case, can be fatal. Nothing significant, the psychiatrist might have added, except loss of weight: Danquah had lost 40 lb since being imprisoned a year earlier. Nothing except chronic bronchial asthma, which woke him up repeatedly in the middle of the night, and made him sweat and strain for breath till it felt as if the blood vessels would burst. Nothing significant as regard's Danquah's mind: but Danquah's body had been deliberately and systematically reduced to the point where every hour of life had become a gamble with death. With a weak heart and high blood pressure Danquah could easily succumb to an attack of asthma, a fall in the bathroom, or even a sudden emotion of anger or sorrow.

On 20 January Mrs Elizabeth Danquah was able to visit her husband after a gap of nearly three months. She had been told that Danquah had been writing "annoying letters" to the President, and she felt compelled to rebuke him for acting, as it seemed to her, against his own best interests. At the time when Danquah needed most of all the comfort that his wife alone could give him she was so distressed that the interview was extremely painful to them both.

*   *   *

On 4 February Mabel Dove, Danquah's former wife, rose early. Nine days before she had had a message from the President summoning her to an interview at 10 am. She guessed it was in connection with the recent letter she had sent to the President, requesting Danquah's release.

That same morning in the cells at Nsawam the usual routine was followed. At 6.15 Danquah was called from his cell and

64

marched to the bathroom to wash and brush his teeth. While he was out of the cell a prison officer entered to carry out a check on the contents. Instead of the usual cursory glance at his few belongings, the officer overturned the bedding, threw everything into confusion, and left several of Danquah's things, including his Bible, scattered untidily on the floor.

A few seconds later Danquah returned to see the state of his cell. The petty outrage was too much for him. He lost his temper and began to shout at the warders and prison officers. "Who did this?" he demanded. "You are a lot of cows and fools. . ." His voice rose and reverberated around the block. The other occupants wondered what was happening. Then Danquah's heart missed a beat.

Suddenly one of Ghana's greatest sons fell down across the narrow bed in the narrow cell, never to rise again.

*　　　　　*　　　　　*

Mabel Dove arrived at Flagstaff House promptly and was ushered into the Presidential presence. As she sat down by the President she noticed that he looked scruffy and that his eyes were bloodshot. Then he spoke, fixing those reddish eyes on his visitor.

"I have bad news for you. Can you take it? I feel I should be the one to tell you." "What is it?" she asked.

"Danquah died last night!" The announcement was sudden, dramatic, infinitely painful, like a knife thrust. Nkrumah quietly gazed at his visitor.

"Didn't I tell you to release him? Didn't I tell you to release him?" Mabel Dove burst out, fighting to keep back the tears.

"I see you are upset," said the President. "The interview is over." Mabel Dove stumbled away from Flagstaff House and took a taxi to Ghana News Agency to break the news to her son, the child of her marriage with Danquah. Through the tears she was conscious of a sinister thought: her interview had been fixed nine days before. Did Nkrumah know that Danquah would die before the interview? Or was it just a strange coincidence? [18]

65

Radio Ghana announced Danquah's death briefly in the one o'clock news. Next day the *Daily Graphic* and the *Ghanaian Times* carried the bare facts in small paragraphs tucked away in obscure corners; but those tiny reports moved the heart of the nation more deeply than a hundred pages of news or ideology. "J B" was dead.

*   *   *

Danquah had been an all-round nationalist, not only as an orator and practical politician, but also as an author; as a scholar and one of the first sons of black Africa to qualify for a doctorate; as an authority on Akan religious beliefs and practices; not least, as a fighter for the right of the Gold Coast to a university of its own.

During the late 1940s the British Colonial Office was debating the establishment of a second university in British West Africa. Fourah Bay College, in Sierra Leone, had conferred its first degrees of Durham University in 1879, but it catered for only a very small proportion of those West Africans who wanted a higher education—the rest flocked to British universities in ever greater numbers, most of them coming from Nigeria. If the Colonial Office decided on one additional university, it would probably be in that country.

Danquah was intensely loyal to his native land. He also had a conviction that the movement for independence would lead to more widespread education and an infinitely greater demand for university places; so he persistently demanded that the Gold Coast should have its own institution, and not be forced to share it with any other territory.

The news of his death hit Ghana's university students like a bombshell. He was a familiar figure at Legon; right up to his recent detention he had often been invited to join the panel of judges at inter-hall debates. Lawrence Cantey, a member of Commonwealth Hall debating team, determined that Danquah's death should not pass unmentioned in the institution which owed so much to him—but he knew very well that any kind of public tribute would call down certain retribution from the

Party. A year ago Lawrence had drafted that resolution protesting at Korsah's dismissal, and five of his fellow students had spent a term and a half in detention as a result. This time he would take a step in which there was no possibility of concealment.

He made for the dining hall with a spring in his step and a look of determination on his small, sharp features. Dinner had already started and 500 of his fellow students were seated in their gowns at the long tables of shining West African timber. Lawrence Cantey stood up on a chair and waited as the buzz of conversation and the clatter of knives and forks subsided into an expectant silence. They did not need to be told that it was because of Danquah that he was standing there. At last he spoke:

"Let us observe one minute's silence in memory of the late Dr J B Danquah. It will be recalled that this man was one of those who fought for a separate university college for the Gold Coast. May he rest in peace!"

For a minute not another word was spoken. Apart from the crowd of family, friends, and fellow-lawyers at his burial in Kibi, this was the largest public tribute to Danquah until after Nkrumah had fallen, perhaps the only one. The CPP group at Commonwealth Hall did not profane the solemn moment, but as soon as the meal was over the secretary-convener of the Party at Legon, a classmate of Lawrence Cantey, phoned in to Accra. Next morning at six o'clock a distinguished trio came to Commonwealth Hall porter's lodge and asked for Cantey; they were Kofi Baako, N A Welbeck, and Kweku Akwei. But Cantey combined study for his second law degree with teaching English literature at an Accra secondary school, and he had left fifteen minutes earlier to reach the school in time for his morning classes.

They left him in peace for a month. Then on 8 March he was summoned to the Special Branch and after perfunctory questioning about the one minute's silence he was locked in a cell eighteen feet by thirteen which was already occupied by a Frenchman held for alleged spying, and an army officer whose only crime was that he had visited Danquah's house. The "cell" was really just a spare lavatory, and contained a water closet and a tap under which he and the two others could wash; two beds were the only furniture. It was to be his home for the next nine and a half months.

Sometimes it was crammed with as many as fourteen prisoners—smugglers caught by the Border Guard with contraband, rebel Malians and Togolese temporarily locked up during the October Organisation of African Unity conference to avoid embarrassing protests against visiting heads of state. Sometimes the number dropped again to a mere handful.

Fortunately Cantey was allowed to study for his LL B finals, due to start on 29 May. The senior tutor of Commonwealth Hall and the acting head of the Faculty of Law visited him and arranged for him to get his books, notes, and paper to write on. The sense of purpose made detention bearable and even in such strange surroundings he managed to revise for the ten-day final examination.

On 29 May a party of three came to the Special Branch from Legon, to bring the examination papers for the day, and to invigilate while Cantey answered the questions. At the last minute Cantey was told he would not be permitted to sit for the examination after all.

For another four months he continued to get his meals sent in from the university, but after this disappointment he began to lose weight. He could not summon up enough interest to go on reading; the mosquitoes which swarmed into the cell each evening began to irritate him and he fell ill with malaria. His only relaxation was to read a copy of the Qur'an brought in by a Muslim teacher from Tamale Secondary School, detained like himself without any legal basis.

After the OAU conference the rebels and refugees from other African states were let out again, and Cantey and two of his companions determined to draw attention to their plight in the only way open to them—by going on hunger strike until they were told the reason for their imprisonment. The other prisoners agreed to join in, and on 9 November they sent their

68

breakfast and lunch back uneaten. "We have nothing to fear," argued Cantey. "If we're going to be detained we might as well be detained properly under the Preventive Detention Act: that can't be worse than the place we are in now."

There was an immediate reaction. All the prisoners at the Special Branch were interviewed. Some of the older ones were released at once: Cantey and several others were taken to Ussher Fort and formally detained.

The prison superintendent read the order: ". . . in these years you, Mr Lawrence Otu Cantey, have engaged in activities prejudicial to the security of the State. It is therefore necessary for you to be detained under sections 1 and 4 of the Preventive Detention Act . . ." Then he told Cantey he could petition the President, and gave him the appropriate form; and he was introduced to the mode of existence designed by Nkrumah and his lieutenants for those who opposed him—solitary confinement, two blankets and a pillow to sleep on, a prison cloth to wear, and the bucket in the corner.

The only book he was allowed was the Bible, so he read it consecutively from cover to cover. After studying the Qu'ran at the Special Branch he was glad of the opportunity to read the Christian and Jewish scriptures. He approached them as law books: Exodus to Deuteronomy, which most detainees had read but found incredibly dull, were full of interest for the young LL B student. He related what he had been studying at Legon to the Mosaic law of tort, to Old Testament family law, and the law of marriage and divorce. Paul's letters were fascinating texts for the study of conflicts of law and international law.

To his surprise the Bible also spoke about his own condition—it seemed to be full of accounts of unjust imprisonment: Joseph in Egypt, Samson in Gaza, Daniel in Babylon, John the Baptist in Galilee, Paul in Philippi and elsewhere. The psalmist prayed, "Bring me out of prison, that I may give thanks to thy name!" There were many outstanding trials in the Bible too; no one was punished without some sort of trial. Even Adam in the Garden of Eden had a fair trial and a right to defend himself—God asked him, "What is this that you have done?"

Then through all the legal requirements, the historical accounts, and the poetic outpourings of Scripture, the perfect standards of God shone like a clear light on his predicament. The Bible stood for truth, justice, integrity, love: he was dealing with people who seemed to stand for the very opposite. His enemies were God's enemies too. That thought encouraged him.

For a long time he had been wondering what to do about that form he had been given to make his petition to the President. He had kept it by him, thinking that he might use it one day. But why trust in clemency, when God was on the side of justice? He took his pencil and filled the blank spaces with an obituary notice on Dr J B Danquah.

4

THE COUP THAT DIDN'T HAPPEN

1965

A HIGH-RANKING police officer stepped boldly out of the chemist's shop and as he did so he wrapped the brown paper a little more tightly round the bottle he carried in his left hand. He had been compelled to make the purchase himself—he could not explain the reasons to anyone else; fortunately he had a friend in the pharmaceutical profession, and he had told him a convincing story to justify the purchase. Now he must do his best to look like a law-abiding citizen and regain the privacy of his car before anyone spotted the label and asked him, "What does John Harlley, Commissioner of Police, want that for?"

He did not breathe easily again until he was back in his office at Police Headquarters and had locked the bottle away in his desk. Then he thought over once more their plans for using the contents; but again he had to face up to the inevitable problem—every plan demanded the cooperation of other people, and he didn't know whom he could trust.

Perhaps there were other groups in other parts of the country, in other units of the Police or the Army, who were thinking the same thoughts, examining the same possibilities, coming up against the same obstacles. Perhaps even Otu and Ankrah, leaders of the army, were secretly plotting like himself yet unable to reveal their plans to anyone else, and hence unable to act.

Three years ago, just after the bomb-throwing of August 1962, Ankrah had been named in the British press as "the strong man for this grave crisis".[19] Accra had been full of rumours that Ankrah would stage a coup, even that he had already arrested Nkrumah and made him a prisoner in Flagstaff House. That particular rumour had proved false; it might be true that Ankrah didn't approve of Nkrumah's actions, but Harlley could never discover his real intentions without compromising his own position.

So he continued to discuss the country's plight with a few close friends—Deku, Lt-Col Emmanuel Kotoka (Quartermaster-General in the Ministry of Defence), and Captain Kwashie of the Military Hospital. Kotoka persuaded them to abandon the old idea of an ultimatum to Nkrumah: to drive into Flagstaff House in an armoured car would be suicidal, for the President's Own Guard had anti-tank guns that could pierce straight through the armour plating. They had discussed shooting down the plane next time Nkrumah left the country, or on his return—they had rejected that because it would involve killing innocent people. The latest plan was to kidnap the President at night, during a visit to one of his "girl friends". This could be done with a small force if the girl chloroformed the President in his sleep. No one else could be trusted with the secret, so the Commissioner of Police had to go and buy a bottle of chloroform himself. But at their next meeting this plan too fell out of favour.

"Kidnapping the President would cause confusion but it would not stop others carrying on his administration, so long as they were backed up by the President's Own Guard and Radio Ghana," said Emmanuel Kotoka, leaning back in an arm-chair at Kwashie's house. He had just been playing tennis and was still in white shirt and trousers. "All we have done for the past twelve months is talk, talk, talk, but nothing comes of it. Why? Because, as I learned in the Congo, you've got to meet force with force." Kotoka had done three tours in the Congo, serving with the Ghana contingent of the United Nations forces. For his part in the battle of Katanga less than two years before he had been awarded the Ghana Service Order.

"That means risking civil war," said Harlley, who was anxious to avoid bloodshed at all costs. "In any case, where can we get force from? We have no troops, and since the shooting incident at Flagstaff House the police have been disarmed." "It's true," replied Kotoka with quiet annoyance. "It's a pity that I am not in a command where I have, say, a battalion of troops under me. For the past eighteen months I have been stuck at the Ministry of Defence as Quartermaster-General. Why, even Kwashie here commands more troops than I do." "Oh dear," moaned the secretary of the Military Hospital, "I hope I shan't have to lead my medical orderlies into battle armed with hypodermic syringes."

"I'm convinced we can get troops if we go to the top," said Kotoka, at last. "Why don't you see Major-General Otu, the Chief of Defence Staff, and Brigadier Ankrah too? They're good men. Even if they didn't think the time was ripe for a coup, we could rely on them to keep their mouths shut."

"And how would you advise me to introduce the subject— 'Good evening, Major-General; I propose that we conspire together to overthrow Osagyefo'—will that do?"

"Oh, I know it won't be easy to raise the subject, but you'll have to find some way to do so."

Harlley had an idea on the spur of the moment. "You know Amegashie—principal of the College of Business Administration? He was talking to me only the other day about the nation's balance of payments: I'll get him to prepare a kind of economic situation of the country for me, then I'll go and discuss it with Otu. That will give me a chance to sound him out."

A week or so later Harlley paid an unexpected visit on the Chief of Defence Staff in his office at Burma Camp and gave him Amegashie's economic situation to study. Otu came from Adukrom, Akwapim, and thus was a Twi speaker. He was the first man outside Harlley's own circle of Ewe friends with whom he had dared to discuss the plight of the nation. Otu read through the statement and threw it on the desk with a sigh. "Oh, yes, John, I know the state we're in. Why, the army can't even get boots for our soldiers to march in! The crash is bound to come sooner or later."

Harlley saw his opportunity and followed it up like lightning. "But we are so involved by reason of our position that if Nkrumah falls we shall fall with him. It would be very sad for some outside organization to overthrow Nkrumah's régime while we sit here doing nothing about it. Besides, unless we act we cannot avoid responsibility for what he's doing—we are the people who keep him in power!"

"We and the President's Own Guard," said General Otu, thoughtfully. "If we acted against the President we should have to be ready for a battle with the President's Own Guard and the security forces."

"But if we had the advantage of surprise . . ."

"Do you realize what you're suggesting?"

Harlley knew he must go ahead now even if he were to be shot for it. "I realize exactly what it means. I've been thinking of it ever since the Old Man sacked Korsah. The nation looks to us to do something."

"Of course, you're quite right, John."

"Do you mean you agree with me?"

"Nearly every month I get half a dozen letters begging me to overthrow Nkrumah. I do believe most of the nation would be behind us. But it's not so easy for me to act."

"You? But you are the Chief of Defence Staff!"

"Yes, and I have a deputy! Do you imagine that Ankrah would be for it?"

"Of course he would."

"No, I'm afraid he's loyal. That's why Nkrumah planted him on me. I dare not go to him with a proposal like this."

Yes, thought Harlley, that just shows how difficult it will be to find anyone who would risk even talking about it. Nkrumah always appoints two people with overlapping responsibility, and leaves the rest to human nature. Sooner or later each one feels that the other is spying on him. Besides, Otu is a Twi speaker and Ankrah is a Ga; no doubt Nkrumah had intentionally appointed two men of different tribes, to make it more difficult for them to plot against the government.

But there was a way out of it this time.

"Never mind," said Harlley, "I'll go myself. I brought this economic survey to you—now I'll take it to Ankrah too."

"Be careful!"

"It can't do any harm. And if there really is a risk, then it is a risk we have to take."

"Are you going to Ankrah now?"

"This very moment!"

Brigadier Ankrah reacted in very much the same way as his chief, but when it came to the question of a coup and how to get troops he said he was quite powerless; the Chief of Defence Staff was bound to get wind of it. "That's my whole trouble, you see," said Ankrah mournfully. "If I went to him with a proposal like this I should be in Nsawam Prison tomorrow."

Harlley pulled out his trump card with a curious feeling that his success was too good to be true. Had he really cut straight through the military leaders' mutual suspicion in an hour and a half? It seemed too easy. "Otu is on our side," he said. "I've just come from his office. His only worry is that he imagines you are fanatically loyal to the President."

Ankrah's eyes opened perceptibly wider as he took in the implications. "If that is really so," he said eagerly, "we will get to work."

For the time being there was nothing more that Harlley could do; the army men must be left to develop a plan, and his task was simply liaison. So it used to happen, by pure coincidence of course, that the paths of Harlley and Ankrah would cross in unexpected places. It would have been extremely suspicious if Harlley had paid even a second visit to Burma Camp, or if Otu or Ankrah had started making calls at Police Headquarters; but nothing could be suspected if, when Harlley went out for an evening run, he met Ankrah at a lonely spot on the Aburi road, returning from an exercise. While their duty drivers relaxed in their seats, the two revolutionaries would greet one another with a great show of surprise, and discuss the latest developments. By May 1965 they had finalized everything. The coup would take place in June, at the end of the Commonwealth Prime Ministers' conference. Otu was in full agreement so long as he was not expected to assume any political responsibility after the coup.

May 1965

The month preceding Nkrumah's departure was a busy one. In 1960 the life of the national assembly had been extended by a clause tacked on to the referendum on the declaration of a republic. The extra five years had nearly elapsed, and even the genius of Geoffrey Bing found no way to extend the powers of this parliament beyond 1 July 1965.

The public had long since ceased to bother their heads about constitutional correctness, and if Nkrumah had seen fit to let the same old parliament go on until the members died of old age, few would have dared to raise any objection. However, the President liked to preserve an outward appearance of constitutional legality, so he gave instructions for a general election.

He recollected that in 1954 and 1956 the opposition had captured 43 per cent of the votes. In 1960 the devices by which he had reduced their share of the poll had could not really be repeated. So at the same time as giving instructions for the elections he told his civil servants to arrange things in such a way that there would not actually be any voting.

The public received their first hint of an approaching general election on 18 May 1965 when the papers announced that the last session of the parliament elected in 1956 was just beginning. A week later, on 26 May, the National Assembly was dissolved and Nkrumah gave notice that a general election would be held on 8 June. The closing date for nominations was to be the following Tuesday, 1 June, at two o'clock in the afternoon.

It was soon clear that only those candidates on the CPP's official list of 198 could be nominated. Since no one except District Commissioners could provide nomination papers, and only four working days elapsed between the announcement of the election and the closing date, there was little time to argue about the list, and none at all for a non-Party candidate to find ways and means of getting legally nominated. Even CPP candidates who happened to be out of the country when the announcement was sprung on them had difficulty in getting home in time to complete the formalities.

Alex Quaison-Sackey, chosen president of the United Nations General Assembly by the most democratic procedure the nations of the world could devise, was conducting negotiations with several European governments in connection with article 19 of the UN charter. He was in Paris, dining with Dr Bossman, Ghana's ambassador to France, when he learned he had been nominated for election in a village which most people even in southern Ghana had never heard of. His wife, Elsie, said it was ridiculous to accept such a nomination. How could he hold up his head in the councils of the nations if everyone knew he had accepted a seat in Ghana's parliament without a fair election? Dr Bossman could only give dire warnings of what would happen if he refused—it could well be that the President was already jealous of his fame and popularity. It was a choice between becoming an MP, going into voluntary exile, or returning home to face Nkrumah's suspicion and displeasure.

Quaison-Sackey tried to get Kojo Botsio, the foreign minister, by radio telephone, and he sorted out his ideas as he sat and waited for the call to go through. Of course he held a CPP membership card—many civil servants did—but he regarded himself as a "technocrat" as well as a politician. He had adopted as his motto at the United Nations a Churchillian sentiment: "When I'm abroad—My country, right or wrong! When I'm at home, I fight."

He suddenly had an awful premonition that the first was very much easier to live up to than the second.

Botsio came through faintly on the telephone across two thousand five hundred miles of space. Quaison-Sackey pictured him at his desk in his comfortable, air-conditioned office on the top floor of a building in the Ministries, Accra, in steaming, tropical Accra. He gathered that he was on the list whether he liked it or not. "Will I have to prepare an election campaign?" The traditional Ghanaian reply to an embarrassing question is a peal of ecstatic laughter, and Botsio was a traditionalist. So Quaison-Sackey was resigned to becoming a Ghana MP, a totally unexpected addition to his duties. He sent off a telegram formally accepting nomination and returned from Paris to New York. If he was to comply with the regulations he would have to make time for a lightning visit to Ghana, arriving next Tuesday morning, to complete his nomination papers before the deadline. Then events moved quickly:

Saturday, 29 May Most of the 198 candidates met at the CPP headquarters and passed a resolution thanking Osagyefo the President for having been kind enough to choose them.

Tuesday, 1 June It was announced on radio and in the Press that the 198 CPP candidates had been returned unopposed and consequently there would be no voting on election day. (On that day Quaison-Sackey was busy completing his nomination papers at the office of his local District Commissioner in Winneba, so he had not actually submitted them yet.)

Tuesday 8 June "Election Day"—with no campaigns, no polling stations, and no voters.

By **Sunday 13 June** the National Assembly had met and re-elected Nkrumah President, and he in turn had named a cabinet of 14, and 16 additional ministers of non-cabinet rank. Quaison-Sackey found himself appointed to succeed Botsio as foreign minister.

A silent wave of shock passed through the nation. There was something strangely unreal about a "general election" in which new MPs had been elected and new ministers appointed without a single citizen actually casting a vote. Why, even in Soviet Russia they went through a pretence of going to the polls when they had a general election! But once again the Ghanaian people looked on helpless while the opportunity to question the procedure, or lack of procedure, passed out of their reach.

Monday, 14 June Nkrumah inspected a guard of honour formed by the President's Own Guard at Accra Airport and left

78

for London to attend the Commonwealth Prime Ministers' conference.

The chiefs of the army and the police watched with satisfaction as the wheels of the President's plane took leave of the runway. That would be the last time the dictator stepped on Ghanaian soil before his powers were stripped from him and he was disgraced before the world. Now there were days of hard work to be done: double work, for in addition to detailed arrangements for the coup d'état everyone had to carry on with his normal job as if nothing else were imminent. It was all the more difficult as so far only half a dozen people were in the know; that made the burden much heavier for each of them. Besides, the team of plotters was one short—Deku was in London on security duties.

Each time Nkrumah went abroad, Tony Deku went ahead and made arrangements with the police of the country for the President's safety. He had been doing this for six or seven years now. The fact that when Nkrumah moved him out of the Special Branch to head the CID he had asked Deku to carry on doing this job indicated the President's confidence in him. Owusu-Sekyere could head the Special Branch and make political arrests, but when it came to Nkrumah's own personal safety, he relied on the old guard.

Deku covered everything with his usual meticulous care; he was, if possible, more careful than ever. He checked the routes by which Nkrumah would travel, the places he would visit, the people he would meet. After all the preparations they had made in Accra to give Nkrumah a warm reception on his return, it would be tragic if something happened to him in London.

Then, on the day the President was due to arrive in London, Deku left for Rio de Janeiro to attend a meeting of Interpol. He tried to show appreciation of the honour done to Ghana and to himself when the meeting proceeded to elect him chairman; but he wished heartily that this had not happened just now—he was expecting an urgent cable from Harlley at any moment, recalling him to Accra to help in the coup.

He conducted the business of the conference day after day with growing impatience, but still no word came from the Commissioner of Police.

The Commonwealth Prime Ministers' conference opened on Thursday, 17 June with a proposal by Harold Wilson, the British prime minister, which in the long run proved Nkrumah's undoing. Nkrumah's name was included in a group of five Commonwealth heads of government who, it was proposed, would form a mission and try to bring about peace negotiations in Vietnam. The other heads of government were Wilson himself, Tafawa Balewa of Nigeria, Eric Williams of Trinidad, and Dudley Senanayake of Ceylon (now Sri Lanka).

On Friday President Nyerere of Tanzania attacked the peace mission as an attempt to "put China in the dock." Mr Murumbi, Kenya's foreign minister, said Harold Wilson should not be a member as Britain was already committed to the American side. Mr Senanayake, who was not present himself, sent a message from Sri Lanka to say that for health reasons he would be unable to take part, and Ayub Khan of Pakistan refused to take Mr Senanayake's place in the team. It was widely reported that Kwame Nkrumah himself was on the brink of withdrawing.

Between three and four on the morning of Saturday, 19 June two tanks moved into position in front of the presidential villa. The police on duty at the gate were replaced by a military guard and the president was deposed by the chief of the armed forces. The place was Algiers—the president was Ben Bella, and the chief of the armed forces was Col. Boumédienne.

Nkrumah heard the news next day in London and trembled inwardly under the impact of this attack on a fellow-president. Ben Bella was an old collaborator in the cause of African unity and Afro-Asian solidarity. He remembered the Twi proverb, *Obi de aba, obi de nam kwan so*—"One man's has come, another man's is on the way". He was trying to put the thought out of his mind as he drove through the Sabbath emptiness of the capital of Great Britain on his way to call on the Chinese chargé d'affaires. He reached his destination and was given a respectful welcome. He had come to find out whether the Chinese government would be willing to receive the peace mission either in its present form or in some other. The Chinese chargé d'affaires could say very little, but next day the Peking *People's Daily* gave the answer: "China has already banged the door in Gordon Walker's face," screamed the editorial*, and it accused the British Labour government of "once again offering its services to the United States on the Vietnam question." Speaking about Harold Wilson's initiative the paper commented, "This is the action of a nitwit making trouble for himself."

* *Gordon Walker was Commonwealth Secretary in the British Labour government.*

Nkrumah's advisers wondered what kept him interested in the peace mission in the light of China's violent opposition. Was it the hope of gaining a reputation for peace-making? Was it the prestige he might gain from personal negotiations with the leaders of the great nations? Or was it a fascination with the problem of Vietnam itself—a fascination which was to lure him on inexorably to disaster?

As the Commonwealth Prime Ministers' conference went on to discuss Rhodesia, the press continued to speculate over the Vietnam peace mission and Nkrumah's part in it. Soon the heads of government would meet to haggle over the wording of their final communiqué, and it would all be over for another year.

Nkrumah got a shock when he returned to his hotel. Brigadier Hassan to see him. The director of military intelligence! What could have brought him to London?

He listened gravely as Hassan told him he thought a coup was being prepared back in Accra, but he seemed to have no definite evidence. Sometimes he thought this man concocted plots and coups every few months just to prove that he was doing his job. He had ignored rumours of this kind many a time; besides, there had been no attempt on his life for eighteen months, ever since that shooting at Flagstaff House in January last year—all the same, after the fall of Ben Bella in Algeria, Nkrumah did not feel like taking chances. He held a consultation there in the hotel room and sent Hassan back with urgent instructions for Otu and for the security services.

The plotters in Accra were shocked to receive Nkrumah's unexpected instructions, and, under the impression that Nkrumah had been too clever for them, called off the proposed coup at the last moment. The President flew back into Accra airport exactly a fortnight after he had left. Among those who met him were John Harlley and Major-Generals Otu and Ankrah—all simmering with rage at the missed opportunity, all fearing that there would never be another chance. Within a week both of them would probably be in detention.

On the contrary, at the end of the week they celebrated "Armed Forces Day", and Nkrumah decorated Otu and Ankrah with the "honour of Officer of the Most Distinguished Order of the Volta". Nevertheless the rumours stirred up by Hassan's suspicions continued to reverberate in cocktail parties and in offices at Flagstaff House (where the President had taken up residence again after living at the Castle while improved security equipment was installed). Nkrumah decided to get rid of Otu and Ankrah and put a stop to all this gossip. On 28 July they were forced to resign and Brigadier N. A. Aferi and Brigadier C. M. Barwah were promoted major-generals; Aferi became chief of defence staff, and Barwah army chief of staff.

If only the plotters had known that Hassan had no real evidence they could have carried out the coup in spite of the false alarm. Instead, another moment of opportunity had slipped away and there could be no retrieving it.

In the reshuffle following the dismissal of Otu and Ankrah, Kotoka was made colonel and sent to Kumasi to replace Aferi as commander of 2 Brigade. It was an advantage to have troops under his command, but that was outweighed by the fact that he was now 130 miles from Accra. If he was to plan a coup, it would demand close consultation between the army and the police over a period of several weeks. How could he hope to manage that at such a distance?

5

NKRUMAH IN CONTROL OF THE NATION'S LIFE

NKRUMAH had no idea how effectively he had scattered the first conspiracy that had ever seemed likely to oust his government. But in dismissing Otu and Ankrah, Nkrumah had acted more on instinct than on suspicion; if he had had definite evidence against them, they would have suffered a far worse fate than mere dismissal.

But Ankrah and Otu knew they were marked men. Ankrah's house, in Asylum Down, Accra, was so obviously surveyed by security men that he had difficulty in restraining himself from driving them away. Their constant surveillance could not uncover the thought that was uppermost in Ankrah's mind; but on those rare occasions when he met anyone who was in a position to help, the conversation would drop to a low tone and the question would be, "How can we make another attempt?"

Another group of plotters continued to meet periodically on the first floor veranda at the back of the commissioner of police's house. Colonel Kotoka was now based in Kumasi, 130 miles from Accra, but most of his troops were in Tamale, 250 miles further north, and a total of 380 miles from Accra. Kotoka was not often in Accra, but whenever he was there he gathered the small circle of friends who had been discussing a possible coup: Harlley and Deku of the police; Kwashie of the military hospital, and another soldier who was so strongly opposed to carrying out a coup in Nkrumah's absence that when this proposal was adopted later on he was not asked to help.

"If we do it while he's away there will be no bloodshed and we are free to choose the time that suits us best."

"Yes, that's what went wrong in June: we pinned ourselves down to one moment, the moment of the President's arrival in Ghana after the Commonwealth Prime Ministers' conference. If he had changed his plans—if he had arrived a day earlier or a week later—the whole thing would have failed. You can't hide troop movements in daylight; the secret would have leaked out: result—chaos, perhaps even civil war."

"As it happened he didn't even have to change his plans; Brigadier Hassan's scare was enough to overthrow the whole operation."

"I still think it could be done in broad daylight with Nkrumah sitting in his office in Flagstaff House if we planned it properly."

"Too many people would get killed."

Someone else questioned whether there was any need to remove the President at all: "If he goes on much longer as he is now, all we need to do is sit tight and Nkrumah will fall by the weight of his own top-heavy, incompetent administration. The economy of the country will collapse."

"As long as Ghana produces cocoa and the world eats chocolate the economy won't collapse, however many millions Nkrumah spends on ambitious projects with East European governments. The economy is not as weak as that or it would have collapsed long ago!"

"I agree. Nkrumah will not fall unless he is forced out, and the army is the only power left that can do it. He controls everything else—the administration, the farmers, the trade unions, commerce; through the Young Pioneers he indoctrinates the youth; and the young intelligentsia are being systematically brainwashed at Winneba Ideological Institute. The army is the only power left."

"The army has very little power, my friend. Nkrumah is virtually master of the army too."

"What do you mean? He is the commander-in-chief but he can't take the day-to-day control out of our hands."

"He can do so, and he is doing so! Phase one is to starve the army of clothing, equipment, spare parts, and advanced training—he's doing that already, isn't he?"

"Admittedly, he's doing that."

"Phase two can start as soon as Ian Smith declares independence in Southern Rhodesia. Nkrumah then begs or charters a fleet of transport aircraft to move the army over to Zambia. The shortages will get unbearable, morale will drop and there will be a mutiny. That will give Nkrumah an excuse to get rid of all the officers he doesn't like and to have a purge of the troops."

"And then?"

"Why, in comes the Workers' Brigade, which is Nkrumah's own creation. They have had paramilitary training and political indoctrination. With the President's Own Guard as a nucleus they could form a new army."

"It would be a shambles."

"Yes, it would be a shambles at first, but remember Nkrumah could keep any officers and NCOs he wanted from the present army. They have their families to support and they would not be likely to refuse a job."

"It means we ought to move quickly."

"I think we should go ahead and carry out a coup at once. Instead we seem to be going backwards."

But when they came to discussing dates and details they could make no progress. Every scheme foundered on the basic problem that they could not trust anyone else. Every scheme demanded a strong military force and active police co-operation, but they knew the army and the police were sprinkled liberally with informers in the pay of the security service. Kotoka might in theory have a brigade under him, but he could not act without his three battalion commanders and his headquarters staff. If he breathed a word of his plans to them, someone was sure to report him at once. Brigadier Hassan, director of military intelligence, was inclined to see

85

plots even where they did not exist; if his activities had no other result, at least they served to make those who really were plotting extremely cautious.

That very month, November 1965, Hassan's monthly intelligence report accused Kotoka of a deliberate attempt to transfer Ewe officers into 2 Brigade. Kotoka made several protests, and finally went to see Major-General Barwah, the army chief of staff. He knew that Barwah and Hassan worked closely together; both were firmly behind Nkrumah, and Nkrumah had absolute confidence in them. But they were two very different kinds of person.

Barwah was the orthodox soldier, rooted deeply in British traditions. He had joined the army as a young man in 1947 and had climbed up the ladder of promotion by merit: the British themselves had sent him to Sandhurst*, Britain's Royal Military Academy, in 1952, long before independence. Barwah was soft-spoken and courteous and would never tell you to your face what he thought of you. He had the finest collection of military buttons in West Africa.

----

* The Royal Military Academy in England, one of Britain's officer cadet training units, to which at that time the Ghana Army sent their best candidates for training.

Hassan, on the other hand, had a chequered background. He spoke Arabic and Hausa much better than English, having spent most of World War 2 in Northern Nigeria and the Sudan, and had not enlisted in the Ghana Army until 1960. At that time he was said to be a captain in the Sudanese Army, and on the instructions of Flagstaff House he was given a commission in the Ghana Army with the same rank. The following year, when General Alexander and all other British soldiers were removed from the Ghana Army, Hassan was promoted lieutenant-colonel. Four years later he became a brigadier. He put on an outward appearance of joviality, but he felt thoroughly out of place amid the sophisticated conversation of the officers' mess, and was seldom seen there.

Charles Mohamed Barwah listened politely to Colonel Kotoka's bitter complaints about the intelligence report. He sympathized, and advised Kotoka not to take it seriously, but his visitor was in a fighting mood. "I fail to see why we should have a director of military intelligence," said Kotoka, "if his reports are not to be taken seriously." Barwah had to admit that Kotoka was in the right, and a few days later Hassan withdrew the accusation that Kotoka was trying to turn 2 Brigade into an Ewe stronghold; but still Kotoka was conscious that every move he made was being watched.

*　　　*　　　*

On 11 November 1965 Ian Smith rebelled against the British crown, and declared Southern Rhodesia independent. A fortnight later Nkrumah stood in the Ghana National Assembly, concluding the presidential address with which he had opened an emergency meeting of parliament. From his speech it seemed as if those dire warnings about Nkrumah's intentions towards the army were just about to be fulfilled:

"Mr Speaker, Members of the National Assembly," he said, "if a cry for help comes to us from the victims of oppression in Southern Rhodesia, we, the African States, must answer it. It is for this reason that the National Assembly is being asked tomorrow to enact legislation to give the government power to prepare for any military eventuality. The bill which will be introduced upon a certificate of urgency seeks to give the government general powers to make all laws necessary for mobilization. Already the first steps in this direction have been taken. Members of the armed forces who have completed their time of service are being retained in the forces. As a precaution all military leave has been stopped.

"Under existing law we are going to establish a militia. This militia will be a voluntary force. Its members will not be paid. Their training will be on a part-time basis and their enrolment is to start on Monday next.

· "Under the bill which you will be asked to pass the government is given power to requisition Ghanaian aircraft and

87

ships. You may remember that at the time of the Congo crisis the Western powers failed to provide us with air transport which they had promised. The government cancelled all internal and external services of Ghana Airways and used the aircraft to transport our troops. We shall not hesitate to do the same thing again. The bill also enables airports, seaports, and roads to close in whole or in part in order to facilitate troop movements. I must warn that a mobilization on the scale which we have in mind must entail considerable disorganization of civilian life but in a crisis of this nature we must put military necessity first . . ."

Next day the National Assembly heard thirty-three patriotic speeches, well laced with oldfashioned quotations and boring tirades. Kofi Baako, introducing the African Defence (Ghana) Bill, quoted Shakespeare's "Henry V" and J M Barrie; he ended with the lines of Norman Macleod:

"Courage, brother! do not stumble,
Though thy path be dark as night;
There's a star to guide the humble:
Trust in God, and do the Right."

Alex Quaison-Sackey, recalled at a few day's notice from New York to take part in the debate, seemed at first appalled by the boisterous interruptions which prevailed among Ghana's legislators. After his experience at the United Nations it seemed strange that there could be no opposition and no division at the end of the debate. He began, halting, like a new boy on his first day at school:

"I arise to support the bill, although I understand that bills introduced here are not supposed to be passed automatically. But this House is the master of its own procedure; therefore any moment that there is a crisis the House can take its own procedure, and that is why I rise to support and bring out the implications, political and otherwise, of the bill which this house has been asked to vote for unanimously . . ."

Then he went on to argue persuasively for the use of force in Southern Rhodesia, his confidence returning as he proceeded. When he read his speech in *Hansard* next day he found that the

Ghana parliamentary reporters' flair for spotting historical allusions was not quite up to United Nations standards. In his reference to a former prime minister of Southern Rhodesia the name of Sir Godfrey Huggins had been replaced by a mysterious "Hawkins"; and the Roman Cato, who lived two centuries before Christ, was credited with the prophetic demand, "The Catholics must be destroyed!" [20]

Professor Kojo Abraham, first African fellow of All Souls College, Oxford, made a witty and polished attack on British indecision:

" . . If the Gold Coast had posed any similar threat to the British government before 1957, the British army would have been brought in to prevent the deed, and a charge of treasonable conduct would have been brought against our leaders. Indeed, they were imprisoned for much less; and for much less a veritable British Armada was raised against British Guiana in 1953.

"Of course, Britain may have some reason for the mildness of its offence and for the even greater velvetiness of its as yet uninflicted retribution. We have been looking for the iron first inside the velvet glove. Alas, it is sawdust—which we must prevent being thrown into our eyes. Of course, a British government has tried before to over-ride by force an illegal declaration of independence. Mr Speaker, you would recall that the British forces were badly defeated by the arms of the original members of the United States of America. Perhaps, for a country that lives so much by its history, that experience two hundred years ago unsteadies the nerve of Britain.

"It is sad for us who have been ruled by the British lion for over a century to find that in the face of Ian Smith's insolence, the only reaction evoked is an incomprehensible appeal to 'think again' . . ."

Mr J K Twum, the member for Asankrangwa, contributed a story which as he said contained food for thought (though the moral was not very clear):

"A Young Pioneer, after attending a Young Pioneers' meeting where he had been ideologically equipped, was going home. On reaching the Kaneshie bus stop he heard two ladies engaged in a serious argument. One of the ladies, who was staying at Nima, was trying to blame the Accra-Tema City Council for having spent too much money in erecting a wall around the Awudome Cemetery. The other woman, who stays at Kaneshie, contended that the wall around the Awudome Cemetery would save the children from fright and so was perfectly in agreement with the Accra-Tema City Council for erecting that wall. But the woman who comes from Nima stated that they had no clinic and that the money spent on erection of the Awudome Cemetery wall could have been more profitably used for a clinic for the people of Nima. After this argument the Young Pioneer came in and asked these ladies why they were quarrelling. When the ladies had stated their case, he said to them, 'My mothers, why are you arguing on this point? Whether a wall has been built around Awudome Cemetery or not, those who are in the cemetery are not prepared to come out and those who are not in the cemetery are not prepared to go in . . ."

The minister of justice, Kwaw Swanzy, offered to serve in the militia, and Kofi Batsa, editor of the weekly *Spark*, called on journalists to help with their pens and typewriters; but in spite of speech after speech and quotation after quotation, from the writings of Kwame Nkrumah, from Patrick Henry, and even from such dubious friends of African rights as Winston Churchill and "Rule Britannia", the total effect was unconvincing. If the relaxed atmosphere on the U-shaped benches of the National Assembly was any guide, Ghana was not really going to war.

The Africa Defence (Ghana) Bill duly became law. District Commissioners' offices up and down the country were crowded by thousands of unemployed youths who hoped that they would reap some benefit from enrolling in the new militia. But even if Nkrumah could have found any other African government to join him in a crusade against Ian Smith, his own policy of starving the army had already made it impossible for Ghana to participate. Every year the director of ordnance services placed orders worth C1,200,000 with the Supply Commission. The money was always voted but very few goods had actually arrived for several years. Some said this was due to the lack of foreign exchange: others pointed to the fact that the President's Own Guard Regiment, which had its own independent supply arrangements, was provided with the latest and most modern equipment, and suggested that funds were being diverted to build up this rival force: but whatever the explanation the fact was that supplies were three and a half years in arrears. Many reserves had been completely exhausted, and more than half the army's vehicles were off the road for lack of tyres and batteries. It would take many months to put the army on a war footing.

December and January passed uneventfully. On 1 February 1966 the President opened a new session of parliament with a pre-budget address in which he devoted one brief paragraph to the Rhodesian problem, and made no reference whatever to the bold and warlike preparations of two months before.

One of the plotters had said that Nkrumah controlled the administration, the farmers, the trade unions, and commerce; that he was indoctrinating the youth through the Young Pioneers; and that the intelligentsia were being systematically brain-washed at the Winneba Ideological Institute. It was a fair summary of the situation. If he put the farmers near the top of his list there was logic in that.

Controlling the farmers

Cocoa had been one of Ghana's main exports for nearly fifty years and Nkrumah started trying to control the cocoa producers in the early days of the CPP. Farmers' co-operatives were already flourishing at that time; they were run on sound co-operative principles and their independent spirit of enterprise and self-help did not encourage interference. Nkrumah's first move was to found a rival organization, the "Farmers' Council", which was officially inaugurated in 1954. Two years later the Farmers' Council started marketing cocoa in competition with the co-operatives, and the economic struggle between the two farmers' organizations became a part of the political struggle between the CPP and the opposition. Then

Nkrumah used his executive power to kill the old co-operative movement and to replace it by what he now called the United Ghana Farmers' Co-operative Council. In 1961 this Council took over cocoa-buying from the foreign companies which had previously bought on behalf of the national Cocoa Marketing Board, and having established a monopoly of cocoa-buying the UGFCC had the farmers at its mercy—the Council could even withhold payment for their crop, giving them instead a receipt and a note of the amount due.

The Farmers' Council also controlled the sale of gammalin for cocoa spraying, and inflated the price. Towards the end of 1965 it became impossible to buy even a simple cutlass anywhere except through the Farmers' Council, often at ridiculously high prices.

The Council had a democratic machinery of district and regional committees, from which the national body was formed, but in practice the farmers were prevented from using this machinery to express their views. The prospects of promotion in the Council hierarchy encouraged some people to surrender to the Party line, while opponents of official policy were victimized. At a meeting at Kukurantumi the farmers were warned that photographs would be taken of the voting; those who voted against the Council's policy would thus be easily identified and might be detained. By such means farmers were even forced to vote for a lower price for cocoa, and their patriotic decision was reported in the national press with a great show of enthusiasm. Thus Ghana's economic life-line, cocoa production, was subordinated to the CPP government's desperate need to increase income and cut expenditure.

Controlling the TUC

The old-established trade union movement was undermined in a similar fashion, and in 1959 a new Trades Union Congress was inaugurated. Among the objectives laid down in Article II of the constitution were these, in the following order of priority:

To maintain the Trades Union Congress as one of the wings of the CPP, dedicated to the building of a Socialist State in Ghana;

To uphold the aims and aspirations of the CPP through financial and organizational support in its struggle to create and maintain a Socialist State in Ghana.

Another objective mentioned in the same article, but which soon ceased to play a great part in TUC policy, was this:

To assist the national unions of the TUC in securing improved wages, shorter hours, and better working and employment conditions for workers within their jurisdiction.

It was soon clear that the Party regarded the TUC as its slave. In 1962 thousands of agricultural workers were suddenly dismissed by a radio announcement. Two or three thousand were sent to Accra by their fellows to stage a massive protest and to present their case to the Ministry of Agriculture. Instead of assisting them, TUC officials joined with police in stopping the marchers some 17 miles from Accra on the Kumasi road. The press and radio completely ignored the incident.

Sometimes the TUC national executive would receive instructions in these terms: "The Party has directed that Mr So-and-so should become executive secretary of such-and-such a union". It was left to the national executive to fix the election. Most members of the executive feared to resist because they themselves were involved in corruption; the Party would not allow the police to take action against them because the threat of prosecution was such a useful means of blackmailing the TUC leaders into obedience.

Mr B A Bentum was one of the few men who sometimes resisted Party pressure. He had been an active trade unionist for twenty years: he founded the Agricultural Workers' Union in 1949, became national organizer of the Union of General Agricultural Workers in 1959, and worked his way up till in 1964 he was elected chairman of the executive board of the TUC. Bentum used his key position to resist Party control of the TUC.

He reported misuse of funds by TUC employees to the police in writing. But he soon paid the inevitable penalty—in March 1965 he was dismissed from all his many offices in the trade union movement on Party instructions.

The Ideological Institute at Winneba

If Nkrumah controlled the farmers and the trade unions, he was equally anxious to control the intelligentsia. Up to the time of independence this was no problem: no one likes to be ruled by foreigners, and Nkrumah brilliantly personified the national desire to cast off the fetters of colonial status. But to impose autocratic rule on present and future generations of Ghana was quite another matter. If Nkrumah was to carry professional people and university students with him in this bold endeavour, he would have to back up brute force with intellectually respectable arguments.

However, despite involvement with Marxism in his student days, Nkrumah was entirely a pragmatist and not a doctrinaire. His ideological adviser was the West Indian George Padmore, a PanAfricanist, a "communist fellow-traveller" perhaps, but not a master of Marxist ideology. Then from 1958 onwards Nkrumah came in contact with Sekou Touré of Guinea, and was made painfully aware of the fact that Ghana had no political theory, and neither did he himself.

In 1961 he spent two months in communist countries. The same year the Ideological Institute at Winneba was opened.

At first the intelligentsia were not interested. Sixth formers had their eyes on the universities; graduates were out for big jobs with high salaries. Nobody wanted to go to Winneba to study the new philosophy of Nkrumaism (expounded in a book entitled *Nkrumaism* allegedly written by Nkrumah himself though some questioned the attribution). For the first two years of its existence the Institute provided six-month and one-year courses for trade unionists and employees of the CPP and government-controlled organizations. A Hungarian lecturer at the Institute described this period as follows:

The President conceived of the Institute as a mixture of Socratic Athens, the London School of Economics, and the Moscow Institute of Marxism-Leninism.

While not quite up to those standards, it was a very odd hybrid indeed—almost as bizarre as the ideology it was supposed to propagate...

Its catholicity was awe-inspiring; from the rantings of Malcolm X, through the involutions of the African personality, to turgid expositions of the Soviet textbooks on dialectical and historical materialism.

The unfortunate students, who possessed as a rule only the barest of formal schooling, were expected to digest these heterogeneous ideas and to emerge from their studies as fully-fledged and academically trained Nkrumaists. One could not help feeling sorry for them.

No one really knew what Nkrumaism was, not even—I strongly suspect—its professional exegetists.[21]

Then conditions of entry were adjusted to make the Winneba courses more attractive. In 1963 the Institute offered a two-year course leading to a diploma in economics and political science, and many teachers in elementary schools enrolled for it. In October of the following year fifty students with the equivalent of the university entrance qualifications started a degree course in economics and political science; they were attracted by the fact that they would not be bonded to teach in schools or training colleges after the course, as they would have been if they had studied the same subject at Legon.

They settled down to the study of economics, including Keynes as well as Marxist writers, political science from Plato to the twentieth century, philosophy, and government (which covered the constitutions of the USA and various Commonwealth countries as well as that of Soviet Russia, the USSR). One and a half hours of the weekly timetable were devoted to Nkrumaism. During the first year the set book was Nkrumah's autobiography.

95

Only a handful survived the first three terms. In October 1965 the new intake plus the remainder of the previous year's degree students totalled only 38. However there were some 300 students on other courses, including the diploma course and a two-year course in graphic art. Many of them were teachers with a complete elementary education and two years of teacher training (out of a possible maximum of four years).

The lecturers included the English communist Pat Sloan, the Hungarian Tibor Szamuely (who left in 1964), some East Germans, Russians and Poles, a Czech, an Iraqi, and a number of Ghanaians. Ikoku, head of the education department, was a Nigerian and one of the most popular lecturers. As an African he thoroughly understood his students' background and could draw his examples from African and Ghanaian situations. When on the campus he was always ready to see students about their difficulties, even late at night.

The Russian who lectured on history spoke good English and was easy to understand, but the lecturers in political economy found the language barrier a serious obstacle—the Poles could not get their ideas across because they did not know enough English; Mrs Arnold on the other hand (the enthusiastic East German with greying hair) knew too much English for her students' comfort, and used to gabble away at top speed and enormous length, leaving them following far behind.

Whatever its shortcomings, it looked as though, over a period of years, the Ideological Institute would make a serious impact on the nation's thinking about political questions. Several hundred teachers, for instance, were now going out into the elementary schools to teach Nkrumaism to the youth with a new dedication and new professional skill.

The Young Pioneers

At another level, in the elementary and secondary schools, the Young Pioneers—the CPP-inspired national youth movement—were doing their best to impart a Socialist outlook to the youth. Unfortunately the young Pioneers did not have the quality of leadership they needed. Many of the paid posts were occupied by self-seekers who had no interest in the work and scarcely visited the local groups for which they were supposed to be responsible. School and college units were led by volunteers from the staff, and their effectiveness depended entirely on those individuals.

Often they were conscientious and the high-sounding aims of the Young Pioneers were in some measure fulfilled:

To train the mind, body and soul of the youth of Ghana;

To train them up to their civic responsibilities so as to fulfil their patriotic duties;

To train their technical skills according to their talents;

To foster the spirit of voluntaryism, love and devotion to the welfare of the Ghana nation;

To inculcate into the youth "Nkrumaism"—ideals of African Personality, African Unity, World Peace, social and economic reconstruction of Ghana and Africa in particular, and the world in general.

In other cases, lack of the right leadership led to disastrous consequences. Take the case of the Women's Teacher Training College at Kibi. The local Young Pioneer organizer was incapable of running an effective programme even in the elementary schools; he hardly dared show his face at the training college, where the principal, a Swiss lady who had first come to Ghana ten years earlier as a Basel missionary, was intolerably efficient and businesslike. She had an unfortunate habit of talking him into fixing the date and time for a meeting with staff members to discuss the Young Pioneer programme in the college, and when he quite understandably failed to turn up because he was visiting a friend in the next village she could make him feel distinctly guilty at their next encounter. Fortunately for everyone, a new member of staff arrived at Kibi Training College in October 1965 and he took up responsibility for a Young Pioneer unit in the college with great enthusiasm. We will call him Mr Mensah.

Seven students from each class were asked to join, and for a time it seemed that Mr Mensah was capturing their enthusiasm. Each day after classes the growing band of Pioneers gathered on the grass in the cool of the evening, and after the "institutionalization of Kwame Nkrumah" they devoted themselves eagerly to a varied programme of singing, drumming and dancing, games, and lectures on socialism by the indefatigable Mr Mensah. When the time for the inauguration drew near they were provided with sticks shaped like rifles, and in addition to the evening meetings they held parades at six every morning and called in the local police to instruct them in rifle drill.

The first sign that anything was amiss was towards the end of that term, when Mr Mensah took the Young Pioneers on a hike and several of the girls returned very much the worse for drink. No doubt it was just an unfortunate lapse, so the matter was forgotten and in January 1966 the Young Pioneers returned to their games and lectures with renewed enthusiasm.

On the first Friday of the new term the district organizer came to the principal's office with one of the girls, the president of the college Young Pioneers. The local MP and the District Commissioner had sent to ask permission for certain girls to see them in town in connection with the activities of their group. The principal looked at her watch: it was twenty past five.

"It is too late for the students to go into town this evening," she said, "but if the MP and his party will come here of course the girls can see them. What a pity that all the students are washing their clothes, otherwise we could have arranged to receive them in style!"

For a moment the district organizer did not know how to reply. The principal did not like the way he glanced furtively at the Young Pioneer president. But when he finally spoke, her worst fears were confirmed: "Perhaps . . . perhaps they wish to see them privately . . ."

The principal refused firmly but promised to wait till six o'clock in case they decided to come to the college. Then she returned to her bungalow on the other side of the town. At seven thirty that evening the MP arrived at the college and presented the Ghanaian housemistress with the same request that the Swiss principal had refused a couple of hours earlier.

"I'm sorry," said the housemistress, "but our rules about going out of the college are extremely strict. I can't take the responsibility of letting girls go into town at this hour of the day."

"Not even with the DC and the MP?"

"This is an institution and we have to stick to the rules . . ."

"Look here—I am a representative of the government of Ghana. This college is the property of the State. I can come here whenever I like and nobody can query me. Send those girls along."

"I can't do that."

The MP marched out of the college and summoned the principal from her bungalow to face a barrage of abuse and accusations in the presence of the DC, the district organizer of the Young Pioneers, the local chairman of the Party, two local elementary school headteachers, and some Young Pioneer officials. She had been interfering with the Pioneers, she was told. She was making the work of Mr Mensah and the district organizer impossible. Sinister imperialist influences were at work. She must be very careful.

The principal was allowed to go back to her half-eaten dinner in the solitude of her bungalow—no, not the solitude, for she committed the problem to God and knew he was with her. There was another thing too. She felt at home in Ghana: she spoke the people's language and ate the people's food; she did not feel alone among a strange people because she was no longer a foreigner. At the same time she knew the people of Kibi could not protect her against the might of the Party; with a few more trumped-up charges of the kind she had faced that evening it would not be difficult for the MP to get her deported and to put an end to the work she was trying to do for her adopted country.

At the next staff meeting there were complaints all round of a strange and rebellious spirit among the students. Discipline seemed to be breaking down. Unknown to them, Mr Mensah had for some time been attacking his fellow members of staff during meetings of the Young Pioneers. From a distance he appeared to be busily expounding an obscure point of political theory; but what in reality held those girls so enthralled was Mr Mensah's eloquent denunciations of their teachers, delivered with prophetic fervour and apocalyptic warnings: "They are not properly qualified," he declared. "That's why they bully you so mercilessly—they are only trying to hide their own weaknesses! But Osagyefo has sent me here to save the college. Bring your grievances to me and I will see that they are dealt with. And as for any student who does not join the Young Pioneers, in that day she will run away and leave her shoes behind her . . ."

The discussions and decisions of staff meetings were becoming common gossip in the whole college, because Mr Mensah revealed them at the next gathering of the Young Pioneers. It was no wonder that students began to challenge their teachers openly; breaking bounds became a regular habit. It was even said that at the week-ends some students went without leave to the DC's bungalow and entertained his guests late into the night.

At another staff meeting Mr Mensah introduced a new suggestion. "The members of the Young Pioneers wish to organize a visit to Kulungugu at the end of term." The principal as usual treated the proposal with all seriousness but the whole staff recognized the dangers in a flash. "We want to go during the final week of term—just the third year students. We wish to pay homage at the place where the enemies of the State tried to assassinate our beloved Osagyefo." The other tutors began to ask awkward questions:

"Who will accompany the students?"

"Oh, I will!"

"But you are a man—a female member of staff should go too."

"Are you accusing me of something?"

The principal cut into the discussion. "No, Mr. Mensah, no one would think of accusing you of anything. But it is well recognized that when female students go on an excursion, they should be accompanied by a female member of staff."

"There will be some female Young Pioneer officers accompanying us," said Mr Mensah, with a flash of inspiration.

"How will you travel?"

"We shall get transport from the Young Pioneers."

"But what about food and accommodation?"

"Accommodation?"

"Yes, how far is it to Kulungugu?"

"I'm not quite sure, but we shall stop at different places of interest on the way. It will be a most educational trip. Other colleges do it, you know."

"It is five hundred miles to Kulungugu. You will have to make arrangements for accommodation at Tamale and other places on the way. Where do you intend to stay?"

"We shall make arrangements through the Regional Commissioners..."

"What about food?"

"That will be provided by the college. Or if not, the Young Pioneer organization and the Regional Commissioners will look after us."

One thing at least was becoming very clear. Mr Mensah proposed to go away with some 20 female third-year students for a whole week, during term time when the college was entirely responsible for their welfare. The staff could not agree to it. He was told to come back later with the idea more fully thought out. But he could not mistake the note of hostility that had crept into the remarks made by some of his colleagues.

On Sunday 6 February on her way back from a meeting the principal thought she saw a student in a stationary car many miles away from Kibi. The girl at once clambered into the back of the car and buried her head in the luggage. The principal asked the driver the girl's name. "She looks like one of my students!" she explained. The man gave a false name and for a moment the principal's suspicions were allayed; but on her return to the college she found this student and two others were absent. The staff took the case very seriously, and imposed a long period of suspension on all three girls.

The incident might have brought the wave of indiscipline to an end but for the persistence of Mr Mensah, who continued to foment rebellion. "The day of reckoning draws near," he chanted with evangelistic fervour. He spoke truer than he knew.

HOW THE COUP WAS PLANNED

"But for God, who had already finished the job, it would have been impossible for the army and police to overthrow Nkrumah."—Emmanuel Kotoka, addressing a military parade in Kumasi on 20 March 1966.

TUESDAY 8 FEBRUARY 1966

COLONEL Kotoka's staff car swung out of 2 Brigade headquarters, Kumasi, early on the morning of 8 February 1966, and turned past Wesley College, its domes and pointed arches inspired by the architecture of India and East Asia; how did an Englishman design such an exotic building to house the training of Methodist teachers?

On through the chain of small villages, where Kumasi's office workers were queueing up to catch tro-tros into the city. (In Accra, back in the 1950s, they nick-named these lorries "trotro", *tro* being the Ga for "threepence", the normal fare. People still called them "trotro" although the fares had more than doubled.) When would this inflation, and the Nkrumah government's financial policies, which must have something to do with it, be halted?

At one time the thought of a 125-mile drive to the dry grassland of northern Ghana would have filled Emmanuel Kotoka with pleasurable anticipation. Now practically everything he saw as the car flashed through the tropical forest on its way north reminded him of the country's plight. He saw the ranks of vigorous youngsters, boys in khaki shirts and shorts, girls in simple coloured dress, parade outside each school as he sped by. He glanced at his watch: it was eight thirty am. At this time, throughout Ghana, nearly a million children in the primary and middle schools, and 25,000 secondary school and training college students, were reciting the Young Pioneers' pledge:

I sincerely promise

To live by the ideals of Osagyefo Kwame Nkrumah, Founder of the State of Ghana, Initiator of the African Personality:

To safeguard by all means possible the independence, sovereignty, and territorial integrity of the State of Ghana from internal and external aggression:

To be always in the vanguard for the social and economic reconstruction of Ghana and Africa:

To be in the first ranks of men fighting for the total liberation and unity of Africa; for these are the noble aims guiding the Ghana Young Pioneers.

As a Young Pioneer, I will be a guard of workers, farmers, co-operators, and all the other sections of our community.

I believe that the dynamic Convention People's Party is supreme and I promise to be worthy of its ideals.

So help me God.

Many would repeat the liturgy:

Leader	Nkrumah does no wrong
Response	Nkrumah is our Leader
Leader	Nkrumah does no wrong
Response	Nkrumah is our Messiah
Leader	Nkrumah does no wrong
Response	Nkrumah never dies

and cap it with a children's chorus borrowed from the churches and invested with a rather different meaning:

If you follow him, if you follow him,
He will make you fishers of men
Fishers of men, fishers of men;
He will make you fishers of men
If you follow him.

Most adults, thank God, had not lost their independence of mind, even though it was impossible to speak out publicly; but after years of such indoctrination, what would the next generation be like? And if Nkrumah succeeded in brainwashing the nation, how many generations would it take before, as was already happening in the Soviet Union and in communist eastern Europe, the first rumblings of youthful dissent would be followed by open defiance, and eventually a change in the whole system?

Was this young fellow, sitting next to him in the car, infected with it? Kotoka asked himself.

Young Afrifa—he was only 29 years old—had been promoted major last August at the same time as Kotoka became a full colonel and took over 2 Brigade. Kotoka strongly suspected that he had been planted on him to watch his movements. But at Christmas Afrifa came to Kotoka's house and was the heart and soul of the party. Francis Kwashie was there and commented on the fact: "He's a good chap, no doubt about it," Kwashie said; "don't fear him in the least!"

Kotoka stole a side-long glance at his lanky brigade major, who was deeply engrossed in a paperback with a lurid picture on the cover. He still looked just a boy, with his round face, small features, and close-cut hair. If he shaved off that moustache you could imagine that he was back in the sixth form at Adisadel. They said he did classics there—Latin and Greek! What could modern Ghana politics mean to a young fellow like this? One could hardly blame him if he was infected with this blind enthusiasm for Nkrumah.

Afrifa got to the end of a chapter, slammed the book closed, and turned to Kotoka with a smile. "Dreadful stuff, sir," he said apologetically. "It reminds me of the rags we used to have at Sandhurst. Somehow I always got into the task force." "What task force?" asked the colonel, out of courtesy rather than curiosity. "When we de-bagged anyone—in fact whenever there was a bit of fun—three or four boys were picked for the first die-hard party; and I was usually among them. I think they liked a black face in the gang to frighten the others!" (Afrifa was being a little too modest; he knew they chose him because of his boisterous sense of humour.) "But you could forget about colour at Sandhurst, sir; you got real comradeship there, wherever you came from. It's a damn fine place; I wish more of our people could go there." "Is that so?" Kotoka pricked his ears up. Was this an attempt to lure him into saying something that could be turned against him? Better make no comment.

"Who else was there in your time?"

"Why, old Nzegwu—he led the party who shot Sir Ahmadu Bello in Northern Nigeria three weeks ago. He was in my company, Normandy Company; six months senior to me . . ."

" . . . and a member of the task force?"

"Oh no, not Nzegwu. He was a funny type: a devout Catholic, wouldn't drink or smoke; and the moment he got a week's leave you could trust him to be sightseeing in Moscow, or Rome, or Stockholm, or somewhere."

"Quite a traveller!"

"He once landed on me for the night at Tamale. I hadn't seen him since Sandhurst. He drove up in a brand new Volkswagen, cool as you please, as though he'd just come round from the next road on an evening call. He'd driven straight from Lagos—800 miles in a couple of days. 'What the hell are you doing here?' I asked. 'I've bought this thing in Lagos,' he said casually: 'thought I'd better make sure it works. How about coming back with me by the northern route—there is a northern route, isn't there?' 'You'll find it if there is, Nzegwu,' I replied, 'but you can have it all to yourself!' You wouldn't have thought a man like that would assassinate a regional premier, would you?" [22]

106

"I suppose you wouldn't."

"Don't you find these coups interesting, Colonel? Take Castro's coup in Cuba. It was too brutal. They made prisoners dig their own graves, shot them, and bundled the corpses in . . ."

"So the American papers said."

". . whereas the military take-over in the Sudan was a tea-party."

Afrifa paused for a long, deep breath. He must move a little nearer the subject. "I've often wondered if we're going to have a coup in Ghana. When the President goes away from the country we have a Presidential Commission. Supposing something happened to the Presidential Commission and they were no more in power, would the President have any claim when he returned?"

Kotoka reflected on the question as if it had never occurred to him in his life. "It's rather a technical point, but I suppose you could argue that if the Commission represents the President, whatever happens to them has happened to him. But why do you ask?"

Afrifa took another deep breath and looked his commanding officer in the face. The car had just passed through his home town, Mampong; his mother was probably out weeding her yam farm, a little patch cleared from the mighty forest. "I don't like the way things are going, sir. Somebody must do something to save the country before it's too late."

"When did you come to that conclusion?" Kotoka's voice hardly sounded encouraging, but Afrifa had gone too far now to turn back, even if he was going to be reported and spend the rest of his days in Nsawam Medium Security Prison. "It's been in my mind for years, sir; especially since the three judges were dismissed a couple of years ago. And that farcial election last June is making Ghana a laughing-stock all round the world."

Kotoka smiled a little self-consciously; the tension of the past six months was rolling away like a bad dream. "I haven't been able to tell you about it, Afrifa," said the colonel, "but it has been in my mind even longer."

By the time they reached the site of the proposed exercise, near Yendi, their eager discussion had covered almost every aspect of Ghanaian life, and each was relieved to find that the other shared his views.

The conversation had to be interrupted; there was work to do. They decided on various details of the exercise—the "start point" of defenders and attackers, the most likely movements, and the number of umpires required.

That night Kotoka stayed with Lt-Col John Addy, garrison commander of Tamale. Although Kotoka's 2 Brigade headquarters was in Kumasi most of his troops were here in Tamale, some 250 miles further north (and thus 250 miles further away from Accra). Addy commanded 3 Battalion, in addition to being garrison commander for Tamale. 5 Battalion and the Parachute Battalion were also in Tamale. As Col Kotoka, the brigade commander, sank into an armchair in John Addy's comfortable house, he started weighing up the advantages and the possible dangers of discussing the coup with him. It would be helpful to have an ally up here where the troops were but, at this early stage of planning, was it worth increasing the danger that the secret would leak out?

Last year's attempted coup had been an inter-tribal effort—Ankrah, a Ga: Otu, an Akuapem: Harlley and Deku, both Ewe. But ever since Kotoka had been involved in practical planning for a coup, the plot had been confined to his own intimate companions, all Ewe. Until this morning. This morning he had revealed the secret to Afrifa, an Ashanti. Now he was on the point of telling a Ga. Was it wise? Something calmed his doubts, perhaps a recollection of Aggrey's story of the piano—"You can play a sort of tune on the black notes, and you can play a sort of tune on the white notes, but to get the best music you must play both of them together". Later that evening he suddenly blurted out, "John. I'm fed up with the kind of government we have. It would be fine to overthrow them. What do you think?"

Addy was so delighted he hardly knew how to reply. He pledged his co-operation, and after briefly discussing the troop movements involved they both retired for the night. Next morning they finalized arrangements for an exercise which was never to take place: it was scheduled for 23 to 31 March.

WHERE UNITS OF GHANA ARMY WERE STATIONED IN EARLY 1966
from north to south (units and officers mentioned in this book – not a complete record)

TAMALE
2 Brigade: Major Afrifa, Brigade Major
    2 Battalion: Lt-Col Addy
    5 Battalion:
    Parachute Battalion:

KUMASI
2 Brigade HQ: Col Kotoka, Commander

ACCRA-TEMA
1 Brigade HQ: Col Ocran, Commander
    2 Battalion: Col Asare, Burma Camp, Accra
    4 Battalion: Michel Camp, Tema
Reconnaissance Regiment of armoured cars: Major Dontoh
Engineers squadron: Col Coker-Appiah, Teshie
President's Own Guard Regiment
    Battalion at Burma Camp (defending Flagstaff House)
    Artillery squadron at Shai Hills Camp: Major Tetteh, Commander

TAKORADI
1 Brigade:
    3 Battalion

There was plenty of routine work to keep Kotoka and Afrifa busy on their return to Kumasi: for a couple of days they had no time for subversion. Besides, Kotoka was in no hurry to take the initiative. Afrifa had spoken far too frankly for Kotoka to believe any longer that he was spying on him, but would he have the resolution to carry this through to its logical conclusion? School-boyish pranks at Sandhurst were one thing, but this was a matter of life and death and the issue in the balance was no less than the fate of the whole nation Ghana.

On the other hand he had seen in the papers only last week an announcement that Nkrumah was going to Hanoi on a peace mission. He might leave at any moment; he always moved unexpectedly, for fear of attempts on his life. Nkrumah's absence in Hanoi would be the perfect opportunity for their coup.

FRIDAY 11 FEBRUARY

The night of 11 February was warm and sticky, nearly 80 degrees Fahrenheit at ten thirty even in the "garden city" Kumasi, more than 500 feet above sea level. Afrifa decided to pay a social call on his brigade commander; good—Kotoka was alone. He made himself comfortable in an armchair as the colonel went to the fridge and pulled out a bottle of beer. Afrifa came straight to the point. "What can we do about our discussion the other day?" he asked.

Kotoka was glad to see his subordinate's eagerness to get down to positive planning. Together they began to assess the situation. They would have to rely principally on the troops under Kotoka's command, the two infantry battalions at Tamale and the parachute battalion in the same town; unfortunately Tamale was over 400 miles from Accra and most of the vehicles in 2 Brigade were off the road for lack of tyres, batteries, and other essential spares. "How many vehicles can you get on the road, Akwasi?"

Akwasi Afrifa made a quick calculation. "We can't send every single vehicle to fetch them: that would bring everything to a standstill here in Kumasi, and it would look suspicious too. We might manage 40 vehicles, including 3-tonners and Landrovers."

110

"40 vehicles. They won't carry more than five companies and our HQ staff. Is that enough to overthrow the government of Ghana?"

"It doesn't sound much, sir. Can't we get in some troops from Accra?"

"Whom can we trust?"

Accra was the base of 1 Brigade, commanded by Colonel Ocran, a contemporary of Kotoka's at Eaton Hall Officer Cadets Training Unit, Chester, England, where both of them received the Queen's commission in November 1954. Ocran was three years younger than Kotoka, but had followed close behind his colleague up the ladder of promotion, till in August last year they had both become full colonels and each had taken command of one of Ghana's two infantry brigades. What could be more natural than for Kotoka to approach his old friend and suggest a coup? Yes—and what could be more hazardous?

Then Afrifa remembered that Major Coker-Appiah of the Field Regiment was coming to see him the following day. Coker-Appiah, six feet two and commander of the Engineers, had been at Sandhurst just before Afrifa. "He's the man for this type of job," said Afrifa. "I guarantee he'll be with us. He'll be here tomorrow to plan the Engineers' part in the exercise."

"Yes, and I shall have to tell Major Dedjoe; if I try to get stores for this kind of operation without saying what's on, he's sure to suspect something." They began to list the points which had to be secured when the coup took place. Flagstaff House and Radio Ghana were obviously the most important points—"Once we've captured those, the battle is fought," said the colonel. They would have to seize the Post Office, Ghana News Agency, and the External Telecommunications Department. Anyone capable of organizing resistance would have to be arrested beforehand: that involved a formidable list of ministers, parliamentarians, party workers, and a handful of soldiers— Barwah, Hassan, and Zanlerigu at least.

It was beginning to look like a large sort of operation for a mere five companies, but there was another factor that they had not yet thought of: the two battalions of the President's

111

Own Guard Regiment, one at Burma Camp in Accra, the other some 32 miles away to the north-east in an old camp near the Shai Hills. If they proved to be loyal to Nkrumah they would completely upset the balance. They were bristling with first class Russian equipment, including anti-tank weapons and armoured personnel carriers which were not available to other battalions. In addition the Shai Hills battalion had artillery which could make short work of the rebellion.

"We haven't thought of the airport . . ."

" . . . nor of the security forces—they live in those blocks of flats just opposite Flagstaff House."

"The whole thing is hopeless. We can't begin to do it with five companies. Of course if we had the armoured cars and Ocran's battalions. . .

". . . which is very unlikely. . . "

The discussion went on late into the night, but by the time they finished they had drawn up a master plan, which Kotoka summarized on a small leaf of paper tucked in his diary. Afrifa made a copy in Greek characters, to avoid detection, and chuckled as he wondered what the ancient Greek military historians whom he had read at Adisadel would have made of it.

The commander of 2 Brigade retired to bed in a cheerful frame of mind. Maybe all that Latin and Greek had its merits after all.

SATURDAY 12 FEBRUARY

Major Coker-Appiah was not in the best of moods when he left Accra for this conference with Major Afrifa. Why should he have to work daily from Monday to Friday and then spend his week-ends in Kumasi planning exercises? Hitherto the Engineers had been as short of equipment as everyone else: that involved improvising, crises at the last moment, and always waste of precious time. Now they had permission to order large quantities of equipment from East European countries, so things would ultimately get better; but the necessity to prepare their orders imposed an enormous extra burden on all concerned, not least on the major commanding the Field Regiment. He was holding equipment-ordering meetings from three to five o'clock three afternoons a week, and there was detailed preparation to be done for each meeting.

Then there were these young officers to train for their promotion exams; that meant staying up late at night studying textbooks and preparing lectures. Always in the background was a host of projects in various stages of completion, such as the ammunition store for the President's Own Guard Regiment, or costing and surveying for the sports stadium at Burma Camp. And then on top of it all they must plan exercises!

Exercises! Major Coker-Appiah had enough exercise in one day's normal work to last some Army officers for a couple of months. All the same he had to admit that he enjoyed that last exercise, with 1 Brigade. They had done river crossings, bridge building, demolitions with high explosive—it had been exhausting, but fascinating too. The 2 Brigade exercise would involve the paratroops, so there would be air drops to add to the fun. Maybe it was worth giving up his Sunday morning to work this out with Afrifa: he was not often seen in church anyway.

He got to Kumasi and Afrifa took him to the City Hotel for some booze. Then at ten o'clock on the night of Saturday 12 February they set to work on the exercise. They'd been at it for an hour when Afrifa pointed out that it was four weeks to the day since the Nigerian coup. Coker-Appiah wasn't particularly interested, so Afrifa tried the direct approach:

"What about having one here?"

"When?"

"The President is supposed to be going to Hanoi next week..." and Afrifa explained the plan in full detail, while Coker-Appiah sat at the desk hardly believing his ears.

Then he started making suggestions. They were the suggestions of an expert in demolition, and involved attacking some key targets with dynamite. Afrifa was confident that the whole thing could be done quite easily even in broad daylight, provided they had the element of surprise in their favour, but Coker-Appiah insisted that this or that must be blown up, and his companion began to fear their discussion would end in a

113

heated argument. Vainly did he insist that they mustn't waste the taxpayers' money: at length he wondered if they had stayed a little too long at the bar of the City Hotel. Just before midnight Coker-Appiah gave way and pledged his full support. "I believe in a simple plan; can't go wrong with a simple plan," said Coker-Appiah, a little wearily.

Afrifa heaved a sigh of relief. They went back to planning the exercise which would never take place, and went to bed in the early hours of the morning. Coker-Appiah returned to Accra after breakfast. He had accepted responsibility for arresting the army chiefs and for taking over the Post Office, Ghana News Agency, and the External Telecommunications Department; in addition he was to be the liaison between Ocran in Accra (commander of 1 Brigade) and Kotoka in Kumasi. He had detachments of Engineers with 2 Brigade, and he could run up and down between Accra and Kumasi without arousing any suspicion. Without arousing suspicion, yes: but not without upsetting either the equipment conferences, or the promotion exams, or the construction projects for which he was responsible up and down the country. Ah well, that's life; and provided the coup was successful, it probably wouldn't matter much anyway.

Afrifa brought the news of Coker-Appiah's involvement to his commander. Colonel Kotoka thanked him in a matter-of-fact sort of way, and after he had gone, sat down quietly to overcome his excitement and to consider the implications. It's two and a half years since I first discussed a coup with John Harlley, he thought to himself. The first attempt fell through at the last moment, but this one must not be allowed to fall through and it seems that even if I wanted to stop it, I could not do so. Until last Friday all that had happened was that three Army officers and two policemen, all linked by ties of long and intimate friendship, had been chatting: that is all. But in the past two days things have been moving faster than I realized. On Friday I discussed a detailed plan with a man whom I suspected of being a spy until a few days earlier. On Saturday that man, Afrifa, passed part of the plan on to Coker-Appiah. Well, Afrifa

114

seems to have confidence in him, but heaven alone knows whom he will talk to in the next few days: and I wonder if John Addy up in Tamale has kept the secret. Emmanuel, my boy, life begins to look a little dangerous; if this plan falls through, you'll certainly fall with it.

Really, though, I've done nothing yet. I've just been waiting, waiting for something to happen. Suddenly young Afrifa comes out with his feelings on the way to Yendi–I didn't ask him to! Then this Coker-Appiah man: It would never have occurred to me to call in the help of the Engineers! Somehow I feel like a mere spectator. But now the time has come for me to act. Let's see: I have this Army Commander's conference on Wednesday in Accra, haven't I?

That is another gift! Surely God is in this, and I didn't know it! He's even arranged for me to go down to Accra on a routine visit that cannot arouse the least suspicion; but it will give me all the time I need to contact Harlley, Coker-Appiah, and anyone else I need to see. It all seems so easy . . .

TUESDAY 15 FEBRUARY

Tuesday evening, the day before the Army Commander's conference, saw Colonel Kotoka lurching round the military camps of Accra and Teshie in Captain Kwashie's ancient car; for the use of his own car might have aroused suspicion. They passed the police on duty outside Harlley's house and found the Commissioner at home. The customary drink was provided, greetings were exchanged, and then they got down to business. "There's no backing out now," said Kotoka. "Too many people are in the know already. But what worries me is that there is more to do than my five companies can possibly cope with."

"And the police have no arms," commented Harlley.

"Precisely. We're fortunate to have Coker-Appiah of the Field Regiment; he's agreed to do the military arrests."

"My boys can look after the ministers and party men."

"Won't they put up a fight?"

"Maybe one or two of them; but in any case there will be complete surprise, so we have nothing to fear."

With this reassurance from Harlley, Kotoka pulled out his diary, and ticked off another section of the master plan: "Civilian arrests–Harlley".

"And what about the date?" asked the Commissioner.

"I've been thinking of next Monday, the 21st. What do you say?"

"The Old Man leaves for Hanoi on Monday, but there can always be last-minute changes. No. Wait till you know he's gone before you move. It'll be a bloody affair if we attack Flagstaff House while he's in."

"Then," replied Kotoka, "I'll have to come down again on that day; and if everything goes all right it shouldn't take us more than three days to move the troops. We can be ready on Thursday morning."

They were vaguely conscious that their hurried decision could give 24 February a memorable place on the Ghanaian calendar for centuries to come—or it could make next Thursday the most disastrous day of their lives. Quickly Kotoka and Kwashie took leave and rumbled on to their next call.

It was not till they reached Coker-Appiah's house in Teshie that things began to go wrong. Kotoka stepped through the dark front garden, knocked at the door, and was admitted. Kwashie waited with the car, and thought he would turn it round while he was waiting; but instead of carefully negotiating a three-point turn, Kwashie's mind was preoccupied with the question, whether the commander of 2 Brigade, Kumasi, had been observed paying a surreptitious visit to an officer in Teshie, with whom he had no official connection. As he turned, there was a lurch, an awful screech of metal on concrete, and one wheel came to rest in a narrow open drain, right down to the hub.

Fortunately Kotoka did not stay long inside. He told Major Coker-Appiah that Afrifa wanted him to go up to Kumasi to do some more work on the exercise. "He wants advice on a river crossing," said Kotoka, mysteriously. He still could not bring himself to speak openly about the coup even to Coker-Appiah. As he came out to see the colonel off, Coker-Appiah dearly wanted to ask whether the coup was on or not, but their conversation was cut short by Kwashie's call for help; the tubby little captain was trying vainly to lift the wheel out of the drain, single-handed. The major commanding the Field Regiment would have liked to recommend a suitable charge of high explosive, which would have put a convenient end to the car and all its problems once and for all. Instead he consented to be pressed into service, and added his six feet two inches of manpower to that of his fellow-plotters. At last, with the help of a couple of passers-by, they lifted the car till the wheel came clear of the drain and rolled back on the road.

Kwashie drove his weary passenger home, and the engine spluttered to a stop. He was horrified by a cry from Kotoka: "My diary—where is it? The master plan is inside!" The interior light of the old car didn't work. They fetched a torch and searched the floor and the rear seats. It was not there. As they pulled out the seat and poked in the dust underneath, Kotoka suddenly realized he was sweating with shock. They examined the odds and ends in the car pocket, checked and rechecked them. Not there.

Immediately Kotoka sent a messenger to Coker-Appiah, to see if he'd left the diary there. A few minutes later Kwashie himself went all over the route from Appiah's house to his own bungalow at the military hospital, but he saw nothing. He spent ten minutes searching every inch of the place where they had lifted the car out of the gutter—the diary was not there. Two young men had helped them get it out: Kwashie tried to remember what they looked like—were they likely to realize the significance of Kotoka's master plan? One thing was certain: if Kotoka's diary fell into the wrong hands, they would all be in Nsawam Prison in a matter of hours. Next day Kotoka had a conference at the Ministry of Defence. As he arrived he couldn't help looking out of the corner of his eye to detect the slightest sign of anything unusual. He thought the security men might be waiting for him at the entrance. "Now for it," he said to himself, "keep calm!" But nothing happened. Everyone greeted him as usual.

117

All through the conference he was ready to be whisked away to explain the notes on that tell-tale piece of paper tucked in the diary. At the end of the day nothing had happened, and Kotoka returned to Kumasi a little reassured. As soon as he got there he rang Kwashie to check on whether the diary had turned up: it had not. Harlley, who would have been implicated if the diary had been discovered, forced a laugh when Kwashie told him about it. "That man Kotoka is too learned," he said: "he likes putting things on paper. A simple chap like me wouldn't have written a single word!" Inwardly he felt a rude shock. He began to long for the moment when the suspense would come to an end and the real action would begin.

Back in Kumasi, Kotoka managed to forget about the diary by wrestling with a different kind of problem: how to get those five companies away from Tamale without revealing the plan to a still wider circle. The battalion commanders were sure to be sympathetic, but it would take at least 24 hours to move the whole force over 400 miles from Tamale to Accra, and to brief them before they moved was asking for trouble.

On Friday 18 February, the day after Kotoka's return from Accra, he and Afrifa hit on a perfectly natural plan. There was an exercise in progress at Kintampo, which gave them an opportunity to call the battalion commanders down to Kumasi for a conference without exciting the least suspicion.

Major Afrifa simply informed them that Kotoka, the brigade commander, wished to test the troops' state of readiness for a sudden move to Rhodesia or Zambia, and that he would start with five companies—two from 3 Battalion, two from 5 Battalion, and one from the Parachute Battalion. They would be told when to send these companies down, and transport would be provided. Not a word was said about a coup—the only man who saw the connection was Lt-Col John Addy, garrison commander of Tamale, to whom Kotoka had spoken just over a week before; and he was not accompanying the troops lest his presence should draw attention to the importance of the move.

Once again, it all seemed so easy. Cold chop indeed. While most other men would have spent the week-end in an agony of apprehension, Kotoka was suffering from a bout of over-confidence.

7

PEACE IN VIETNAM—REBELLION AT HOME

EDITORIAL NOTE: Pages of chapters 7, 8, 9, and 10 will have headers as necessary giving the date and / or time of day of the events recorded on each page. Ghana time is given on the left of the page, times in various lands, from North Africa to East Asia, are given on the right.

TUESDAY 8 FEBRUARY

WHILE Kotoka and his fellow officers were seeking a military solution to the autocratic rule of Kwame Nkrumah, one bright flame of democratic expression was snuffed out in the National Assembly. If the flame burned bright at the end, that only hastened the decision to extinguish it.

Mr S I Iddrissu, the member for Gushiegu, in Northern Ghana, had always been a fiery speaker and a fearless critic of corruption and mismanagement within the CPP; but during the past week his burning invective had scorched rather too many people of standing in the omnipotent Party. In addition, he had a series of hot exchanges with Kofi Baako, the Leader of the House.

On Tuesday, 8 February, he made an impassioned plea for Muslim feasts to be counted as public holidays in the same way as Christian festivals. He also spoke out boldly on behalf of labourers: "At present the average labourer is paid about 6 shillings a day but he was promised some time ago that very soon he would be able to live on 2 shillings a day as a result of the development of our agriculture. But when the Minister of Agriculture comes here he is not patient and ready to listen to our advice and suggestions . . . Rather the Minister of Agriculture likes to come into this House to propound philosophic theories . . . I regard this Parliament as signifying the dictatorship of the proletariat; this Parliament cannot signify the dictatorship of the proletariat unless the workers' needs are met, or they have to seize power and hand it over to those who they think can do it better . . ."

Two days later he introduced a private member's motion "that this House regrets that the Ghana National Trading Corporation has not yet been able to satisfy the demand of the masses for essential goods." He bitterly attacked ministers, senior Party and government officials, and the chairman of GNTC, Sir Patrick Fitz-Gerald—"a capitalist has been appointed to advise on socialist economy," declared Iddrisu. Then he quoted some comments on the evils of neocolonialism from the President's latest Sessional Address, and applied these remarks, not to the foreign states of which Nkrumah was speaking, but to Ghana itself. "You will be surprised to learn, Mr Speaker," he said with a touch of sarcasm (for Mr Speaker was in an excellent position to know all about it) "that it was rather some of the lieutenants of Osagyefo who monopolized trade so that they and their families would become rich at the expense of the masses. Despite their great fortunes in Ghana, these people have property abroad and have refused to bring it home, and yet still they want to continue the exploitation of the people even in the face of Osagyefo himself . . . Nine of them, apart from being members of this House, are in places of the highest trust that Osagyefo can graciously give to a comrade. I shall not mention their names, for I hope that they will either change or apologise to the nation for adopting a corrupt attitude towards the nation's economy. If they do not regret or repent and change their shameful attitude, their names will be mentioned in this House later during this session."

TUESDAY 15 FEBRUARY

Exactly 7 days later Iddrissu was once again on his feet introducing another private member's motion, "that this House appreciates the government's housing policy and asks that the housing programme should be pursued with greater vigour". At first members thought they were going to be entertained to a harmless historical study of housing in Ghana, but many faces began to register acute discomfort as Iddrissu blazed into battle once again on the way MPs were sub-letting their houses in Kanda Estate at exorbitant rents. "We are members of parliament and before we speak we must examine ourselves. How many of us in this honourable House who are staying at the Kanda Estate can dare get up to say that they are not grateful to the government for providing them with such luxurious houses for ten pounds a month? How many of us can dare say that we do not preach Nkrumah in the presence of Kwame Nkrumah whilst we exploit the people? How many of us members of parliament can dare say that they do not rent their boys' quarters at exorbitant rents? Before we speak of others we must examine ourselves. It is likely that Iddrissu is renting his boys' quarters, but Iddrissu hopes and Iddrissu has the belief that he and other comrades have seen that it is a dirty thing to do in a socialist state . . .

"The President said that everybody should take stock of his actions. Those of us who are renting our houses to the Lebanese and Syrians must repent. They should go to the Party headquarters and say, 'We are sorry, we did not know that it was bad, now we have known it through a motion which was introduced in Parliament recently'. If this is not done I am prepared, armed with facts, to reveal everything during the debate on the budget, and no one should blame me for that . . ."
There was a lively discussion lasting an hour and three quarters, and then the deputy speaker asked Mr Iddrissu to wind up the debate.

Mr Iddrissu: The debate has been very interesting and from the interest members have shown in it, it is quite clear that they have the interest of the people and of the nation at heart. Mr

122

Speaker, at this moment I have no right to address this House. I was born in a humble home, born with a strong heart and born with honesty, and for that matter I follow the Leader of the nation. Mr Speaker, there is a letter here signed by Osagyefo Dr Kwame Nkrumah. I wish to read it; it is dated 15 February 1966—

Mr Deputy Speaker: Let me see the letter . . . (there was unusual silence in the chamber as Inkumsah, the deputy speaker, peered at the piece of paper) . . . As deputy speaker of the House, I have read this letter and I find it is not necessary for the member to read it to the House. The reply of the Minister of Housing is sufficient. The question will now be put . . . (Mr Iddrissu rose to interrupt, but Inkumsah went on speaking) . . . On the strength of the letter addressed to the member, which I have read, I am not going to allow him to wind up.

Mr Iddrissu: That is the reason why I want to tell the nation the contents of this letter. I have to quit my estate house at Kanda and before I quit I have to tell the reason why I have to quit.

Mr Eric Heymann: On a point of order. I think the member is doing great injustice to himself.

Mr Iddrissu: I have never done injustice to myself. I only stand here for the people because the Leader of the nation is for the people. I will wind up . . .

Mr Deputy Speaker: The member will not wind up.

Mr Iddrissu: I will wind up because as the mover of the motion I have to. If you refuse me permission to wind up you will see how the debate will end . . .

Hansard did not describe the uproar that followed; it did not describe the consternation on most of the members' faces, the sense of injustice that pervaded the chamber—for by this time everyone knew the contents of the letter: it was Iddrissu's dismissal from the CPP, and under the new one-party system that meant automatic expulsion from the National Assembly. *Hansard* demurely recorded the House's procedure, and left it at that:

123

Mr Deputy Speaker: I will put the question on the motion forthwith.

Question put and agreed to. Resolved: That this House appreciates government's housing policy and asks that the housing programme should be pursued with greater vigour.

ADJOURNMENT

The House was adjourned at Fifteen Minutes before One o'clock pm till tomorrow Wednesday, 16th February, 1966 at Nine o'clock in the forenoon.

*   *   *

All through the exchanges over the letter, Quaison-Sackey had been itching to get up and defend Iddrissu's right to speak. At the same time he was a newcomer to the Assembly and he did not know if there was some rule or procedure which gave the Speaker power to prevent a member from reading a letter; he did not want to look ridiculous—if only someone else would get up to defend Iddrissu, he, the Foreign Minister, would leap to his support.

No one else did.

Quaison-Sackey went home for lunch with a heavy heart. He knew well that a crucial moment had passed by and he could not forgive himself for having failed to throw the weight of his reputation and his experience into the balance on the side of freedom and justice.

That afternoon he went to Flagstaff House for the weekly Tuesday cabinet meeting. The President was late; he had been busy with Ambrose Yankey, studying an anonymous letter which implied that David Zanlerigu, commander of the President's Own Guard Regiment, was not keeping to the security regulations. At last he entered the long room with the wood-panelled walls, the maps at one end, and the elegant polished table, The ministers rose as he entered, then they were seated and business began.

The President bluntly announced that the central committee of the Party had decided to dismiss Iddrissu for bad behaviour and drunkenness. Once again Quaison-Sackey wanted to protest but he knew what Nkrumah's reaction would be, because he had raised objections of this kind before: "Oh!" he would say, with an impatient gesture, "Sackey, you've only just come. That's just United Nations stuff—don't talk like that here!" and the other members of the cabinet would grin at him condescendingly, as though he were still a new boy and much could be forgiven him. He was failing again and he hated himself for it.

He left quickly after the meeting and tried to forget Iddrissu in an orgy of work. He was due to leave with Nkrumah next Monday for China, to try and negotiate a Vietnam peace settlement. There would be plenty of hard talking to do in Peking and Hanoi and he must prepare for it. He went back through the files and meticulously studied the background of the mission.

It was not easy to negotiate with the Vietnamese: after the Commonwealth conference last June, Harold Davies, a British parliamentary secretary and a personal acquaintance of Ho Chi Minh, had gone to North Vietnam but was not even given an interview with the North Vietnamese President. His visit seemed to have been a complete waste of time.

However it apparently had one result. Harold Davies returned to London on 14 July; two days later Ho Chi Minh invited Kwame Nkrumah to visit Hanoi. Within a week Kwesi Armah, formerly Ghana's High Commissioner in London, who had just been appointed minister of trade in the new cabinet, was in Hanoi, and as soon as he returned Alex Quaison-Sackey left for Washington with a personal message from Nkrumah to President Johnson. He returned with Johnson's reply, then sent a second message from Nkrumah to the American President by cable, asking him to halt American bombing of North Vietnam during Nkrumah's visit; but all in vain—Johnson would only promise that the Ghanaian President would be in no danger from the United States air force if he made a planned trip to Hanoi in search of a peaceful solution; he would not agree to halt the bombing. He could hardly have been more uncooperative without actually threatening to shoot him down. The fact that he had not gone to that extreme was no compensation for the many thousands of miles covered by the two Ghanaian cabinet ministers.

For six months Nkrumah gave up any ideas of carrying out the peace mission, Then about a month ago he had revived the idea and Quaison-Sackey had been working on it ever since.

For the hundredth time the minister of external affairs carefully analysed the American 14 points and the four points of Ho Chi Minh. There were two problems: the American refusal to have the VietCong at the conference table, and the North Vietnamese demand that the United States should withdraw its troops before negotiations started. China was unfortunately pouring scorn on the whole idea of a Ghanaian initiative, but in Quaison-Sackey's opinion there was nothing to be lost by a sincere peace overture, and if by some remote chance Ghana were able to pave the way to effective negotiations it would be a remarkable diplomatic triumph.

Ghana's foreign minister spent the next two days in bed. He had reacted rather violently to one of the inoculations given in preparation for his trip to East Asia, and his last chance of raising the question of Iddrissu's expulsion in the National Assembly while it was still a live issue had been lost. Then he gathered together several boxes of documents, marshalled his arguments, trying to foresee how the negotiations would develop, and made ready for their departure on Monday, 21 February.

*　　　　*　　　　*

Up in Kibi Women's Teacher Training College the hatred and tensions were mounting, to a point where an explosion must follow at any moment. During the past week there had been warning messages in the columns of the Party press—a fairly sure sign of detentions and deportations to come. Mr Mensah, the district organizer, and the DC had probably called in the MP and it seemed that it could be only a matter of a few days before the Swiss principal was packed off home and several of her staff were in jail. To bring this about the district organizer of the Young Pioneers had circulated a letter to the Party, the Young Pioneer headquarters, and the regional commissioner, demanding action.

Teachers on the college staff had contacts in the district organizer's office, and an extra copy of the letter was smuggled out to them. They knew that once they were in detention they would be unable to speak; now was the time to defend themselves. So they held a private staff meeting and drafted a reply to the accusations that had been levelled against them. They did not invite the principal, for fear of involving her in Ghanaian politics, nor Mr Mensah.

SUNDAY 20 FEBRUARY

The senior prefect, a third year student whose father was a well-known personality in the CPP, came to an agonizing decision. She had been elected by the student body, but she was consulted by the staff on disciplinary matters and took her responsibility seriously. At the same time, she was a member of the Young Pioneers and saw how Mr Mensah's behaviour was disrupting the whole life of the college. She also knew more than any members of staff how many students were in the habit of breaking bounds. The decision was not made any easier by her desire to please her parents; but in the end she saw it was quite inevitable. She resigned that Sunday from the Young Pioneers.

It seemed that hell was let loose for the next couple of days. The senior prefect was ostracized by her fellow students. She was called a sneak and a traitor to Osagyefo. They gathered round her bed at night to threaten her; some were bold enough to boast of their intimate relationships with MPs who, they said, would see to her downfall. On Mr Mensah's instructions they laid ambushes for the senior prefect as she moved about the compound, but she managed to evade them.

127

WEDNESDAY 23 FEBRUARY

On Wednesday morning a group of town ruffians set on the senior prefect and tried to beat her up at the Anglican Primary School, where she had been sent for teaching practice. The other teachers protected her; police were hurried to the scene, and managed to arrest two of the young men.

When the principal returned that afternoon from supervising teaching practice in some outlying villages she received a summons from the DC. This is it, she thought. I shall be deported now. I wonder how long they will give me to pack my things. Please, God, help me to take it patiently.

The interview lasted nearly an hour. Once again the DC sat in state, surrounded by Young Pioneer leaders and the headmasters of local elementary schools. The actions of principal and staff were exaggerated, their motives were misrepresented, and she felt sure that she would be taken straight from the room to the cells. Her fears were confirmed by the arrival of a policeman, who waited for a few minutes outside the room before interrupting.

"Why don't you want to co-operate with the Young Pioneers? Don't you realize that these days we have plenty of new training colleges? so that if you don't like to do as we say we can close your college straight down at any time and nobody will miss it?"

The principal dearly wanted to answer. The DC, even the regional commissioner himself, could not possibly close down a training college—that was the prerogative of the Ministry of Education alone. As for the numerous new colleges, she knew very well, and so did the DC, that the number of students seeking entry each year, and being turned down, was becoming a national headache. There were tens of thousands of candidates for only a few hundred places. But it was best to keep silent as far as possible.

Then the superintendent of police stepped into the room.

"Yes, officer, what do you want?"

"We have arrested two young men in town, sir. We found their conduct was liable to lead to a breach of the peace."

128

"What happened?"

"According to the statement taken they called a student of the training college out of the classroom where she was engaged in teaching practice and accused her of saying the Young Pioneers were useless, and as such they should teach her a lesson. There was a sharp quarrel and they attempted to lay hands on the young lady. I wish to charge them with insulting behaviour."

"What are these young men?"

"One is a typist, the other is a clerical assistant. Both are employed in the office of the Young Pioneers' district organizer. They claim that he sent them there for the purpose of beating up the young lady."

Slowly the DC turned to the Young Pioneer leader:

"But did you really do that?"

"Yes, sir," he said, without a word of explanation.

The DC frowned impatiently. "You mustn't do such things," he said, in the tone of a man who rebukes a favourite child for going out in the morning without combing his hair.

"I won't do it again," said the district organizer.

The DC seemed to regard that as the end of the matter, so the police superintendent spoke again. "What shall I do about the young men, sir?"

"See me about it later, officer,'" said the DC; "I'm busy just now." And with that he returned to the matter in hand, and went on scolding the principal for a good fifteen minutes more before he let her go.

That night the students did not sleep. There was pandemonium in the dormitories. They sang and shouted. They drummed noisily on their wooden beds. One girl got up in the middle of the night and rang the college bell. They trusted implicitly in the words of the prophet Mensah. The day of judgment was at hand.

8

OPERATION COLD CHOP—ROUND ONE

ONLY a matter of minutes after the President's VC 10 swept out of Accra International Airport on Monday, 21 February, "triumphantly swift, silent, and serene", as the advertisements said, a little military plane flew in, bearing a colonel from Kumasi on his way to the military hospital for a medical check-up. The medical orderly reported that the doctor he was to see was away in Bolgatanga, in the farthest north of Ghana, and feared that he would have to bear the colonel's wrath; but Kotoka took the news quite cheerfully. As it happened, he had other things to do in Accra.

MONDAY 21 FEBRUARY — MORNING

He discovered from Captain Kwashie that the diary was still missing. He phoned Coker-Appiah, who abandoned half a dozen urgent jobs to come for an informal chat in the military hospital, on the road outside the reception office. Soldiers with arms or legs in plaster of Paris were pushed by in wheel-chairs (there will be more like that by Thursday evening, thought Kotoka) and privates came in to report sick or get medicine, as the two officers carried on their conversation in low tones. This time there were no more attempts to hide what they were talking about. They used the code name "Operation Cold Chop", but they frankly discussed the arrests and seizure of the important points in Accra. Kotoka decided to relieve Coker-

130

Appiah of one of the arrests, for he had too many assignments already, and he made a mental note that he must send down an advance party to take care of Major-General Barwah.

"There's one thing I'd like you to do for me," said Coker-Appiah when they had finished. "My second-in-command is a friend of yours. You know how it is—a commanding officer has to put a bit of fear into the others, so I'm not sure of him. Anyway I think you could put it to him better than I could. How about it?"

"Yes, I know what you mean," said Kotoka, with some understanding. He had been in exactly the same position with Afrifa a few weeks ago. "Call him on the phone; I'll speak to him at once."

When the second-in-command got back to the Field Regiment lines after talking to Kotoka, Coker-Appiah contrived to meet him casually. "Well," he asked, "which side are you on?" The man grinned. At long last he was in his CO's confidence. "I'm all for it," he replied.

Meanwhile Kotoka was chatting with Harlley, asking eager questions about his side of the planning.

"Have you seen Ankrah?"

Major-General Ankrah was the Deputy Chief of Defence Staff dismissed together with Major-General Otu in 1965, after the coup attempt was cancelled. Harlley had kept in touch with him over the intervening months, and he seemed the best person to head the new government. He had been very popular with the troops. He was known for speaking his mind frankly, yet without being rash.

There was no alternative national leader within the CPP, and most of the former opposition leaders were in detention and so out of touch with the present situation. In any case there was much to be said for a non-political administration—a military régime, in fact.

"Ankrah? Yes, he's ready to help. I've seen him twice in the past few days and he's a hundred per cent behind us."

"When will he come in?"

"He'll join us at Police Headquarters as soon as the operation begins on Thursday."

"Have you told anybody else yet?"

"Not a soul. It can wait till three or four o'clock on Thursday morning—that's when I propose to call my officers in and give instructions for the politicians to be arrested."

In Kumasi Major Afrifa had just heard that Nkrumah was safely out of the country. He despatched a column of some 30 vehicles northwards to pick up the troops from Tamale; then he sent signals to five companies instructing them to proceed to a rendezvous ten miles north of Ejura at one o'clock on Wednesday afternoon, and he awaited developments.

* * *

EGYPTIAN TIME
MONDAY 21 FEBRUARY — 3.00 pm

The Presidential party flew into Cairo airport in jet-propelled luxury at three o'clock Egyptian time. Nkrumah was in the best of spirits, and sent a telegram to Fathia suggesting that she should come to Cairo for a short holiday and await his return from Hanoi. They met Nasser, who asked Nkrumah with a mischievous look in his eye, "And what are you doing with that beautiful conference centre?" "We shall find a use for it; it will be a hotel or something," said Nkrumah.[23]

EGYPTIAN TIME
TUESDAY 22 FEBRUARY — 8.0 am

The Ghanaian party slept in one of Cairo's former royal palaces, magnificently furnished by the former King Farouk, and left at nine o'clock next morning, Tuesday 22 February.

At the same time as the delegation to Hanoi was gathering to proceed to Cairo airport for the flight to Hanoi, eight o'clock Egyptian time, Colonel Kotoka's car was standing outside the house of his counterpart in 1 Brigade, Colonel Ocran. In Ghana it was 5.30am.

At the very last moment, less than 48 hours before the coup was due to begin, Kotoka had seen the impossibility of carrying out the whole operation without the help of 1 Brigade.

Ocran threw on his dressing gown and met Kotoka in the garden, in the shade of the trees. Kotoka greeted him and proceeded straight to business. "I have come to ask for your help," he said. "I have agreed with the officers under my command to stage a coup. My troops will come down from Tamale under Major Afrifa." And with that he handed Ocran a tiny scrap of paper on which were written a few small words full of big meaning: '2 *Battalion*—Capture the airport, attack Flagstaff House: *Reconnaissance Regiment*—block exits from Flagstaff House . . .'

"We need your help; you must help!" said Kotoka.

Ocran had both hands deep in the pockets of his dressing gown, and was gazing through the branches at the freshness of the tropical morning. He was filled with a strange elation and excitement.

"Of course I'll help—you needn't worry about that. This thing is long overdue. But isn't it better to wait till Nkrumah is back in the country? Nkrumah is the fellow we want; at any rate, he's the most important one: while we're doing it we should take the head, not the tail!"

"We decided to do it without Nkrumah being here because this way there will be less bloodshed. But we can't postpone it now—I've ordered the troops to move already. We meet at four o'clock on Thursday morning, at the Dodowa road junction. All right?"

"All right; I will inform my commanders. But can you look in again this afternoon so that I can let you know what they say?"

"I'll be in." With that, Kotoka turned to go, and Ocran for a split second had a recollection of the sergeant-major at Eaton Hall OCTU,[24] Chester, England, swearing at the Africans in his platoon. That must be the last time he shared a crisis with Emmanuel Kotoka, until today. Unfortunately, it proved impossible for Ocran to see the commanders of 2 Battalion and of the Reconnaissance Regiment. He was busy with a court-martial until the early afternoon, and then he had to entertain a visitor in his house, so that when Coker-Appiah came in to know if he should pay another visit to Kumasi he had to ask Ocran the way to the toilets in order to speak to him without being overheard. They decided that he should go up the following day, Wednesday, the eve of the coup itself; meanwhile Ocran drafted a signal to Kotoka asking for the "exercise" to be postponed.

*   *   *

The court-martial which prevented Ocran from passing on the vital orders at once to his commanders had one other result. Lt-Col Addy, garrison commander of Tamale and commanding officer of Kotoka's 3 Battalion, was called down to Accra to take part in the courtmartial, so although he did not travel with his troops he left for Accra on legitimate business a couple of days before they did.

GHANA TIME
TUESDAY 22 FEBRUARY

During Tuesday morning Coker-Appiah had had a ring from Colonel Zanlerigu, the man in charge of the President's Own Guard Regiment, and the principal defender of Flagstaff House. "Can't you speed up work on my magazines?" he enquired, wearily. "I've got a consignment of ammunition due and nowhere to put it. Your men are supposed to be building magazines for me, but they are held up by a shortage of corrugated roofing sheets; come on, man; get a move on!"

"Haven't you heard there's not an asbestos roofing sheet to be had in the country?" countered Coker-Appiah, a little more belligerently than necessary. "You'd better get on to Osagyefo and see if he can bring some back with him from China!" Then he gave way and promised to see what he could do about it. Whatever happened he mustn't let Zanlerigu suspect that anything was up. So he strode out to the car and went in search of roofing sheets.

134

He did not get far. The road was covered with troops armed with light machine guns, who ordered his car abruptly to a halt. Then it was all up! How on earth could the plot have leaked out? He looked quickly round the car; there was nothing there which could possibly betray their plans for a coup; the plans were not on paper but in his head. He would see it through calmly and with dignity.

"What's all this palaver? Can't you see I'm in a hurry"

A corporal of the Military Police came to the car door. "We're carrying out a routine check, sir. Can you open your boot?" Major Coker-Appiah gave the corporal a murderous look, and got out to open the boot. The Military Police glanced inquisitively inside, and waved him on. Help! thought Coker-Appiah as he drove away, still a little shaken, you're getting a bit on edge, aren't you, son?

He was not the only one. Brigadier Hassan, Director of Military Intelligence, had a similar experience, and as he was in the habit of uncovering a plot against the President every few weeks, he made a note to call a meeting for tomorrow.

As the day wore on the Presidential VC 10 touched down at Karachi, New Delhi, and finally Rangoon, dispensing large doses of African Personality, Afro-Asian Solidarity, and Non-Alignment to Ayub Khan of Pakistan, Mrs Indira Gandhi of India, and General Ne Win of Burma. Since they were flying east they met the shadows of nightfall five or six hours before Ghana did, and they had already had a night's sleep on the plane, over India and the Bay of Bengal, when they arrived at five on the morning of Wednesday 23 February in Rangoon.

When the court-martial was over on Tuesday afternoon John Addy had a sudden impulse to go over to the Shai Hills camp, 32 miles from Accra, and visit his old friend Major Tetteh, commanding officer of the second battalion of the President's Own Guard Regiment. Addy knew that his own troops would be attacking Flagstaff House early on Thursday morning. He knew that Tetteh and the Artillery Regiment might well be called in, with all the heavy fire power which they could command, to blast the Tamale troops off the ground. He knew too that the

President's Own Guard Regiment had a reputation for fanatical loyalty to Osagyefo.

Half-way there he had doubts about this visit. He used to know Tetteh well: they had served together. But an unguarded word to him might undermine the whole operation. How would he ever look Kotoka in the face again if that happened?

The dry bush was flying past all too quickly as he came in sight of the rough flimsy buildings that housed Major Tetteh's troops. The camp had been put up by Parkinson Howard, builders of Tema harbour, to accommodate workers in the nearby stone quarries, but had been taken over by the Army. Beyond the camp, the Shai Hills rose mysteriously against a misty sky. There was the sweet smell of bush fires in the air.

"I'll go through with it,'" muttered John Addy to himself as he turned into the main gates. "Surely Tetteh hasn't changed!"

He was very careful about his approach. He said nothing about a coup. He treated it as a casual social call. He sympathised with Tetteh over the delay in his promotion. "It's a disgrace," he declared. "Here you are, taking all the responsibility of a battalion, and yet they have not even made you a substantive major! And meanwhile these people are promoting themselves!"

They had a drink together and Addy retailed the latest gossip from Kumasi. He gave his friend an affectionate look and then glanced at his watch. Time to go. Within thirty-eight hours or so he and Tetteh might be engaged in a battle to the death.

"Well, old man," he said, as if it were an afterthought, "if ever anything were to happen—you know what I mean—don't move your troops. That's my advice." They shook hands and parted. All the way back to Accra Addy wondered uneasily whether he had said too much—or whether he hadn't said enough.

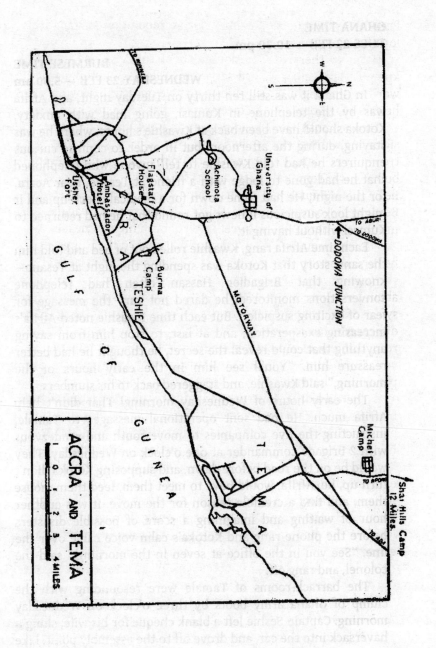

In Ghana it was still ten thirty on Tuesday night, and Afrifa was by the telephone in Kumasi, going mad with anxiety. Kotoka should have been back at Kwashie's house, where he was staying, during the afternoon; but in order to confuse curious enquirers he had told Kwashie to tell anyone who telephoned that he had gone to lodge with a friend at Tesano, near Accra, for the night. He had come down for a medical check-up and it might look suspicious if news got round that he had returned to Kumasi without having it.

Each time Afrifa rang, Kwashie rolled out of bed and told him the same story that Kotoka was spending the night at Tesano—knowing that Brigadier Hassan often had telephone conversations monitored, he dared not vary the message for fear of exciting suspicion. But each time Kwashie noted Afrifa's increasing exasperation, and at last, to stop him from saying anything that could reveal the secret, he thought he had better reassure him. "You'll see him in the early hours of the morning," said Kwashie, and staggered back to his slumbers.

The early hours of Wednesday morning! That didn't help Afrifa much. He had sent operational messages to Tamale, instructing the five companies to move south and rendezvous with 2 Brigade commander at one o'clock on Wednesday. They would be on the road before dawn, and supposing Kotoka didn't turn up, he, Afrifa, would have to meet them, feed them, house them, and find a credible reason for the move. It was another hour of waiting and imagining a score of possible disasters before the phone rang and Kotoka's calm voice came over the line. "See you in the office at seven in the morning," said the colonel, and rang off.

The barrack-rooms of Tamale were resounding with the clump of Ghana army boots by three o'clock on Wednesday morning. Captain Seshie left a blank cheque for his wife, slung a haversack into the car, and drove off to the assembly point. Like

138

one or two others, he couldn't see the reason for this sudden move. The CO had said it was "to test the troops' state of readiness for a possible move to Central Africa". But the President was out of the country—could it possibly be that . . . no, one must not think about that kind of possibility, still less discuss it with anyone else.

GHANA TIME
WEDNESDAY 23 FEBRUARY — 5.00 am, 8.00 am

By five am the vehicles were on the road, and by nine they were crossing the Volta at Yeji ferry, the troops exchanging humorous remarks at the expense of a long line of commercial lorry drivers who would have to wait a couple of hours before their vehicles would get access to the ferry.

Kotoka was in the middle of final instructions to his company commanders in Kumasi at eight am, when the phone rang. It was Ocran's brigade major speaking from Accra. "Colonel Ocran told me to contact you last night, but I couldn't get through," he said. "He says the exercise will have to be postponed, because his umpires are already engaged." This was too bad—it was monstrous to agree to the thing one moment and let your fellow-soldier down the next.

"Tell Colonel Ocran," said Kotoka, crisply, "that the exercise has already commenced. The question whether his umpires can take part or not will not stop it," and he slammed the receiver down and went on with the briefing. A few minutes later the Kumasi party left for the rendezvous with the Tamale troops, which was to be ten miles from Ejura, about sixty miles north of Kumasi on the Tamale road. In Accra Ocran's brigade major reported the result of his phone call, and rang Coker-Appiah for a quick conference. They chatted for a while about "taking the tail" and "taking the head", and finally agreed that Coker-Appiah should make the trip to Kumasi as they had planned the previous day, and report back in the evening.

Meanwhile Ocran announced Brigade Commander's Orders at seven in the evening, and determined to go through with his part in the coup whatever happened.

139

The commanders of all the main units in 1 Brigade would be in his office that evening, except for the Takoradi battalion: Asare of 2 Battalion, Dontoh of the Reconnaissance Regiment (both in Accra), Okai of 4 Battalion (Michel Camp, Tema) and Coker-Appiah of the Engineers (Teshie).

BURMESE TIME
WEDNESDAY 23 FEBRUARY— MORNING

Nkrumah had a day to spare before his party was due in Peking, so he decided to do a little sightseeing around Rangoon. In the military cemetery, half an hour's drive from the centre of the city, dozens of the Gold Coast's bravest sons, killed fighting the Japanese in World War 2, lay in neat anonymous rows. Then there was the famous mausoleum containing the tombs of the twelve Burmese cabinet ministers assassinated at one stroke in the 1950's. Kwame Nkrumah, Alex Quaison-Sackey, and Kwesi Armah, three members of the Ghanaian cabinet, dutifully admired the building and looked at the dead men's photographs, but not without feeling just a trifle uneasy at the thought of their fate. Quaison-Sackey as usual rose to the occasion with a diplomatic quip: "Life is more dangerous than I thought; anyone can walk into the cabinet and shoot the lot of us! Osagyefo, don't you think we poor cabinet ministers should have more protection?" The President was not in a joking mood. "Nothing can happen," he barked; "our defences are impregnable!"

On the way back, Quaison-Sackey was buried in the air mail edition of *The Times*. There had been a coup d'état in Syria, cabinet reshuffles in Morocco and Mauritania, and Milton Obote had assumed full powers in Uganda. "Well," said Kwesi Armah, who found *The Times* a little heavy going, "and what does the imperialist press have in store for us today?"

"Africa and the Middle East are in turmoil!" announced Quaison-Sackey in the tones of a United Nations speech-maker; and he began to enlarge on the situation. And Ghana too, he would have added, if he could have seen the convoy pounding down the magnificent highway that Nkrumah had built between

Tamale and Kumasi, to arrive at the meeting-place north of Ejura at one o'clock with military precision.

GHANA TIME
WEDNESDAY 23 FEBRUARY — 1.00 pm

Colonel Kotoka was waiting for them, his vehicles drawn off the road in a clearing that had once been a tobacco farm. The day was oppressive, with a haze in the air, and heat seemed to ooze out of the damp soil and smother them as they stepped across the grass. They were just north of the tropical forest belt, on the southern borders of the northern grassland or savannah. Kotoka was dressed in his favourite jungle green coat and trousers, Afrifa in a camouflaged waterproof operational jacket and a soft khaki hat at such a rakish angle that he looked like a raw recruit. The troops lit up their cigarettes, wandered into the bushes, and found things to laugh and shout about. Kotoka, Afrifa, and Dedjoe gathered the five company commanders from Tamale and two officers who had come up from Kumasi into a small circle, and all eyes turned to the brigade commander.

"Gentlemen," he began, speaking in English, "I am addressing you as company commanders, and as fellow-Ghanaians. You all know what has been happening in this country. Quite recently two generals were sacked without any explanation being given. Not long before that a number of top-ranking judicial officers were also removed from office for doing their legitimate work. Just a few days ago a member of parliament was kicked out without the consent of his constituency.

"Gentlemen, we have reached a point of no return. As has now become quite normal, the President has left the country just when the budget was about to be presented. Therefore we are going to end his tyranny. I am prepared to die today for my country and if there is any one of you who is not prepared to die with me he is at liberty to take his Landrover and go back to Tamale."

The little group was conscious of sharing in a historic moment. They would not spoil it by theatrical behaviour. "We

141

are prepared for it," said one of them with quiet determination, and all nodded their agreement. Discussion was unnecessary. They had been dreaming of this moment for many months. No one could wish for a better man to be at the head of the operation than their brigade commander, Colonel Kotoka.

"Now it's getting late," said Kotoka, glancing at his watch. "I have to return to Kumasi to put the finishing touches to one or two things. Major Afrifa will give you the detailed plan of campaign. Major Dedjoe has arranged for food to be brought up from Kumasi: it is nearly ready now, and that meal will have to last you till tomorrow. For the time being you will say nothing about the operation to the troops—we shall meet again, and rendez-vous with units from 1 Brigade at four o'clock in the morning at the Dodowa Junction, 12 miles from Accra. I wish you a good journey."

Kotoka walked smartly to his Landrover, and Afrifa saw him off. Just as he moved away drops of rain began to fall and there were cries of dismay from the troops. Everyone ran for the lorries to get what cover they could. "You know what this means?" Major Dedjoe asked one of the Tamale officers as he clambered into the Landrover and pulled down the canvas roof. "It means we've won already! Rain is a sign of blessing!"

After fifteen minutes the rain eased off and the more adventurous souls jumped out to sniff the fresh scents and to watch the steam rising from the road surface. Major Dedjoe's admin group were busy with the rations, and yams and stew were soon shared out. The officers were huddled in Afrifa's Landrover getting their detailed instructions. One company was to take Radio Ghana, and another was to enter Flagstaff House. A third would occupy the security flats overlooking the entrance to Flagstaff House, to prevent the security men who lived there from interfering. One company would make for the Castle and occupy it. That left the fifth company in reserve; it would take up a position in the Information Services compound right next to Flagstaff House.

Company commanders were given 50 rounds of ammunition each and were told to load their weapons before starting.

By four o'clock the meal was over and by five they were ready to move. A few of the officers who had not taken part in the company commanders' conference with Colonel Kotoka caught the atmosphere of impending action from their colleagues who were in the know. "What is happening?" they asked. "You'll be told when we reach the exercise area," was the reply, but their guesses and their hopes alike suggested what was happening: Nkrumah had lost his hold on his people's support.

*   *   *

WEDNESDAY 23 FEBRUARY— 4.00 pm

From his long experience of suspected plots and coups, Brigadier Hassan, Director of Military Intelligence, could tell that these road-blocks did not really look like an attempt to overthrow the government. If there had been anything in it he would have heard more of it by now. The little meeting, scheduled for Flagstaff House at four o'clock on the afternoon of Wednesday 23 February (by which time Afrifa's convoy was well south of Ejura) would probably be rather an anti-climax. They met and asked David Zanlerigu what he thought about it. He said road-blocks of this kind were quite normal. The camp commandant of Burma Camp might easily have ordered a check—there had been a lot of thefts lately. Eric Otoo was worried about the fact that the men were armed. "That isn't normal, is it?" he asked. It was not, and Hassan promised to investigate.

Zanlerigu suddenly had an ominous feeling that this might be more serious than it looked. He didn't want to be taken by surprise in Flagstaff House with an insufficient force of defenders.

"I can bring in the second battalion of the President's Own Guard Regiment from the Shai Hills," he suggested. "They have plenty of heavy weapons. Nobody can touch Flagstaff House if they are inside." He was quite right. If he were to bring in reinforcements at this stage to defend Nkrumah's citadel they would be a match for any attacker, even for a regiment of

144

armoured cars and a couple of battalions of infantry. As for the single company of Tamale troops which, unknown to them, Kotoka had allocated for the attack on Flagstaff House next morning, the second battalion of the President's Own Guard Regiment could reduce them to mincemeat in five minutes.

On the other hand the movement of the battalion from the Shai Hills, 32 miles away, would be a big job and it would give an impression of emergency. Some foreign journalist might get hold of the news. Nkrumah would hear all about it in Hanoi and there would be a fine row when he got back, in which some one would probably lose his job. Besides Zanlerigu vividly remembered how, only last Friday, the President had asked him searching questions about security, arising out of an unpleasant anonymous letter produced by Ambrose Yankey. He didn't want to face another crossquestioning on Nkrumah's return.

They decided to give Hassan time to make his investigation, and to meet again the following day. The meeting broke up before five o'clock.

WEDNESDAY 23 FEBRUARY — 6.00 pm

Just at that time Major Coker-Appiah was having a madly frustrating experience in Kumasi, trying to get final instructions. 2 Brigade headquarters was deserted. He directed his driver to Kotoka's house—he was not in. He tried to find Afrifa: the same story. Even Major Dedjoe was out, the only other man, so far as he knew, who was aware of the coup. His driver was hungry and thirsty, and obviously couldn't know why this frantic search should take precedence over the demands of the stomach. Of course the men Coker-Appiah was searching for had been at Ejura, meeting the troops from Tamale and providing them with a meal; Kotoka was on his way back but did not arrive till just after Coker-Appiah had left.

By a stroke of luck he saw Colonel Ashitey at Brigade headquarters, just when he had given it up and was preparing to return empty-handed. "The Accra people greet you," began Coker-Appiah in Twi; he was too good an African to neglect the traditional greetings even in a moment of extreme stress. "I'm

145

grateful to them," returned Ashitey, responding, though himself a Ga, with the traditional Twi reply. "How are the Accra people?" "They're all well." And then to business. "Do you know anything about this exercise?"

"See that lorry?" asked Ashitey; "I'm just taking the ammunition out to the troops. Yes, I know all about it."

"Is it on?"

"Yes; the brigade commander said you might be coming, and he told me to confirm that he will look after Barwah."

WEDNESDAY 23 FEBRUARY — 6.30 pm

Coker-Appiah didn't waste any more time in Kumasi. He and his driver had a bite to eat from a roadside stall and were off for Accra again, nearly 130 miles, as fast as they could go. They passed Peduase Lodge, the President's hill-top retreat at Aburi, at a few minutes to eight; the driver glanced a little enviously at the security men lolling about at the gates and windows—and being paid five or six hundred pounds a year for doing so. Army drivers were lucky if they got two hundred. "Are they on holiday, sir, when the President is away?"

He was a good chap, this driver, thought Coker-Appiah. He had entered the army through the Boys' Company. He drove well and was absolutely reliable. He had an irrational impulse to share the mighty secret which he carried in his mind with his driver: maybe it was crazy, but at this stage it could do no harm. "Kweku,'" he said, speaking in Twi, "they're in for a good long holiday this time. By tomorrow evening Osagyefo Dr Kwame Nkrumah will no longer be the President of Ghana!" Kweku faltered slightly, and slowed down. "What do you mean, sir?" Crazy or not, Afrifa would have to explain the whole thing now; so the major told his driver what was going to happen.

There was no mistaking Kweku's enthusiasm. He told Coker-Appiah that his troops had been discussing this for months; and since the events in Nigeria five weeks ago they had been waiting impatiently for "our coup"! To them, thought Coker-Appiah, a coup sounded so obvious, so easy. They had no idea of striking a balance between the injustices occurring under Nkrumah's

146

régime and the dangers and possible loss of life involved in a military takeover. How could they imagine the huge difficulty of planning, the shortages of equipment that made problems for any activity at all, or the skill and watchfulness of the security services whose business it was to detect and expose the least whisper of disloyalty?

All the same, Kweku's reactions were an eye-opener to the major of the engineers. Kweku had given him the real pulse of the soldiers, a thing that no one could possibly have ascertained before, and the feeling that his men were already impatient to do the job was worth more to him than an extra squadron. "But you mustn't tell anyone—do you understand?" Kweku understood; more than that, he swore allegiance to his CO and begged to be allowed to drive him throughout the operation—which he did, completing a total of 36 hours on duty without a break, from the time they started that morning till the job was completed.

WEDNESDAY 23 FEBRUARY — 8.00 pm

By half past eight that night the convoy of Kotoka's troops moving south from Tamale was only 22 miles from Kumasi. Near the village of Agona they turned off to the left. With all the hundreds of people around who were in the pay of Nkrumah's security service, it would be fatal to drive thirty or forty vehicles at nine or ten at night through the second city of Ghana, and expect not to be noticed. They must avoid Kumasi, and fortunately there was a convenient route through Efiduase which would bring them out on the Accra road at Ejisu, twelve miles the other side of the city. Even so Major Afrifa tried to confuse anyone who might be spying on them by turning some of the lorries round and sending them back by a more circuitous route so that it would appear that vehicles were going in both directions, not all moving south.

At about nine o'clock, while they were by-passing Kumasi by this rough, untarred rural road, they were met by a party from brigade headquarters bringing ammunition. Every man got 60 rounds, and there was a spare box for each company. The troops

147

were told to fill their magazines but not to load. The drivers checked their oil, water, and tyres, and filled up with petrol where necessary. The order was given to move operationally— among other things, that meant no more singing. The time was about ten.

Still nothing was said to the troops about the object of the journey, but by now even the most unimaginative private knew what they were in for. Everyone had heard of last month's military coup in Nigeria; Radio Ghana, with news not only in English but also in five Ghanaian languages, had made sure of that.

Coker-Appiah reported straight to Ocran on his arrival back in Accra at eight thirty, after his visit to Kumasi. He was an hour and a half late for Brigade Commander's Orders. Ocran, despite his earlier doubts, had briefed Major Dontoh of the Reconnaissance Regiment (who had the armoured cars) and Lt-Col Asare of 2 Battalion, at four in the afternoon, so all was ready. He would see these two commanders again during the night to pass on final confirmation. Lt-Col Okai of 4 Battalion was still with Ocran when Coker-Appiah arrived from Kumasi. Ocran gave them their assignments and they dispersed into the night.

To Asare, Dontoh, and Okai, right at the far end of a very fragile and fallible line of communication, the whole thing looked extremely precarious: whoever thought out the code name, "Operation Cold Chop", was evidently an optimist as well as a humorist. These three commanders, whether they liked it or not, were implicated in an operation in which they might well lose their lives, and for which they would certainly die or be detained for life if it were to fail. They had no idea of the planning behind the operation, except for the part which they had been called on to play; they did not know the ultimate objectives, or who would assume power if Nkrumah were displaced. Each of them was bound to have serious doubts about the operation; each of them was bound to be sorely tempted to report the whole mad scheme, landing a few rash colleagues in

148

detention rather than risking their own lives and the well-being of their families.

They had no one to discuss it with, nowhere to turn for more information. At any moment they might be arrested for complicity in a plot about which they had not even been consulted. Yet every one of them, privately and independently, welcomed the chance of putting an end to Nkrumah's rule, and resolved not to be the one through whom the attempt should come to grief.

23 FEBRUARY — 9.00 pm to MIDNIGHT

Major Dontoh took particular care not to do anything that would worry his wife. Mrs Dontoh was very friendly with Mrs Acquah just across the road, and Colonel Acquah was Deputy Director of Military Intelligence. Immediately after the briefing Dontoh went down to the Reconnaissance Regiment barracks, called the RSM and checked on the readiness of his vehicles. He knew that his armoured cars were ready for the road. He did not know that the light aid detachment of the Electrical and Mechanical Engineers had chosen, that very morning, to remove and check the wheels of every Landrover in the regiment. At midnight, when the alarm was given, the staff-sergeant responsible for the vehicles came in with a guilty look to report the situation. There was thirty minutes of hectic activity in the vehicle sheds, and then he came back to report that the wheels were safely back in place.

Lt-Col Asare decided at nine o'clock to check the number of vehicles available to lift his troops, and the number of wireless sets, but it was too early to reveal why. Fortunately he had some good reasons: a driver had recently damaged his lorry through sheer carelessness, and the Military Academy had put in for some wireless sets for a training exercise due to take place next day.

The troops were noisily enjoying a film in the cinema as Asare drove into the dimly-lit barracks. He called the adjutant and said he wanted to check the state of the vehicles—the brigade commander was annoyed about the one that had been

149

damaged. With numerous vehicles right off the road because of the shortage of spares the most he could raise was nine 3-tonners and six Landrovers; with those he could lift only two companies at a time.

Then the signals staff sergeant was summoned at the double from the cinema. "What have you done about the wireless sets required by the Military Academy, Teshie, for seven tomorrow morning?" asked the colonel with a harshness that he did not really feel. The staff-sergeant's face told that he had done precisely nothing, even before he had started to stammer out his excuses.

Asare exploded in the manner of colonels and all the mechanics were soon hurrying from the cinema to the stores to collect every set in the battalion and make as many as possible operational. In his desire to please, the staff sergeant now wanted to send the sets over to the Military Academy within an hour or so, as soon as they were ready. "No," said Asare, coldly, "they go tomorrow morning, on my orders. On my orders, do you understand?"

*   *   *

Nine-thirty. In Ussher Fort the last detainee had long since been locked up for the night, and a few duty warders were tramping the bare corridors; one of the twelve men in Modesto Apaloo's cell got up to use the latrine bucket in the corner, and Apaloo reminded himself for the hundredth time that tomorrow, 24 February, would be his birthday—the eighth he had spent in prison. Colonel Ashitey was handing out the ammunition by the side of the Efiduase road; another box for you, captain, sixty rounds per man. The ladies on the staff of Kibi Training College were making arrangements to dispose of their belongings in case any of them were detained on the morrow; Mr Mensah and the district organizer of the Young Pioneers were trying to ensure that the police would detain them: the noise in the girls' dormitories was horrible to hear. Kwame Nkrumah was fast asleep in Rangoon, dreaming of impending diplomatic triumphs.

Nine-thirty. Charles Mohamed Barwah, Army Chief of Staff, was sitting in his bungalow with a worrying problem on his mind. Just a month ago he had had a letter from Trinity College, where Methodist and Presbyterian ministers were trained, inviting him to attend the missionary garden party on Saturday 26 February; and the very next day the Principal had phoned to know his decision. It is not Ghanaian to refuse an invitation without a very good excuse; if one does not want to go it is better to accept and then send a last-minute apology. So although Barwah was a Muslim, and the garden party was in aid of Christian work in the largely Muslim north of Ghana, and although Osagyefo would surely not like his senior officers supporting religious mission or evangelism, he could not turn the invitation down flat; he was too courteous a man for that. He told the Principal he hoped to attend, and then, together with his secretary, he devised a letter which would enable him to miss the occasion without giving offence. It read as follows:

Dear Sir,

Missionary Garden Party

I am writing to thank you for your letter of 22nd January 1966 and to confirm my verbal acceptance of your kind invitation.

I consider it an honour to be thus invited and shall be there unless my military duties to the State take me elsewhere on that day.

Yours sincerely,
Barwah

As he signed it he chuckled over that pompous phrase, "my military duties to the State", but he thought no more of it till a few days ago he saw bright yellow posters stuck up round the town with his name in large letters, advertising his support for the occasion. Fortunately the President had not heard of it up to the time he had left for Hanoi, otherwise he would have been told off the other day, together with his friend Zanlerigu. He did

151

not intend to go, but he could not think of any convincing excuse at the moment.

The telephone rang. It was a young lieutenant of counter-intelligence, ringing for the second time to say that he had heard a convoy of troops was moving south. Barwah smiled sadly as he thanked him politely for the information and hung up the receiver. What with the Special Branch, the Presidential Detail Department, and Hassan's Military Intelligence boys, he was incessantly getting false alarms of this kind.

Why, this afternoon Hassan thought he had detected a coup d'état, and it was only the camp commandant of Burma Camp checking on petty thieves. A convoy of troops moving south! What nonsense! One couldn't send a dozen lorries off on a night exercise these days without twenty secret agents sending in highly coloured and contradictory reports about troop movements. He had long since ceased to bother his head about this kind of thing.

Now what was he going to do about this Trinity College missionary garden party? He must find some excuse . . . Well, maybe he'd better sleep on it, and see if the morning would bring inspiration.

WEDNESDAY/THURSDAY 23/24 FEBRUARY — MIDNIGHT to 2.00 am

At midnight Major Coker-Appiah of the Field Regiment summoned his officers to the regimental office. He had called in some of his men from projects in various parts of the country, and before leaving for Kumasi he had asked his second in command to announce an early morning route march, starting at two o'clock, so the whole regiment was alert. There was nothing unusual about the early morning route march; a series of route marches at awkward hours was Coker-Appiah's favourite method of shaking everyone up a bit and keeping discipline at a high level. Engineers had to be tough.

By half past twelve all his officers were there, and the commanding officer began the briefing. It was characteristically brusque and to the point.

152

"There's a special job on tonight: we're going to overthrow the government. The different tasks have been divided among various units, and we have been allocated six jobs, that is, three arrests and three buildings to be occupied. We will arrest Brigadier Hassan, Colonel Zanlerigu, and Musa Kuti of the Workers' Brigade; and we will seize the Post Office, Ghana News Agency, and the External Telecommunications Department.

"I will assign two officers to each party. The troops will be armed, but as there are not enough arms to go round the whole of the unit, those without arms will be sent out on the route march, which they are expecting.

"They will leave first, knowing nothing of what the others are doing. They will march into Accra to the Post Office and return. They have often been seen marching through the town at night, unarmed, before; so the route march will allay suspicion that anything strange is going on. Now you may ask questions, but let it be understood that there will be no discussion as to the rightness of this operation; we are going to carry it out and anyone who hesitates will be shot."

Major Coker-Appiah looked round at his fellow officers, most of them summoned from bed and still blinking in the bright light of the office. He had taken the precaution of mounting a guard outside in case someone should take fright and attempt to get away or raise the alarm, but personally he had no fears about any of these men. They were engineers, used to dealing with explosives, which meant that they had common sense and plenty of guts; and a glance at their faces told him that they were behind him.

There were a few questions, and then he named the leaders of the various parties and those who would assist them. He knew his men and each one was carefully selected for the particular task he would perform. He had worked with most of them on dangerous operations, and knew he could trust them.

"This is an operation where you either live to see the light of day, or you don't live," said the commanding officer, concluding the briefing. "We shall either complete the operation

153

successfully or we shall be wiped out—there cannot be any surrender. Select the men you trust for your parties."

Then drinks were served. Some of them wrote cheques for their wives, they shook hands with one another and wished each other the best of luck, and then dispersed to position their vehicles, check the equipment, and get the ammunition ready. The route march left at half past one and the other parties left one by one soon after.

The men who had been sent to the Post Office, Ghana News Agency, and the External Telecommunications Department had no difficulty in getting into the buildings and marching the occupants outside under guard. They used sufficient ferocity to ensure that the telephonists, journalists, and radio operators came out quickly and quietly, but they expected no resistance and none was offered. The men of Ghana News Agency looked rather disgusted, though: while their telex machines were lying idle inside, the correspondents of foreign newspapers in Accra would get all the scoops.

The party sent after Brigadier Hassan got lost in the maze of officers' bungalows, and the one in charge had to arouse several unsuspecting officers before he found the right house. Hassan made no attempt to resist and was taken to the guard-room of the Signals Regiment. Colonel Zanlerigu and Musa Kuti were not in, but Musa Kuti's wife, not suspecting the purpose of this nocturnal visit, accompanied the officer to some of Musa's favourite night-spots in Accra, without success. The party waited at his house and arrested him on his return after half past three.

Zanlerigu's party at last suspected that he was inside his house and was phoning for help, so rather than break open the door and be shot as they entered they put down a charge of Coker-Appiah's beloved dynamite and blew a hole in the wall. The troops rushed in, prepared for a desperate defence, but found no one besides Zanlerigu's wife and children, who were suffering from bruises and shock after the explosion; so they took them to the Arakan barracks guard-room and reported back to Major Coker-Appiah, empty-handed.

154

Meanwhile Kotoka had arranged for a platoon to come down from Ejura ahead of the main party; he had briefed them at the Dodowa Junction at one o'clock, and they had now reached Barwah's house. One of the two officers knocked at the door, his companion keeping him covered from behind.

The officer detailed to disconnect the telephones had failed to do so, and as a result Brigadier Hassan's son had phoned round to a number of people, including Barwah, to alert them. Barwah was awake and waiting for his callers. When he went to the door he placed a loaded pistol within reach, just behind him. He opened the door a few inches and said, "Yes? What do you want?"

The caller made sure that he was speaking to Major-General Barwah, then replied, "You are under arrest. Open the door wide and come quietly . . ." but in a flash Barwah had swung round, seized the pistol, and fired a shot which missed the officer. His companion, unseen by Barwah in the darkness, returned the fire, and a few seconds later they were helping the major-general, mortally wounded, into the waiting vehicle. He died in the Signals Regiment guard-room not many minutes after arriving there.

At the time of the Trinity College missionary garden party, on Saturday 26 February, the body of Charles Mohamed Barwah was conveyed to Osu, where it was laid to rest with full honours in the military cemetery.

At the precise moment when his top soldiers were being arrested, the President of Ghana was leaving Rangoon on a Russian jet bound for Peking.

Round One of Operation Cold Chop had gone to the opponents of Kwame Nkrumah.

155

9

OPERATION COLD CHOP—ROUND TWO

THURSDAY 24 FEBRUARY— 2.00-4.00 am

AT THREE o'clock on the morning of Thursday 24 February, Commissioner of Police John Harlley was sitting in his house waiting for news that Kotoka's troops had arrived from Tamale and that they were ready to launch the coup. No such news had arrived; all he knew was that Kotoka himself had left for the Dodowa junction to meet the Tamale troops. After half an hour with no message he took the huge decision to go ahead with the arrests anyway, and trust that the troops would arrive in due course.

He gave orders to summon all officers of the rank of Assistant Superintendent and over to the information room at central police barracks. His own office was in the modern headquarters of the Ghana Police on Ring Road, but the five police districts of the Accra area were controlled from the central police barracks, an impressive relic of colonial days, situated today at the intersection of Kwame Nkrumah Avenue and Tudu Road.

Now, in 2010, one can still stand in the spacious quadrangle and survey a scene that has hardly changed in a hundred years—a long time in a country that is developing as fast as Ghana. The two-storey cement-block former police barracks make a rectangle completely surrounding the quad, and the upper floor is reached by wooden staircases and a wooden veranda. The main entrance is a massive gateway embellished with iron spikes and a grill rather like a portcullis. Entering, one passes under the first-floor offices, and on the wall are bronze tablets: one has a profile in bas-relief:

Edward Victor Collins, Inspector General of Police, drowned by enemy action 24th April 1917. Erected by all native ranks of the Gold Coast Police.

The other reads:

In memory of George Arthur Champion, staff officer, Gold Coast Police, late The Royal Berkshire Regiment, who died whilst on leave in England, 19th October 1930; 'A friend to all ranks of the Force'.

A quaint clock tower with sober Roman numerals on the dial looks down on the scene and chimes the hours monastically. Were it not for the palm trees waving gently beyond the rooftops you might have said the atmosphere was quite English—something between that of an old boarding school and a British county jail. Harlley saw none of this as he drove in, for it was four am and still dark. He climbed the wooden steps, worn down from two inches to one inch thick in the middle by generations of black and white feet. There were no more white feet now—the police force had been officered entirely by Ghanaians for the past five years. Harlley stepped into the information room, the nerve-centre of Accra's police force, the walls covered with large-scale maps, beflagged and marked with coloured symbols and boundaries. A couple of blackboards stood there with messages chalked on them, and the duty telephonists sat at their table ready to send out instructions to any station in the city.

Nearly thirty officers in uniform had gathered and were standing shoulder to shoulder in the light of fluorescent tubes suspended from the old wooden ceiling. They had been talking among themselves, and they were already expecting Harlley to announce a coup. That was not merely because several of them had passed the buildings occupied by the Field Regiment and seen the troops: they had been waiting for a coup like everyone else, and Harlley knew it.

157

Here there was no need to threaten anybody, nor was there any sign of emotion or jubilation. When the officers of the Ghana Police get instructions, they know how to carry them out, that is all.

Harlley first checked that the officers in charge of each of the five police districts were present. He announced the coup as quietly as if it had been a weekly routine, saying nothing about the failure of the Tamale troops to appear.

He pointed out that each district had full details of those ministers and party functionaries residing in their areas, and said that all of them were to be taken into protective custody for their own safety. Patrols would be maintained in the town and road blocks would be set up outside Accra to hold any who were attempting to escape. He assigned wireless jeeps and parties of police to each job, and the gathering quietly dispersed into the night.

*   *   *

Kofi Baako, minister of civil defence, was one of the people whom Brigadier Hassan's son had telephoned when his father was taken away. He drove to the house of Nkrumah's security secretary to discuss what was to be done; the security secretary was on the point of leaving himself, and told Kofi Baako that Barwah had been shot. The minister of civil defence slumped in his car; "Oh God!" he said, "we must go to Flagstaff House!" Hurriedly they pieced together the scraps of information they had gathered; Barwah shot, Hassan arrested, and the rebels seemed to have come from the Field Regiment. Only about 50 men were involved. It didn't look too serious. Provided they could alert the President's Own Guard Regiment at the Shai Hills, they should be able to defend Flagstaff House.

24 FEBRUARY — 2.30 am

The time was between two thirty and three o'clock. The lorries carrying Kotoka's five companies were steadily approaching Accra. They had just passed through the dark and deserted streets of Koforidua and had forty miles to cover

158

before they would reach the rendezvous at the Dodowa road junction.

Kofi Baako turned his car and left for Flagstaff House at top speed; but he could not organize counter-measures single-handed. All he could do was to try and phone other people. With Okoh, secretary to the cabinet, out of the country, deputy secretary Impraim was the key man; he dialled the number and heard his heart beating loud as the seconds passed and the "burr-burr" repeated itself calmly. No answer. Then he must go to Impraim's house; no one else could summon the Presidential Commission.

The gate of Flagstaff House swung open for him to leave, and he noted with satisfaction that an armoured car of the President's Own Guard Regiment was standing outside. He turned into Accra towards Impraim's house, and as he gathered speed a car flashed by from the other direction. It carried driver Kweku and Major Coker-Appiah, on their way to report to Kotoka's headquarters in Captain Kwashie's house that the arrests were proceeding and the buildings in Accra had been duly occupied.

Impraim had served in Burma in World War 2 and had been one of the first Africans to receive the King's commission. After the war his stocky figure, in sports coat with leather elbow patches and an army officer's khaki trousers, had stumped the quads and lecture halls and ancient staircases of Oxford University. Now his greying head turned uneasily on the pillow as a motor horn sounded in the parking area in front of his bungalow. Impraim gathered his sleeping cloth round him, and with a glance at the clock, which indicated three thirty, strode out in his bare feet to the living room. His daughter was already there, peering out through the half-opened front door.

So it was Kofi Baako! He opened the door and would have turned to get a drink, but in a second Kofi Baako had blurted out the news in their common language, Fante: "The army is on the move!"

"You mean it's a coup?" asked Impraim.

159

"Yes. They've already got Hassan and killed Barwah. You'd better convene the Presidential Commission at once."

"Where do you want us to meet?"

"Not Flagstaff House, I think," said Kofi Baako: two members of the commission were chiefs whose village palaces were defended by cutlasses and 50-year-old shot-guns: he did not want to be caught in the middle of a sophisticated battle, trying to protect them. "No; we'll meet at the Ambassador Hotel. It's a public place and anybody seeing us there won't suspect anything. How long will it take you to get everyone together?

Impraim made a quick calculation. All the private telephone numbers were in a notebook in his office. He would have to run up to Flagstaff House to fetch it. "Give me forty-five minutes," he said.

He threw on his clothes and screamed up Independence Avenue, lit by brilliantly effective streetlighting, swerved round the armoured car which was still standing outside the main gate of Flagstaff House, and was admitted to his office by a security man with a grim expression on his face.

"What's happening, sir?" he asked. Impraim unlocked a drawer and muttered, "You know as much as I do at the moment," as he put his phonopad on the desk top and leaned down to lock the drawer again. In a moment he had got back to the car and was careering back to his house. He got there only to find that he had brought the telephone directory but left the phonopad, containing the private numbers, on his desk in the office.

An urgent call brought a duty driver to his house, carrying the precious phonopad, and by four fifteen he had rung Kwame Poku, Kwaw Fraiku, and Inkumsah, deputy speaker of the National Assembly. There was no reply from Welbeck.

Then Impraim left for the Ambassador Hotel himself. Kofi Baako was waiting there stamping with impatience at the delay. He told Impraim that Commodore Hansen of the Navy and Air Commodore Otu were at the Ops Room in the Ministry of Defence, Burma Camp, but they couldn't find Ocran, and with

Aferi out of the country and Barwah shot they were having difficulty in getting the army to take any effective action.

*   *   *

After meeting the advance platoon at Dodowa Junction and sending them off with instructions to arrest Barwah, Kotoka drove nine miles in to Captain Kwashie's house to check on developments before returning to meet the main party. One thing had evidently gone wrong—he was getting messages by telephone, though by this time all the phones should have been disconnected. The instructions to the Signals Regiment must have miscarried somehow.

Kotoka, Kwashie, and Col Tevie, dressed in civilian clothes, returned to the junction to meet the main party. It was a simple Y-junction, where the roads from Koforidua and Dodowa convergd to form the principal highway into Accra from the north and northeast. On either side of the tarred surfaces, swaying grass stretched back to the dry trees and thorn bushes of the Accra plains, and brightly painted hoardings erected by the advertising agencies aimed to influence the public's choice of cigarettes and car batteries. These things were hidden in the darkness, and the brigade commander and the hospital administrator were looking over the tree-tops four or five miles to the 1,000-foot scarp which the convoy of 30 lorries must presently descend by a winding road.

Already they were late. The troops from Accra would arrive at any moment to find Kotoka standing there alone, without a single soldier from Kumasi or Tamale. They wouldn't exactly be pleased.

He had to make an effort to keep calm and he passed the time by reminding himself where the various units of the army were stationed at this particular moment. There were two infantry brigades. 2 Brigade, which he himself commanded, had its headquarters in Kumasi and most of its troops 250 miles further north in Tamale. 1 Brigade, commanded by Ocran, comprised a battalion here in Accra (2 Battalion, which should have arrived already from Burma Camp to rendezvous with his

161

own troops from the north). Ocran's brigade also included Lt-Col Okai's 4 Battalion at Michel Camp, near Tema, and another battalion in Takoradi. In addition there was the Reconnaissance Regiment of armoured cars in Accra, with one squadron away in Ho: the Field Engineers Regiment stationed at Teshie, on the coast near Accra: and last, but by no means least, "Nkrumah's private army", the President's Own Guard Regiment, comprising one battalion in Burma Camp in Accra, and another battalion armed with powerful artillery stationed near the Shai Hills.

Flagstaff House was defended by the first battalion of the President's Own Guard Regiment. If they were taken by surprise there would be no artillery to back them up. But if the defenders were really determined to put up a stiff resistance they could possibly hold his force at bay for up to two hours while the battalion from the Shai Hills came in with their heavy weapons. What would happen then did not bear thinking about.

"How's Harlley going to do the civilian arrests?" asked Kwashie.

"I've no idea, countryman," replied the colonel, "but we can rely on him to look after them."

"Do you think Zanlerigu will bring in the other battalion of the President's Own Guard Regiment from the Shai Hills? The message from Coker-Appiah said they hadn't got him yet, so he may be trying to defend Flagstaff House."

"No," said Kotoka, "he won't move the Shai Hills battalion in time; and even if he does, we've got 4 Battalion at Michel Camp, Tema, the whole of 2 Battalion, the armoured cars of the Recce Regiment, and one of my companies from Tamale to throw in against Flagstaff House. It can't stand up to a force like that."

"Not even if they bring up their artillery?"

"No, not even if they bring up their artillery."

Kotoka knew that was wildly optimistic, particularly as there was no sign yet of any of the attacking force, but he regarded it as his job to encourage others and to be prepared for difficulties if they came.

Just then the convoy arrived at the top of the scarp and the line of the black hill-top, silhouetted against the dark grey sky,

162

began to twinkle with the head-lights. "It will be another twenty minutes," said Kotoka, and they settled down to wait.

3.45 am

The convoy arrived at a quarter to four and the lorries parked near the junction. A party was posted to stop anything going into Accra, but vehicles on their way out were to be allowed to pass. In the event the only thing they saw was a petrol tanker which rumbled out towards Koforidua shortly after they moved off half an hour later.

The five companies paraded close together on the road-side and Kotoka spoke to them. He used English but even those whose English was weak needed no interpreter.

"You must be wondering what we are in for. We all know that for many months the shops have been empty, prices have been rising, and at the same time more and more taxes are being levied on us. Kwame Nkrumah and other members of the government don't care.

"The army too has suffered. Soldiers have been going round in rags and tatters," (he indicated a man in front rank whose shirt was so patched and threadbare that it looked shabby even in the darkness) "and we have all been deprived of proper training facilities: at same time the President has been equipping his private army, founded in defiance of the constitution, with the latest things from Russia.

"Today we are going to show the President that he cannot go against the constitution at his will. We have agreed to take over the government from him. The company commanders have already been briefed, and they will tell you what has been arranged for you do. After that everybody will go straight to his target." There were shouts of "We will follow you!" and much noisy and enthusiastic cheering, till the people living in the houses two hundred yards away on the far side of the Koforidua road were aroused and stood in their doorways peering out at the troops.

Kotoka did not mention that the major part of attacking force, 2 Battalion and the armoured cars, had not turned up.

163

When the jubilation had died down, he said, "If we don't meet again, farewell!" and turned for his car. The time was four o'clock. Where on earth could Ocran be? Surely he had not gone over to the other side?

THURSDAY 24 FEBRUARY — 4.00 am

At that moment Ocran was at the Ministry of Defence Ops Room in Burma Camp, together with Air Commodore Otu. At about two in the morning he had passed on final confirmation to Asare of 2 Battalion and Dontoh of the Reconnaissance Regiment, and then he had gone to his office in Burma Camp to await developments. Soon after four o'clock, to his horror, he met Air Commodore Otu hurrying to the Ops Room to deal with the trouble. Otu had been summoned from his bed by telephone. If Ocran refused to accompany him, Otu might take action against his troops, and prevent them from moving off; but by visiting the Ops Room he could allay Otu's suspicions and delay any steps he might try to take to defend Flagstaff House.

Ocran expected Asare and Dontoh to go ahead on the instructions he had given. Unfortunately the two commanders were still confused about the whole operation, and when they got enquiries from the Ops Room and were told that Ocran himself was there they decided not to move till they had further instructions. Kotoka's force was now driving straight into Accra. Only one company was assigned to the attack on Flagstaff House—the support of 2 Battalion and the armoured cars was absolutely essential to the operation. As the precious minutes ticked by and the lorries carrying Kotoka's force neared Flagstaff House, the men of 2 Battalion and the armoured cars were in their barracks, getting bored with waiting for orders.

For a while, Ocran and Otu played out an awkward comedy in the Ops Room, while the duty officer tried vainly to get definite information by phoning round to the various units. Hearing that the troops involved were engineers, he rang the Field Regiment and was told that Major Coker-Appiah was out on a route march—"But I could swear," added the duty officer

164

mysteriously, "that I heard Major Coker-Appiah's voice on the telephone!"

Otu at first thought the trouble originated from the President's Own Guard Regiment, which was a notoriously unhappy unit. It was packed with protégés of people like Yankey, and despite the fine equipment and other privileges it was riddled with intrigues and discontent. Barwah's death was probably due to some internal quarrel.

Later, when it was confirmed that the engineers were involved, they thought it might be a dispute between the Field Regiment and the President's Own Guard, though this was not easy to understand. Then there had been the stories about troops moving south; evidently that was a false alarm, for there was no sign of 2 Brigade.

Nkrumah's large expenditure on the air force and the navy had made available to Otu a dozen training aircraft, some transports and helicopters, and a few jet fighters; Commodore Hansen commanded a navy of two corvettes and a few minesweepers, and a £4,000,000 frigate was on order from a Scottish shipyard. As Otu sat in the little Ops Room at four in the morning to face a practical problem of internal security, with Ocran apparently helpless to bring in the army, Nkrumah's massive expenditure on defence looked irrelevant and a trifle ridiculous. Ocran was busy thinking up excuses to get away and see how Asare and Dontoh were getting on, but he was the senior army officer available; Air Commodore Otu evidently expected him to remain. It would not help the others if he were shot trying to get away from the Ops Room. Meanwhile the hands of the clock crept round to four forty-five, then five o'clock, and Ocran feared that Asare and Dontoh would not move, and Kotoka would have to attack Flagstaff House with a totally inadequate force.

4.30 am

The five companies from Tamale had instructions to carry on alone if the units from 1 Brigade did not turn up. That gave the company allocated to the attack on Flagstaff House an

165

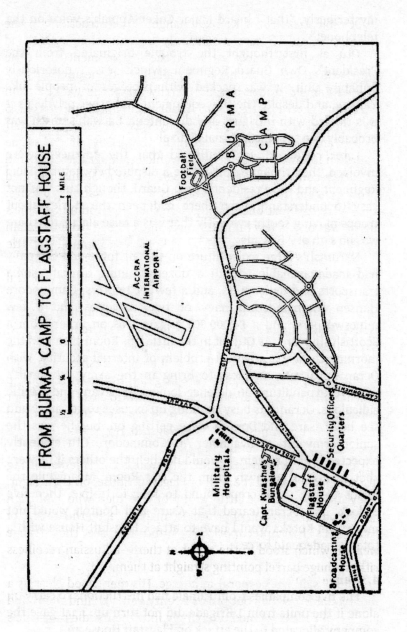

FROM BURMA CAMP TO FLAGSTAFF HOUSE

impossible task, but if Kotoka changed his instructions to the other companies there would only be confusion; Asare and Dontoh would probably arrive at the last moment and if he wasn't careful he would have them all fighting one another.

The Tamale troops bowled merrily down the well-lit main road into Accra with Major Afrifa and "A" Company of 5 Battalion in the lead. This company was to pass by Flagstaff House and seize Radio Ghana. "B" Company of the same battalion followed in the next few vehicles, under the command of a fair-complexioned Ewe officer, Captain Seshie. All had orders to gain their objectives quietly and without opening fire: they were to shoot only if they were shot at. Captain Kwashie's house was only a few hundred yards up the road from the main gate of Flagstaff House, and Colonel Kotoka was standing a little off the road as the convoy passed by. The time was four thirty.

Their hopes that the whole operation would be peaceful were dashed as soon as the first vehicles passed the main gate: immediately they came under heavy fire from inside Flagstaff House. Major Afrifa and "A" Company were held up in the cross-fire but finally got past without serious casualties, and drove on to occupy Broadcasting House. Captain Seshie and "B" Company, whose task was to take Flagstaff House with the help of 2 Battalion and the armoured cars, came up close behind (but 2 Battalion and the armoured cars were nowhere to be seen, and it looked like madness to attack Flagstaff House with a single company of foot-soldiers.)

All their attention was directed towards the riflemen firing at them from behind the wall of Flagstaff House, on their right. They did not notice a little group of five men who had been posted out in the open opposite the main gate, on the tarmac of Nkrumah's helicopter port. They did not see the strange weapon which stood in the midst of them—a Russian recoilless rifle, its huge barrel pointing straight at them.

"Fire!" said the corporal in charge. His men stood clear as a hissing flame belched out ten or twenty yards behind them, and an 82 mm rocket zoomed unerringly into the middle of Seshie's vehicles.

The explosion boomed out into the early morning and startled the occupants of the surrounding houses, including diplomats from all over the world, out of their slumbers. They were entertained to a continuing rat-tat-tat of machine guns and the crackle of rifle fire.

Four of Seshie's men were killed on the spot, three in a 3-ton lorry, one in his Landrover. The vehicles screeched to a halt and half of the men were out and taking cover in a ditch by the side of the road almost before the lorries had stopped. It was not long before Seshie realized that although the rest of the convoy had passed by, many of his men were missing, With his steel helmet facing the wall of Flagstaff House, only ten or fifteen yards away, he raised his head out of the ditch to look for the rest of his company. He couldn't see as many as forty men, but even if a third of the company were dead and wounded, more that should be left. He came to the conclusion that at least one whole platoon was missing. Unknown to him their 3-tonner had had a mechanical breakdown three miles up the road and the driver was vainly trying to get the engine started again.

Captain Seshie did not waste time wondering whether the driver of his vehicle had driven on in a panic, or turned back, or whether they had somehow all been killed. The problem demanding all his attention was how to penetrate the most closely-guarded citadel in West Africa with a shocked and depleted force of rather less than two platoons, with his wireless out of action and his spare box of ammunition exploding in the burning lorry in the middle of the road.

Round two of *Operation Cold Chop* to the defenders.

10

OPERATION COLD CHOP—ROUND THREE

THE six-storey Ambassador Hotel had been built in 1957 as a show-piece for Ghana's independence, and to accommodate some of the hundreds of guests who came to Ghana for that occasion. Since then it had been the venue for countless conferences, dinners, and social gatherings, and the haunt of visiting celebrities from Japanese millionaires to the American Baptist preacher Dr Billy Graham. The luxury of its air-conditioned accommodation, the standard of its cuisine, and the level of its charges, had established it as an international hotel of the first rank. Even so it had suffered the fate of pioneers, and been out-done by the crop of hotels in other West African countries; these had followed in the wake of the Ambassador as each new independence celebration along the coast demanded the same kind of facilities.

In all its nine fascinating years, however, the Ambassador Hotel can hardly have witnessed a meeting at which the whole destiny of the nation was more obviously at stake. Never had such a curiously assorted group—two politicians with secondary education, two chiefs who had only been to middle school, and an Oxford-trained civil servant—been assembled there at such an hour as four-thirty in the morning to consider such an epoch-making crisis.

The two chiefs were already sitting in the brightly-lit vestibule, just inside the main door on the left, when Impraim arrived. Kofi Baako stopped him on the doorstep. "I haven't told them the reason for the meeting yet," he said. "Is there really anything we can do?"

If they could count on the immediate co-operation of the military commanders at the Ops Room in Burma Camp: if they could immediately alert the whole of the President's Own Guard Regiment, and deploy them skilfully in and around Flagstaff House: if they could convince all other units that the rebellion would not succeed: if they could reassure the security forces that help was on its way, and so encourage the defenders of Flagstaff House to hold out—if all those conditions were met, then a military solution to the problem was possible.

But Impraim well knew something that Kofi Baako and most of the other politicians were too blind or too ignorant to appreciate: a rebellion against Nkrumah would have the wholehearted support of the majority of the people of Ghana. Impraim himself, like millions of others, lamented what had been happening in Nkrumah's Ghana but up to this moment, like thousands of others, he had been powerless to intervene and afraid to criticize openly. Now he was suddenly conscious that everything depended on him.

Although he had no idea who was behind the present military action, and during the past hour had had no means of finding out, he was convinced of one thing: they were aiming to end Nkrumah's rule, otherwise they would not have gone for Barwah and Hassan. He knew that by a bold policy, carried out with resolution, it might be possible to halt the rebellion. But it did not occur to him to make such a proposal. He knew Nkrumah's government as well as anybody, and if the coup was aimed at the régime he welcomed it, and he calculated that the best way to help it succeed was simply to let things take their course.

Kofi Baako impatiently repeated his question: "What can we do?"

"If the news is true," replied Impraim, "those responsible must have made certain that they would succeed, they must have made sure they had the support of the bulk of the army. In that case I don't see that we can do anything..."

170

They were interrupted by the driver of the car which Impraim had sent to fetch his phonopad. He had returned to Flagstaff House after dropping the phonopad at his house, but now the car screamed back to the Ambassador and skidded to a halt. The driver came rushing up to Impraim: "There's firing going on outside the main gate of Flagstaff House, sir," he said. "I saw grenades exploding and a lorry in flames outside the gate." Then they saw Inkumsah coming; they had better begin the meeting.

Nana Fraiku took the chair with an obvious sense of the importance attaching to that duty, and Kofi Baako and Impraim outlined what they knew to their astonished listeners. They described the gun-firing and the flaming lorry, and began to discuss how to defend the most important points in Accra. Then an excited American dashed into the hotel vestibule; he felt impelled to tell someone what he had just seen, and the group of people sitting there just inside the entrance gave him a fine audience. He had no idea that he was addressing the highest executive authority in the land. "There's firing going on outside Flagstaff House," he gasped. "Three trucks outside all on fire. One was a jeep I think. Some troops are firing in and the people inside are firing back."

There was a pause as the American recovered his breath and the Presidential Commission looked up at their new informant. The night porter, leaning on the reception desk, was taking a keen interest in the proceedings.

Nana Fraiku felt it his solemn responsibility as chairman to make some kind of proposal for action. "If there is so much fire and firing all over the place, why don't we call in the fire brigade?"

That remark effectively put a stop to the fourth and final meeting of the Presidential Commission. When their laughter had subsided Kofi Baako went on talking about resistance and getting Welbeck to mobilize the Party but he and Inkumsah could already feel the net closing around them. Just before six am they were called to the wireless to hear a special announcement.

171

THURSDAY 24 FEBRUARY — 6.00 am

"This is Major Afrifa," said a strange voice, speaking not with the polished accents of the Radio Ghana announcers' elocution class, but in the rough and ready tones of a military man who has just overpowered the guard at the main gates. "Stand by for Colonel Kotoka." "That's the commander of 1 Brigade," said Kofi Baako, hardly believing his ears. "He should be in Kumasi!"

But the voice was unmistakable:

"I have come to inform you that the military, in co-operation with the Ghana Police, have taken over the government of Ghana today. The myth surrounding Kwame Nkrumah has been broken. Parliament is dissolved and Kwame Nkrumah is dismissed from office. All ministers are also dismissed. The Convention People's Party is disbanded with effect from now; it will be illegal for any person to belong to it.

"We appeal to you to be calm and co-operative. All persons in detention will be released in due course. Please stay by your radio and await further details. Thank you."

Inkumsah and Kofi Baako looked around despairingly. An hour and a half earlier something might have been done; now it would take a miracle to save the situation. Impraim said simply, "I am a civil servant: I serve the government of the day. You are ministers and I suppose you will be taken into custody."

"All right," said Kofi Baako, "then it's each for himself." He drove straight to Bishop Bowers at the Roman Catholic Cathedral and made his confession, then to John Harlley's house to give himself up. Harlley was out and his wife had no intention of trying to arrest the minister of defence, so there was nothing for it but to return to the Cathedral and wait for the police to call later in the day. When they came for him later, they took him to the central police station, where a corporal entered his name in a book and sent him across the road under guard to wait in the Information Room at the central barracks.

*   *   *

When news of the firing at Flagstaff House reached the Ops Room, Air Commodore Otu saw one practical step that he could

172

take—get a helicopter up to take a look at things from the air, and report back. Ocran accompanied him to the airport to send off the helicopter, and they discussed the situation on the way.

"How stupid of this damned Field Regiment," said Otu; "if they had wanted to do something they might as well have done it properly!"

As soon as they reached the airport, just after six o'clock, they were told of Kotoka's broadcast.

The helicopter spotted the lorries still burning outside the main gate of Flagstaff House, and saw soldiers firing at one another inside, but that did little more than confirm what they knew already.

Down below, Captain Seshie's two platoons had quickly overpowered the corporal and four men who manned the recoilless rifle, but they had kept at a respectful distance from the defending force, who were more numerous and far better equipped. From their positions in the road-side ditch his men fired on the guards at the main gate, and had succeeded in capturing some and putting the rest to flight. There was a lull in the firing as the defenders exhausted their ammunition; Colonel Zanlerigu ordered the first party back and replaced them by a fresh platoon. Seshie saw his opportunity and entered the small pedestrians' gate together with his batman and machine-gunner. They found the first courtyard deserted. After checking that the perimeter wall was not electrified, he called a section of riflemen and three machine-gunners to climb over it, and stationed them at the second wall. They kept up steady fire on the two-storey guard-room at the third wall, from which point the defenders appeared to be firing. From time to time he shouted at them to surrender, but there was no reply.

The defences of Flagstaff House had not been designed for a pitched battle like this, and no cover was provided except the concrete block walls. Fortunately for the defenders the open spaces were traversed by trenches dug only a few days before for a new sewerage scheme. Into these trenches Zanlerigu's fresh platoon of defenders jumped. They started to return "B" Company's fire with grim determination.

6.30 am

After 45 mintues large quantities of lead had been shot from side to side but there had been few casualties and no change in the situation. With such a small force it was impossible for Seshie to maintain a position inside the perimeter wall. As there was no way of replenishing their ammunition or of knowing how long the battle would last he withdrew and restricted his men to firing single rounds just to keep the defenders' heads down.

Outside, he found that the remainder of his men were coming under machine-gun fire from the flats on the opposite side of the road, where the security forces had accommodation. Seshie's sergeant-major had told the troops outside to fire at these flats; the company of paratroops from Tamale had arrived at last and taken up positions on the far side of the road, and were firing in the same direction. The men detailed to set up a road block had stopped the traffic, and a long line of vehicles was beginning to form. Several foolhardy drivers ignored the road block, and they and their passengers were shot at; one car was flying the CPP flag and contained an MP, who died on the spot; another was a Ghana Airways mini-bus on its way into Accra.

From the opposite direction a little Morris Minor drove past the security flats and approached the main gate of Flagstaff House. Behind the steering wheel sat Lt-Col John Addy. He held no command in Kotoka's attacking force and the only reason for his presence in Accra was last Tuesday's court-martial: but natural curiosity and a concern for his men's welfare had encouraged the garrison commander of Tamale to carry out on his own initiative a tour of the positions held by the Tamale troops.

He had been up bright and early to start his trip. The Castle, to his satisfaction, was in the hands of the men from Tamale. He searched for them in vain at the CPP headquarters, but the place looked completely deserted and probably was not worth

174

capturing anyway. He found some men from his own battalion outside Broadcasting House

Everything seemed to be going very nicely. It just remained to see how Flagstaff House was getting on.

Lt-Col Addy felt in holiday mood. It was curious to be driving round like this, dressed in civilian clothes, while his men were busy overthrowing the government of the day. There was a deceptive lull in the firing as his Morris Minor impudently approached the main gate of Flagstaff House. Lt-Col Addy got ready to put his arm out of the window and give the troops a cheery wave.

Rat-tat-tat! Rat-tat-tat-tat-tat! There was a hiss as two of his tyres were punctured and the car slewed round, thirty or forty yards from the gate. The windows splintered into fragments and the bodywork was riddled with bullet-holes. Help! thought John Addy: Capt. Lamptey will be furious with me for borrowing his car and getting it into a mess like this.

He decided he would get out of the car. Why should they fire at him—a man dressed in civilian clothes driving an unarmed vehicle? If he got out, perhaps they would stop.

As soon as he got out the firing became more intense. The bullets whizzed past him and grazed the road at his feet. He flung himself down, with wounds over his left eye and on his right arm.

Then they started hurling grenades. Who on earth did they think he was? If they had mistaken him for the devil incarnate they couldn't have given him a more malicious welcome.

He began to crawl across the road towards the security flats, hoping to find cover behind the wall on that side of the road. No sooner did he move than it seemed guns were blazing at him from every corner of the security flats. There was only one thing to do: lie still.

Someone shouted, "He's dead!" A moment or two later he heard the voice of David Zanlerigu: "Stop firing!" It recalled many memories of their service together in 3 Battalion, both in Ghana and the Congo, between 1958 and 1960.

175

How long he lay there he could not tell. His shirt and trousers became a bloody mess, and he had difficulty in keeping perfectly still, for he was feeling pains from a dozen wounds.

At last the nightmare ended as unexpectedly as it had begun. A taxi approached from the other direction, though how it got through the road block is not clear. It drove across the battle area and stopped next to the prostrate form of John Addy in response to a shout from inside Flagstaff House. The taxi-driver looked out of his window, shivering with fright.

"Pick up that foolish dead man," cried a rough voice. The taxi-driver hesitated before complying with such a strange request: then leapt out, dumped John Addy in the back seat, turned his car round and sped off out of the line of fire as fast as he could go. His worst shock was yet to come: for the corpse suddenly sat up and ordered him with a soldier's decisiveness, "Take me to the Military Hospital!"

*   *   *

Ammunition was getting short outside as well as inside Flagstaff House. The men covering the security flats were rapidly exhausting their small supply of ammunition in the attempt to keep the security men's heads down. With no sign of reinforcements and nowhere to turn for more ammunition the situation began to look serious. Just when Seshie was getting desperate, three Russian armoured personnel carriers came rumbling down the road from Burma Camp. The routine of the President's Own Guard Regiment required that the guard at the gates of Flagstaff House should be changed at six o'clock each morning; this small relieving party was therefore despatched from the Guard Regiment quarters and conveniently surrendered to Captain Seshie's men in the road outside Flagstaff House, providing him with additional arms which he did not need, but also solving the problem of ammunition shortage; they had brought four boxes of 7.62 mm, totalling 4,000 rounds—a timely donation that would keep his riflemen supplied all the morning if necessary.

"What's that?" An NCO drew Seshie's attention to another Russian armoured personnel carrier, emerging from the south gate of Flagstaff House itself. This gate was effectively covered from the security flats, and they had not attempted to block it. Suddenly its machine gun blazed out at Seshie's men, who were standing by the wall right along the gunner's line of fire. A man was killed and fifteen of the small force were wounded, including Seshie himself, who received a ricochet in the right eye.

They all spread out on the ground and eventually picked off the machine gunner—the only man of the President's Own Guard whom they saw killed with all the hundreds of rounds they had fired in the past hour and a half. The armoured personnel carrier withdrew and Seshie called for surrender again.

"We are battalion strength," he boasted. "You'd better give in and stay alive; otherwise we shall blast the whole place and you will all be killed." A voice came back from somewhere behind the wall: "You fire—I know I will die anyway!" David Zanlerigu was behind there, cursing his luck. Yesterday afternoon at the meeting with Hassan they had discussed bringing in the rest of the President's Own Guard Regiment with their artillery from the Shai Hills. They had decided against it after a long discussion. What fools they were to have put off a decision!

THURSDAY 24 FEBRUARY — 6.45 am

Just then the helicopter flew overhead, and Seshie told his men not to fire at it unless it fired at them. Somebody from one side or the other did fire though and scored a hit on the airframe, which the crew did not notice till their return. As he looked up, Captain Seshie was conscious of sharp pains in his right eye, He had been unable to see with it since the ricochet hit him, but he had been too busy to think of the numbness that was coming on. Now, in addition to the exchange of fire that was beginning to be monotonous, he had a private battle to fight, between the determination to carry on till help arrived,

177

and the disturbing sense that things were getting blurred and mixed-up.

Air Commodore Otu arrived back at the Ops Room with Ocran, after their visit to the airport, and Otu called Commodore Hanson of the Navy to come and join them. Ocran found it increasingly difficult to keep up the pretence that he knew nothing of the revolt. He was particularly worried that the phones were still working; this meant that the President's Own Guard battalion at the Shai Hills could be called in at any moment, or perhaps they were already coming in of their own accord. If only he could predict the two commodores' reaction to a frank declaration that he himself was participating in the coup!

"The Field Regiment seem to be the only troops involved," said Otu. "The best we can do at the moment is to cut them off at their camp in Teshie. Ocran, you'd better phone 4 Battalion at Michel Camp and tell them to come down to Teshie and block the Field Regiment."

It was Ocran's last chance to tell them that he was supporting the revolt; he decided it was better to keep them guessing than to risk betraying Kotoka. He picked up the receiver and asked for 4 Battalion. Please God the lines are cut, or the number is engaged, or I get a wrong number! Anything rather than that I should give orders that will confuse everyone! Perhaps their phone will be out of order: it usually is. . .

"Hallo! This is 4 Battalion, Lt-Col Okai speaking". No, that's positively unfair. For weeks past I've never been able to get a number I wanted on these internal telephones; now all the phones are supposed to be cut off and I'm desperately anxious not to get through—but the wretched thing works perfectly. "Oh yes, hallo! This is Colonel Ocran. Fine, thanks; how are you? Look, Okai, have you heard what's going on? You heard it on the radio—yes, of course. I'm here at the Ops Room with Otu and Hansen, and we've decided you had better take 4 Battalion to Teshie and block the Field Regiment camp. Is that clear? Yes, just stop them getting in or out. Fine, I'll ring you again later."

He hoped he had sounded sufficiently definite to Otu and Hansen, and at the same time sufficiently vague to Okai to ensure that he would wait until he had rung again before moving. Meanwhile he must bring this ridiculous situation to an end at once, and take all his troops in to help in the battle at Flagstaff House without any more delay. But how could he get rid of Otu and Hansen? Then it came to him in a flash.

"I'm going to call in Asare of 2 Battalion and Dontoh of the Reconnaissance Regiment," he said. "What do you think?" Otu and Hansen agreed, and Asare and Dontoh were called in. Ocran met them outside the Ops Room, and he sent Dontoh back for two armoured cars and a Landrover full of support troops. With this force Dontoh would easily be able to arrest Hansen and Otu and quell resistance from anyone else.

Dontoh arrived back within fifteen minutes, and found Commodore Hansen and Air Commodore Otu sitting in the entrance to the Chief of Defence Staff's waiting room, just opposite the Ops Room. They were quickly arrested and pushed unceremoniously into the waiting vehicles. At first the two commodores were speechless with rage—annoyed not because they had been tricked, but because they had not been let into the secret earlier: there was so much they could have done to help . . .

*   *   *

Otu and Hansen were arrested shortly before seven o'clock. By this time Captain Seshie, after over two hours of confused fighting entirely without contact with any other officer, was stumbling about outside Flagstaff House trying to encourage the remnants of his company, now reduced to a force of little more than a platoon. Unknown to him, and only two or three miles away, the whole of 2 Battalion and a squadron of armoured cars were all ready to join him. They had been waiting impatiently for the past three hours, expecting final orders from Ocran to go into battle.

Lt-Col Asare had paraded 2 Battalion at three thirty a.m. and assigned one company to seize the airport, and the rest to go

179

into Flagstaff House together with Kotoka's men from Tamale. A phone call from the Ops Room had confused him, and his column, already on its way, had been halted by the football field just outside Burma Camp, at about five o'clock.

They could hear the firing at Flagstaff House and were eager to get into the fray, but Asare felt he must first make sure about his commander's intentions; if he just drove up into the midst of the battle without being expected, he might well end up fighting the wrong enemy.

The armoured cars had been in a similar position since the early hours of the morning. Dontoh was aware that many of his men, perhaps even some of his officers, were spies planted by Hassan's counter-intelligence branch. It would be fatal to reveal that they were all involved in a coup d'état until the very last possible moment, and like Asare he had been confused by these phone calls from the Ops Room; it seemed at the time as if Ocran had changed sides.

Now that they had missed the rendezvous at the Dodowa junction he had no means of contacting Kotoka to find out when or where his armoured cars were required. Meanwhile his officers and men were getting tired and critical: "We want to know what we have got to die for," said one of them. They were certainly not going to fight to defend Nkrumah against a coup, and as far as they knew that was what they might be asked to do.

THURSDAY 24 FEBRUARY — 7.00 am

Colonel Kotoka still had no news of either of these two forces, which he so desperately needed to deliver the knock-out blow to the defenders of Flagstaff House. At any moment a battalion of the President's Own Guard Regiment might arrive from the Shai Hills and change the whole situation. Yet at seven o'clock Kotoka calmly returned to Radio Ghana to repeat the announcement he had made an hour earlier. This time everyone in Ghana with access to a radio heard it.

Seshie was still fighting his lone battle. The outcome of the operation still hung precariously in the balance as Asare and

180

Dontoh awaited instructions. But all over the nation rejoicing began as if the coup were already completed. There were shouts of joy in Ghana's cities and homes and villages: schoolboys displayed placards congratulating Kotoka within minutes of the broadcast; ships of the Black Star Line at sea burst into jubilation.

Soon after seven Ocran was at last able to get 2 Battalion and the armoured cars on the move. As soon as he had given Asare and Dontoh their orders he rang 4 Battalion at Tema, hoping to be able to cancel the instruction to surround the camp of the Field Regiment, only to find that they had left already. He sent a message to the Field Regiment telling them to send out a messenger to stop 4 Battalion, but this had no effect and the engineers were duly blockaded in their barracks till Major Coker-Appiah's threats and the belated arrival of Ocran's second message combined to persuade Lt-Col Okai to withdraw his battalion from the camp.

At Flagstaff House Captain Seshie had handed over to Lt Agbledzo and was just being taken off to the Military Hospital when he saw help arrive from two sources: first, his third platoon, which had been delayed three miles up the road by engine trouble, drove up safely; then as he drove off he glimpsed with his one good eye a column of armoured cars and two companies of Asare's 2 Battalion in 3-ton lorries driving up Switchback Road. Thank God be had managed to hold out long enough; if he had lost half his sight, it was worth it.

2 Battalion and the Reconnaissance Regiment, tense and anxious after the long delay, approached Flagstaff House in a long string of lorries, Landrovers, and armoured cars. Though the route was short and simple the leading vehicle had missed the way at one point, and the whole convoy had had to back awkwardly down the road again amid grinding gears and clouds of exhaust smoke. Then as they neared their destination there was renewed heavy firing from inside Flagstaff House. The armoured cars closed their hatches, locked their turrets, and drove into the fire: however it was too much for the vehicles

181

carrying the infantry, and the column retired again leaving yet another 3-tonner in flames outside the main gates.

8.00 am

Asare's men joined two of the companies from Tamale in clearing the flats of the security forces, and soon they had worked out an effective method of co-operating with the Reconnaissance Regiment: the armoured cars turned their machine guns on the flats to keep the security men's heads down while the infantry approached; then the infantry went through each building systematically, bringing out all occupants and separating the men from the women and children.

On the other side of the road, inside Flagstaff House, another mother and her children had spent a harrowing morning. Madam Fathia was now bitterly regretting that she had not taken Kwame's advice to go for a holiday in Cairo. Fathia loved the spacious grounds of the presidential home, with the abundance of shade under the neem trees, the open-air theatre, and the magnificent zoo. But in recent years she had seen wall after wall encroach on the space available for walks and play with the children, and now at last it was left to her, the woman, to look on as Kwame's defences for the first time received the attack they had been designed to discourage.

The noises from the zoo were almost as frightening as the gunfire. Every fresh volley set the lions, the tigers, the cheetahs, and the leopards roaring again with blood-curdling ferocity. The chimpanzee, the monkeys, and the mangabeys shook the grilles of their cages till it seemed the bars must come out of their sockets. Eagles and vultures, pheasants and cranes, pigeons and black swans added to the commotion with their shrill screeches and flapping of wings. There was no sign of the keepers, and at feeding time the whole menagerie went hungry. The President's mother Nyaniba and other relations, to whom he had given accommodation in close proximity to the animals, were even worse off than Madam Fathia herself, but certainly not more frightened than her.

182

Young Gorkeh could not do much to help his mother: but he was valiantly and fearlessly marching round the great house, like the faithful Young Pioneer that he was, vowing in impeccable English to die rather than surrender, and running a risk of being cut by splinters of flying glass. Little Samia instinctively sensed the atmosphere of fear, and the baby cried because the morning feed had been forgotten in the confusion. Madam Fathia rang the Egyptian Ambassador—how reassuring to hear him reply quietly in Arabic at the other end of the line! Unfortunately that did not alter the fact that guns were blazing in between.

"I have nothing to do with politics," she protested. "I married Kwame as a person, not as a president. I want to go home to Egypt. Can't you get me out?" The Egyptian Ambassador arrived at Police Headquarters, where Kotoka and Harlley had now established their base, and found that the question of Fathia's safety was already worrying the coup leaders. They had sent Superintendent Acheampong in search of Fathia's secretary, but he came back empty-handed, to find the Egyptian Ambassador at the headquarters also hoping to rescue Madam Fathia. Harlley gave the Ambassador a letter, and the embassy Mercedes-Benz, flying its Egyptian flag, and followed by Superintendent Achampong, proceeded to drive straight through a road block and up towards the scene of the battle, blissfully unaware that other cars had been riddled with bullets not long before for doing the very same thing. They were stopped before they came to any harm, but the letter was questioned and for an hour the party was tossed back and forth between Dontoh, Ocran, and Harlley, till they finally arrived outside the main gates at about ten o'clock, accompanied by Dontoh and two of his armoured cars.

WEDNESDAY 24 FEBRUARY — 10.00 am
They called out to Zanlerigu using a loud hailer, and within five or ten minutes a large white sheet was hoisted behind the third wall. Fathia came out first, wearing red jeans, a blouse, and dark glasses. She was escorted by a party of soldiers to a waiting

Landrover, together with the three children and two female nurses, shrouded in white sheets to indicate their peaceful intentions. Little Gorkeh had at last given up his single-handed fight and was immediately won over by Major Dontoh's friendly invitation to ride in his armoured car.

As he climbed in he shouted to his mother, "These soldiers are very nice people. They won't do anything to us!"

The little convoy sped off on its way to the Egyptian embassy, and Fathia and the children left by air for Cairo the following day. She told an Egyptian newspaper that her jewellery had been confiscated at Accra airport, and when she got home her mother ordered her straight to bed.

*   *   *

Young Gorkeh, also known as Gamal, after education in Egypt and doctoral studies at the School of Oriental and African Studies, London, served for many years on the staff of the leading Egyptian paper *Al Ahram*. He wrote in later years that his parents' marriage "was not meant to be a marriage made in heaven . . . tranquillity was never on the agenda . . . It was a political union between Mediterranean-oriented North Africa and the rest of the continent. . . . Indeed the political union worked and appeared to be rearing for consolidation when the coup occurred.

"It all began, however, like a fairy-tale . . . it captured the public imagination throughout Africa. The young Egyptian woman who left her country to marry the most illustrious African anti-colonial leader of his time was inevitably invested with iconic qualities."

*   *   *

As soon as Fathia left Flagstaff House, Zanlerigu collected his men together and checked the weapons and ammunition. Twenty minutes later he and other officers, at the head of a company of defenders, marched out of Nkrumah's citadel to give themselves up.

Sporadic firing was still coming from inside Flagstaff House, and those who surrendered had not given up any anti-tank weapons, so it was possible that a few die-hards were planning a hot reception for the first people to get in. The main gates were still locked and would have to be rammed or blasted open before any vehicle could enter; presumably the defenders' guns would be trained on whoever attempted that job.

2.00-5.30 pm

During the afternoon the task of clearing the bungalows and flats immediately round Flagstaff House continued, and an abortive attempt was made to breach the wall in the rear and force an entry there. At five thirty, Major Dontoh ordered a troop of armoured cars under Captain Darkoh back to the front entrance to force the main gates open. Captain Darkoh's Saladin armoured car mounted a gun which fired a 76 mm armour-piercing shell. He ordered the gunner to zero into the wall, to check that the gun was working properly, then got the driver to manoeuvre the heavy vehicle into the best position from which to aim at the metal plate at the centre of the gates, where they were locked together.

The driver shouted out pathetically, "The engine has conked, sir!" New batteries were so rare that hardly a single armoured car started on the self-starter. Darkoh lifted the hatch and called to a support trooper. "Take off the crank lever and come round the front to crank the engine! We will cover you with our machine guns." The engine rumbled into life again, and Darkoh himself took aim on the gate. The turret shook as a mighty boom resounded in the evening air and the shell neatly threw the gates apart.

"Help!" cried Darkoh, as he prepared to reload, "the firing pin has gone out of adjustment!" He was familiar with this fault; it meant dismantling the casing of the gun and reassembling it before it would fire again. "I'm getting out. Cover me, gunner." He leapt outside the metal walls of the armoured car, feeling horribly naked, opened the bin on the back of the Saladin, selected the tools he would need, and set to work to correct the

185

fault. It was five anxious minutes before he had finished and the gun was working again.

Why, oh why, should everything have to happen to him? This was his very first operation, and on the threshold of Nkrumah's fortress the engine had stalled and the gun had gone wrong—it was enough to make a man resign his commission and take up a nice, civilian occupation such as teaching mathematics, like his brother.

6.00 pm

After all that, the armoured cars did not get into Flagstaff House. While Darkoh had been tinkering with the firing pin darkness had fallen with tropical suddenness, and no sooner had he zeroed into the wall a second time to check that the gun was firing than Major Dontoh recalled him. It was no good taking armoured cars into a restricted space in darkness, with support troopers and infantry running round. It would be a death-trap for the armoured car crew and they would probably do more damage to their own men than they would to the defenders. Now that the Reconnaissance Regiment had opened the gates the infantry must be left to finish the job.

The armoured cars parked a little way up the road, and Darkoh suddenly felt an unbearable thirst. Apart from a cup of water he had had nothing to drink for nearly twenty-four hours. He noticed a British warrant officer standing in singlet and shorts, with his arms folded, keenly watching what was going on down at the gate of Flagstaff House. The quarters of the British military mission NCOs were just a few yards away.

"Where can I get some water?" asked the thirsty captain. "What a moment," cried the Englishman, and was back a minute later with a can of iced beer for the commander of each of the armoured cars—the nearest that Ghana's former imperial masters came to having anything to do with the coup of 24 February.

Radio Ghana had had a day of military music punctuated by scraps of Bach and occasional announcements by unaccustomed voices—"We are calling on the security forces to surrender

before eleven thirty, otherwise we shall attack their residences" — "Accra airport will be closed until further notice"—"Citizens are asked to assist the police in arresting party chairmen and secretaries". At one o'clock civil servants were asked to remain at their posts; it was announced that Ankrah had been promoted Lieutenant-General, and that a National Liberation Council had been formed. At six the radio announced the membership of the National Liberation Council and the national economic committee, and said that an administrative committee, publicity committee, and a foreign affairs committee, would soon be appointed.

Harlley could scarcely believe in their success, and Kotoka realized for the first time how overconfident he had been about the whole thing. In spite of the fact that his attacking force was a tiny fraction of what it should have been at the crucial moment, Flagstaff House was in their hands, and so was every other key position. The whole operation had been carried out with the loss of only half a dozen soldiers.

In Accra the people were fêting every army and police lorry that appeared, and the numerous signs of Nkrumah's domination, from the statue outside the National Assembly to the titles of public places named after him, had already disappeared from sight. Former ministers, MPs and party functionaries were hastening to surrender, if possible without being seen by the public.

Where had the famous President's Own Guard Regiment been all day? In particular, where had the much dreaded Shai Hills battalion got to—the battalion that had such a reputation for its vast power of destruction and for its absolute loyalty to Nkrumah? As soon as they heard the six am announcement on the radio, Major Tetteh and his officers, despite the Guard Regiment's reputation for loyalty to Nkrumah, decided immediately to support the coup.

11

CONSEQUENCES OF THE COUP IN CHINA AND GHANA

GHANA TIME
THURSDAY 24 FEBRUARY — 9.00am

CHINA TIME
THURSDAY 24 FEBRUARY — 4.30 am

KWAME Nkrumah's peace mission flew into Peking at four thirty in the afternoon of 24 February: that was nine o'clock in the morning of 24 February by Ghana time. Kotoka's broadcasts at 6.00 and 7.00 am that morning had immediately been picked up by the Chinese radio monitoring service and news of the coup was already appearing in their intelligence reports. But in Flagstaff House the guns were still firing, the lions were roaring, and Madam Fathia was almost driven to distraction. In the Ops Room at Burma Camp Col Ocran was still looking for some way to escape from his predicament with the commanders of the Ghana Navy and Air Force. No one knew yet whether the President's Own Guard Regiment would respond to the emergency by throwing its immense resources into the battle. As Nkrumah and his party flew into Peking, the result of the coup in Ghana was still hanging in the balance.

It was snowing at Peking airport as the party of Ghanaian politicians climbed out of the mighty Ilyushin, but well over a thousand Chinese, mostly young people in the uniform of the Party youth organization, were there to cheer the Ghanaian party. Nkrumah was met by Premier Chou En-Lai and Liu Shao-Chi, chairman of the Communist Party; a girl representing the youth of China presented him with a bouquet.

The Ghanaian visitors could not make out whether the Chinese leaders were looking a trifle bewildered or whether it was merely their traditional inscrutability; but when pressmen gathered to take a group photograph of Nkrumah and the welcoming party, the only people smiling were the Ghanaian president and the girl who had given him the bouquet.

An hour and a half later, Nkrumah's party arrived at their guest house. Most of his security men had suddenly been diverted to the hotel where the press and TV party were accommodated. Nkrumah now had only four of his bodyguard with him, including Ambrose Yankey and the faithful Kosi: all the rest had been disarmed by the Chinese.

Then Huang Hua, Chinese Ambassador to Ghana, came in and broke the news. Nkrumah was chatting with Kwesi Armah, Alex Quaison-Sackey, and the three top civil servants in the group, Okoh, Arkhurst and Dei-Anang. Though Nkrumah was obviously upset, he simply did not believe the report. Then they brought in a cable from the Chinese embassy in Accra, which proved that there was at least some truth in it; but Nkrumah insisted that the mission to Hanoi must go on as planned.

While they carried on their anxious discussion, hundreds of guests were awaiting Nkrumah's arrival at a banquet organized in his honour in another part of Peking. The Ghanaian party arrived 75 minutes late. All the Ghanaians except Nkrumah himself were taken in and introduced to the waiting diplomats and Chinese officials. Then the band played the CPP song, "There is victory for us" and the Ghana national anthem, and the guests moved into the banqueting hall.

For some of the Ghanaians it was a convenient opportunity to celebrate Nkrumah's downfall—but not too openly, for they were being watched. The Chinese security men were alerted even against Quaison-Sackey: when, back at the guest house, he put his hand in his pocket to get a nail-clipper, their reactions showed clearly that they thought he was going to pull out a pistol.

The atmosphere was strained and the speeches were brief. Nkrumah abandoned his prepared address and spoke for a few minutes without notes about his Hanoi visit and the fact that he would be discussing Vietnam while in Peking. As soon as he could get away, Nkrumah returned to the guest house with his close advisers and they went on talking late into the night as message after message came in.

He still did not accept that the report was true: "All this news is monitored from Ghana radio", he said. "A few people have captured Radio Ghana, that's all. But where's Barwah? Where's the security force? Where's Zanlerigu and the Guard Regiment . . ."—for a horrible moment he recollected the aggrieved look on David Zanlerigu's face the other day when he had questioned him so closely—". . . Do you realise my President's Own Guard Regiment have better arms and equipment than the regular army? I did it on purpose: they are invincible. Don't worry. Better news will come."

Then he told members of the party that they would go back to Accra and put down the rebellion. "You," he promised, "I'll make you a colonel; and you can be a brigadier. This party is the vanguard of our army of liberation. We shall bomb those rebels until they give in—we will get help from China and Russia. We will win even if Accra has to be rebuilt . . ."

FRIDAY 25 FEBRUARY

Next morning they heard news on Radio Ghana that Barwah was dead, that a National Liberation Council had been formed, and that the membership of the economic committee had been announced. Armah and Quaison-Sackey, Okoh and Dei-Anang tried to persuade Nkrumah to accept the situation, but he still believed he was popular with the ordinary people and that the coup must be the work of a few discontented officers. He clung with pathetic hope to a news report that firing was still going on in Flagstaff House.

191

When Quaison-Sackey advised him to go and visit Fathia and the children in Egypt he rebuked him bitterly: "Midzi w'akyi a, mebeyew" (if I follow your advice, I'll be lost)—you are a woman, a coward . . ." He wanted to take the whole party back with him to Conakry, Guinea. Later in the morning Nkrumah went for a talk with Chou En-Lai, and the civil servants began busily discussing their plight.

"Have you heard that the Ghana embassy staff in Conakry have all been arrested?"

"Who told you that?"

"Kofi got it on his transistor radio last night, on the Japanese English language news."

"I thought foreign broadcasts were jammed in China."

"Only in the day time; he got it quite clearly. If the Old Man takes us with him to Guinea we shall be in real trouble.

"They can't force us to go."

"Where are our passports?"

"The security boys have them."

"Do you think we could appeal to the Ghana embassy here in Peking?"

"How would you get there? Nobody has any Chinese currency and the road outside is absolutely deserted. I've been watching. The embassy might be miles away. I'd rather be in Conakry any day than get stranded here; better the devil you know . . ."

"Be careful what you say, man: there are microphones in those walls!"

Friday 25 February seemed like an age. They were all thinking out how they could escape, dropping in to the television room periodically to while away the time or to share the latest news. Quaison-Sackey was lucky: he was given a perfect way out by Nkrumah himself. "I am sending you to attend the OAU meeting at Addis Ababa," he said; "you will have to get them to pass a resolution supporting me." Quaison-Sackey's instinctive reaction was to point out that that was unthinkable: it would constitute an interference by other countries in the internal affairs of a sister nation, a thing the

OAU had always been at pains to avoid. But in the same instant he saw in this plan his chance to get away, and wrapped up his intentions in diplomatic jargon: "Yes. It is a question of credentials. The OAU council of ministers will have to take into account the *de facto* situation, and of course the National Liberation Council have a *prima facie* case. But I will go and do my best. When do I leave?" Then Bossman, the high commissioner-designate to London, suggested that he should fly to Britain and organize Ghana students in support of Nkrumah. Dr Badoe, the physician in attendance on the President during the, tour, pointed out that if he was anticipating a prolonged stay in Conakry, he had better lay in a large stock of his favourite drugs. The familiar brands he generally used were available in London; he had better go ahead and purchase them.

The civil servants were vying with one another in their enthusiasm to go to Ghana in order to send back reliable inside information to their leader—but Nkrumah began to get an uneasy feeling that a common motive underlay every proposal. They all wanted to get away. Except for Quaison-Sackey and Bossman, he refused to let them go.

On Friday night Nkrumah sent Quaison-Sackey to the Ghana embassy in Peking to read a statement to the press on his behalf:

"I know the people of Ghana have always been devoted to me, the Party, and the government, and all that I expect at this moment of trial is that all remain calm but also firm in their determination and resistance. If there are officers and members of the armed forces of Ghana who are involved in this attempt, I order them back to their barracks. I am the constitutional head of the Republic of Ghana and supreme commander of the armed forces. I shall soon return to Ghana."

26-28 FEBRUARY

Next day, as Quaison-Sackey started off on his journey, the diplomats inside the Ghana Embassy pledged their full support to the National Liberation Council. Nkrumah left a couple of days later on the first leg of his journey to Guinea. His party arrived by a special Russian plane at the secluded airport of Vnukovo on the outskirts of Moscow, in the early hours of Tuesday 1 March. Newspaper reporters were refused permission to see him. The rest of the 10-strong peace mission, including the bodyguard, journalists and TV cameramen, travelled to Moscow by regular passenger flights. Most of them were back in Ghana a few days later.

Quaison-Sackey had taken a plane to Canton and a train to Hong Kong to catch a flight for Frankfurt via New Delhi and Tehran; at Frankfurt he was to board the next plane for Addis Ababa. But by the time he got to the old German city his brain was in a whirl and he made up his mind to take twenty-four hours to rest and think out the whole situation. He could not do that in Frankfurt, with newspapermen from a dozen countries pestering him for interviews, so he took a car for Bad Soden, an hour's journey from the city, and put up for the night in an obscure guest-house. It was exactly a week since the peace mission had set out with such high hopes from Accra.

He was well aware that in Addis Ababa they would already be awaiting his arrival. That very morning, Monday 28 February, 35 delegations had met in the main hall and Emperor Haile Selassie had delivered the opening address. Ghana's new rulers had quickly organized their own delegation, headed by P E Seddoh of the Ghana Ministry of Foreign Affairs. They reported to Diallo Telli, OAU secretary-general, and then waited alone in the hall as the other delegations adjourned to a committee room and had a heated discussion about Ghana's representation. Guinea, Mali, and Tanzania led the opposition to recognizing the NLC delegation, and hoped to delay a decision till Quaison-Sackey arrived. They knew he was on the way and anxious diplomats waited at the airport at all hours to seize Quaison-Sackey on arrival and produce him in triumph in the debating chamber.

In the little guest-house at Bad Soden Nkrumah's foreign minister was locked in his bedroom, examining the possible courses of action. (He had locked the door when a member of the hotel staff had slipped a piece of paper underneath, bearing the instruction: "Do not come out; the press are here".) By going to Addis Ababa he might prop up Nkrumah's reputation for a few precarious days, but it was a lost cause—a cause he no longer believed in. If he returned to Accra, he would go straight into prison. The most attractive solution was to get his wife and family out of Ghana and find somewhere to live in exile; as a former president of the United Nations general assembly he had plenty of friends and it would not be difficult to find something useful to do. The thought no sooner occurred to him than he turned it down. The only possible course was to go straight home and place himself at his country's disposal. Next morning he flew to London: he caught the night plane for Ghana: and on Wednesday 2 March he slept for the first time within the historic walls of Ussher Fort prison, Accra.

*   *   *

Most of his fellow ministers had been in custody since the previous Thursday or Friday. The arrival in Ussher Fort of a steady trickle of former CPP ministers and MPs was the first indication some detainees had that a coup had taken place. Lawrence Otu Cantey, the student who called for a minute's silence in honour of Dr Danquah, was in A 27, one of the cells labelled "special case". He had at last been formally detained on 15 December and had started his three months' solitary confinement—the usual introduction to prison life for people held under the Preventive Detention Act. He was agreeably surprised when, nearly a month before his solitary confinement should have come to an end, he was moved to a nearby cell where there were four other detainees. It was a thrill to be able to converse with others again, and to share prison gossip; and exciting rumours were flying round, for it was said that all old and infirm detainees were being released.

That evening at six thirty Cantey was peering through the peep-hole of the door when he saw a most encouraging sight: Kofi Baako, the man who had sent him to prison, was marched along the corridor outside and locked unceremoniously in the very cell from which he himself had just been taken; he was accompanied by Kwaku Boateng and Kwasi Amoako-Atta, two of

Nkrumah's other ministers. On Friday more Party celebrities came into residence, including Lawrence Cantey's former lecturer in family law, Dr Ekow Daniels. If this was a purge, thought Cantey, it was certainly a radical one. It was not till later that day, when all detainees on the top floor of the block were moved out, that Lawrence Cantey and his companions learned what had actually happened.

Modesto Apaloo, in another part of the prison, heard distant shots just before six on the morning of 24 February. He was sharing a cell with eleven others and they soon broke into excited discussion about the unusual noise. Apaloo, though he had been deprived of the daily papers for eight years, was better informed on current affairs than many people outside, and thought it might be people looting the stores, driven to desperation by the food shortages. A few minutes later a friendly warder passed along the corridor and made an unmistakable gesture: he held up his left wrist, took hold of it with his right hand, and turned it upside down. What a birthday present for Apaloo! Within ten minutes the news had spread to most parts of the prison—but not to the "special cases".

One of Apaloo's fellow-prisoners received the news with a remarkable lack of enthusiasm. For a long time they had suspected this fellow of being a spy, planted there to listen to their conversation and report back to the security service through the prison authorities. He used to receive extra rations of food, and it was uncanny how people who quarrelled with him soon found themselves in trouble with one of the warders. That morning he lay like a log on the floor, pretending to be deep in prayer. His sudden conversion to religion caused some amusement, and he was mocked all the more mercilessly when it dawned on his companions that they would no longer suffer for quarrelling with him.

A hundred miles west of Accra, at eight thirty on the morning of the 24th, the news reached R R Amponsah at Cape Coast Castle. He was playing with his cat when he heard a policeman in the prison yard below shouting, "RR! RR!" His first thought was to tell the man to be quiet; people had been arrested for less. Then he saw three policemen on the other side of the yard talking excitedly and making signs in his direction. "Tell him!" said one of them; "go on, tell him!" Reggie smiled and nodded towards them, then turned away from the window and fell instinctively to his knees. He still did not know what it was all about, but somehow he felt he must thank God for it. A moment later he was sobbing for joy.

He got up again to find the prison superintendent standing in the doorway, looking rather embarrassed. "What's wrong?" he asked. "Are you ill?" for he knew that Reggie had reported sick that morning and been given permission to see the doctor. Then the superintendent told him Nkrumah had been overthrown by the army and the police. "I'm not supposed to tell you yet, RR, so keep it quiet; but you'll be released tomorrow. Today we are letting out the aged and infirm detainees only."

Later in the morning there was cheering on the verandah of the magistrate's court which overlooked the prison yard. Hundreds of people had crowded on to it and RR had to make an appearance at the window for their benefit. It made him want to weep for joy, and he had to leave the window with the people still yelling their heads off.

At a quarter to eleven next day the great moment arrived for which he had been waiting for eight long years. The open space between Christ Church and the Castle was crammed tight with people; for a time it seemed that the crowds who had come to welcome the detainees would instead prevent them from setting foot outside the prison gate. When RR emerged at last, traditional customs were performed. A bottle of schnapps was broken on the ground, a second bottle was poured out as a libation and a goat was slaughtered at Reggie Amponsah's feet. Like Nkrumah fifteen years before, he walked out of prison to become a national hero. Later that morning, in the ancient Methodist manse, R R Amponsah and the minister joined at the communion table in thanking God for his release.

On the previous day 56 old and infirm detainees had been released: five were suffering from tuberculosis, five were over

197

80 years old, another 33 were over 60. Another 450 were set free the same day as R R Amponsah. By the time they had finished, nearly 800 political prisoners had gone back again into normal life. The release of Nkrumah's detainees was not merely a humanitarian gesture on the part of the new régime—it was a necessity if the prison authorities were to find adequate accommodation for the very people who had detained them.

*   *   *

Only about half of the cabinet ministers voluntarily gave themselves up. Three were abroad: Quaison-Sackey and Armah in Peking, Dowuona-Hammond in Europe. One or two were in the regions, the rest had to be hunted by the police all over Accra.

Dr Ekow Daniels, a lecturer at Legon and deputy attorney-general, was arrested in his car by the police at Achimota. Several others were found hiding in private houses. Some chose more ingenious hiding places: two of the wanted men took refuge for a while in the Russian embassy: one hid in a mortuary.

Then the police were told that Kweku Akwei, secretary of the Party's education and information bureau, was hiding in a private hospital in Adabraka; he was said to be armed and ready to put up a desperate resistance. A small party searched the ground floor of the hospital, firing a shot through each door before entering, so as to put fear into the fugitive.

It seemed that Kweku Akwei had outwitted them. In the world of Party ideology this man had a formidable reputation as a fierce and resourceful fighter, so at any moment they expected to be fired on from some hidden vantage point. They phoned for two trucks of police to surround the area while they continued the search upstairs. On the second floor, under the stairs, was a wooden cupboard crammed with old pillows and soiled linen. A soldier dug his bayonet into the musty heap. "Hey, hey, I beg you!" The muffled cries of the desperate gunman were scarcely audible through the old sheets and dirty towels. The pile of laundry trembled and heaved, the folds parted, and gradually the head and shoulders of Kweku Akwei emerged from the confusion. He was wearing nothing but a pair of white shorts, but he was sweating freely and the stuffing from an old pillow hung grotesquely from his head, looking for all the world like a judge's wig.

"Why didn't you come out when we called from the yard?" asked the deputy superintendent of police severely.

"I was afraid," said the ideological expert, simply. "Will I be killed?"

The little group of his captors were torn between pity and shame: pity, because Kweku Akwei was shivering from fright: shame, because as his compatriots they would have liked to see a leader of Ghana's national party behave with a little more dignity.

At Winneba, centre of the nation's ideological education, students heard Kotoka announce the coup on the radio at six am. By that time three tennis enthusiasts were already on the court, winding up the net for an early morning game, when the fourth player came running up without his racket. Was he crazy? From what he said it seemed he must be. Nevertheless they abandoned their game and returned to their dormitories, where the students were sitting in small groups discussing the news. At seven every radio was tuned in and the rediffusion boxes were at full blast. Still they could not believe their ears.

"Perhaps it's just a way to change the ministers," suggested one student. "Maybe Osagyefo didn't want to throw them out himself, so he got the army to do it in his absence." The European staff said the whole thing was a deception; they thought a few fanatics had captured Radio Ghana but that the army would soon round them up. Breakfast was a miserable meal. No one wanted to eat. At ten thirty a police superintendent came to the compound with 18 policemen, and a crowd of a hundred students gathered round them to hear what they would say.

"We have instructions from Accra to look after this property," said the superintendent. "A lot of government funds have gone into the Institute and on account of the coup some

199

persons might endeavour to remove certain articles." Then it was true. With the police taking control of the Ideological Institute one could not doubt it any longer. The students began to drift home. On Friday there were only 200 left; that evening a large force of police arrived at dinner time and proceeded to eat the food that had been prepared for the students. That was decisive. By the week-end the place was empty.

*   *   *

Ghana's national shipping line was one of the enterprises started by Nkrumah that made a handsome profit every year. When news of the coup went out over Radio Ghana on the morning of 24 February, the ships of Black Star Line were scattered far and wide, unloading cocoa in icy European ports, taking on timber in the blazing heat of Takoradi, or ploughing steadily across the Atlantic.

The *Offin River*, captained by a highly qualified Indian from Bombay, was back in tropical waters after picking up cargo and passengers from Rotterdam and Dunkirk. The ship carried a miniature United Nations; after the Indian captain, the next most senior officers came from Spain and Scotland, Holland and Turkey. The third mate and the heavily bearded third engineer were both Ghanaians; so was the purser, a handsome young man who always enquired with much solicitude whether the passengers had enjoyed their meal. Two Dutch families and a few Ghanaian students were on the ship, returning from Europe.

It was eight am on 24 February when the radio officer, an Irishman, picked up a report of the coup. The *Offin River* was one day out of Dakar. The news was shouted from mouth to mouth round the ship and the officers and passengers sat down to breakfast in holiday mood. "Now that Nkrumah is out, the shops will be full again," said one of the Ghanaians.

"Yes, things will be cheap and plentiful, just as they were six years ago," said another, as he poured out the coffee.

The non-Ghanaians were more cautious. During the years that they had been associated with Ghana most of them had formed the habit of defending Nkrumah, especially against those who attacked him just because he was an African; they could not break the habit in five minutes. Besides, they feared that the Ghanaians were expecting too much too quickly. However good a new régime might be, it could not change the whole economy of the country overnight.

"I'm not sure it's a good thing," said one of the Dutchmen. "We may get a bitter struggle for posts in the new government. With all his faults, Nkrumah did give us stability; even dictatorship is better than anarchy ..."

But the Ghanaians would have none of it. "As soon as Nkrumah is out of the way you will see everything get better." Already they had implicit faith in the new régime, although none of them had so much as heard of Kotoka, and the Irish radio officer could not even be sure that he had got the name right. Breakfast on the *Offin River* that morning was like a second independence celebration. They did not know, as they sipped their coffee and the ship pitched and rolled in the Atlantic swell, that the battle was still going on outside Flagstaff House.

Before they reached the next port, Nkrumah's portrait disappeared from its honoured place on the wall of the lounge, leaving a large rectangular patch of the original colour contrasting with the faded paint all round. The captain tried in vain to find out who had removed it, but when a substitute was put in its place it was appropriately enough on a very much diminished scale. When the *Offin River* docked at Takoradi a customs official spotted the little photo of the former president where the full-scale coloured portrait had formerly hung. "It's still much too big," he said. "Be sure it disappears altogether before I come back in here!"

*   *   *

The students of Kibi Teacher Training College got up on the morning of 24 February weary and angry after the rowdiness of the night before. There was a smell of rebellion in the air as they gathered in the open outside the staff common room, waiting for the principal to come out on the veranda and take morning prayers.

201

The college bus drew up on the other side and the staff streamed exuberantly into the common room. The first one to see the principal cried out, "Have you heard the news?" She had not, but half a dozen eager voices told her. She took her Bible and hymn book and the staff filed out on to the veranda. When prayers were over she asked the students to wait for a moment.

"Everybody should be calm," she said. "I have to give you some important news." There was a murmur and some fidgeting down among the students. No doubt the principal had planned some unpleasant reprisal for their riotous behaviour the previous night. Never mind. Mr Mensah was there and he would help them to bear it.

"Kwame Nkrumah is removed from office and all his ministers will be detained." She paused for a moment. It seemed too brief an announcement for such a large event, but she herself knew nothing more than that. Now that she had spoken, it even occurred to her that after all it might not be true—and there were savage penalties for publishing false news . . . "Now you may go to your classes."

The students went off in a daze, they just could not make sense of the words. It was a full minute before the meaning sank in, and even then they could hardly believe it. The staff went back into the common room. No one spoke a word; then with one accord they exploded into extravagant mirth—rich, satisfying, healing laughter, coming from deep within them, uniting them, releasing them from the fears and tensions of the awful weeks they had passed through together. How long they laughed none of them could tell, but before they stopped Mr Mensah was already far away. He had rushed into town again to collect some papers from his room; then he made for the village where he was supervising teaching practice in the primary school.

In the midst of the morning's excitement his colleagues noticed that Mr. Mensah seemed to be deeply agitated. At last he came to the headteacher's office and asked for the key of his latrine. Later in the morning when the headteacher himself had occasion to go there, he could not restrain his curiosity, and he

202

peered down into the shadows of the ill-smelling bucket. Lying open on the bottom was a packet of papers to do with the Young Pioneers and the CPP, including Mr Mensah's Party membership card.

At the residential area in town the DC was sitting in his bungalow surrounded by local Party activists. Chiefs had come in from several villages on hearing Colonel Kotoka's broadcast and a later announcement that Party officials were to be taken into protective custody. The DC's arrest would be a treasured historic memory, and they wanted to savour all the drama of it, like the members of a family hastening to the scene of a relative's death. The DC himself, like most of his colleagues all over the country, was quite resigned to his fate. One knew instinctively that protective custody under the National Liberation Council would not be half as unpleasant as preventive detention under Nkrumah.

"I have always been saying," remarked the DC quietly, "that how this man was working with us was not good. Only, we could not voice it out. Not so, Nana?

The chief looked back at the DC, trying hard not to show his astonishment. It was certainly not so—he had never heard the DC utter a single word critical of Nkrumah.

"That's right, you have always been saying it," he replied.

"What will happen about the deportation of the principal?" asked one of the others. "Everything is upside down now," said a Party branch secretary. Gloom descended on the gathering. Then one of the chiefs broke the silence with an unwonted venture into English: "As for that woman," he said, with an air of finality, "that woman, she is brick. Oh, she is too bold. Very brick."

The DC was getting impatient with all this waiting. Until a few hours before, his least frown had caused the training college staff to be uneasy, and the villagers to tremble with fear. But he did not dispute the testimony of the radio: deep within him, like many other Ghanaians, he had been half expecting this moment—without believing it would ever really happen. Now that it had come he wanted it to pass quickly.

He lifted the telephone receiver to call his old friend, the police superintendent. "Is that you, officer? Yes, it's me. How are you? Your wife and children? Good, good. Look, officer, I'm all ready here. Have you got your instructions to fetch me yet? No? Oh well, any time you get instructions, you know where I am."

It was only fifteen minutes later that the superintendent drew up outside the bungalow in his own private car and came into the room.

"Ah, you've got your instructions now, officer?"

"Yes, thank you," said the superintendent.

The DC got up and walked down the steps to the waiting car. He was gone before the others had a chance even to shake hands with him. When they came out on to the veranda the car was already turning the corner by the silk-cotton tree.

The Last Word

THE COCKEREL

Where is the red cockerel that fathers the child but feeds it not?

Where is the red cockerel that deceives the hen and leaves it from morning till evening, from dusk to dawn?

Crow to the skies, mighty cockerel, pompous in plumage, vicious in quarrel, cunning in deceit, coward in danger, void of virtue, greedy in plunder from the field it soweth not!

Where is that Kwame Cockerel, the greatest, the loudest lord and heir, Saviour and Redeemer, pride of the farmer?

Art thou become a Guinea Fowl?

Come back home, Kwame Cockerel—home is home!

Lord and earl, humbly born before the wedding, come back home for a belting, and bring with you the Guinea Pig.

from the Accra *Evening News* of 6 April 1966.

A red cockerel was the party symbol of the Convention People's Party.

12

POSTSCRIPT, 2010—WHY DID THE COUP SUCCEED?

THE STORY told in the preceding pages is the story recounted to the author by the main actors in the coup, in interviews given in March and April 1966. It is time to give some kind of verdict on the coup which they described.

It was a simple plan comprising the arrest of all the main military and political leaders by elements of the Army and by the Police before 6.00 am on 24 February; and the simultaneous occupation of a few key positions: Nkrumah's offices and residence at Flagstaff House, Ghana Broadcasting Corporation, the General Post Office, Ghana News Agency, and the External Communications Department.

It was simple, but to tell the truth, it was a coup that did not deserve to succeed, for three reasons. **First** it had no plan to prevent the three battalions of the President's Own Guard Regiment, one based in Burma Camp and responsible for the defence of Flagstaff House, the other based at Shai Hills, 20 miles out of Accra, from bringing their excellent equipment and heavy artillery to bear on the insurgency.

Second, though both Army brigades were involved, the attack on Flagstaff-House depended almost entirely on two platoons of Kotoka's own infantry of 2 Brigade from Tamale, because inadequate instructions were given to the two battalions of 1 Brigade, in Accra and Takoradi. The commander of the Accra Battalion had only verbal instructions, and those were delivered at the last moment, with no effective means of confirmation or communication with Kotoka; the Takoradi battalion simply failed to arrive on the morning of 24 February.

Third, it was not yet the age of mobile phones. Though wireless technology was available, the coup leaders did not set up radio links to keep in touch with one another as the action proceeded.

There were six main actors. The brain behind it was Kotoka, Commander 2 Brigade, based in Kumasi but with most of his troops in Tamale. He alone knew the whole plan, and his personal relationships with two people, Commissioner of Police Harlley and his own Brigade Major, Afrifa, were the foundation stones on which the conspiracy was built.

Kotoka had not spoken personally to Ocran, Commander of 1 Brigade, till two days earlier, and though Ocran agreed to take part in the operation Kotoka did not follow up his original contact with sufficient confirmation. Afrifa passed on verbal instructions to Coker-Appiah, Commander of the Engineers, and Dontoh, Commander of the Reconnaissance Regiment of armoured cars, but again there was no proper follow-up or confirmation.

Coker-Appiah successfully carried out his overnight mission to arrest some key personalities, but both he and Dontoh were confused and delayed a little later when two of the most senior officers of Ghana's armed forces, Air Commodore Otu, Commander of the Air Force, and Commodore Hansen, commander of the Navy, arrived at the Operations Room in Burma Camp and began making phone calls to find out what was going on. Kotoka had not consulted or even informed either Otu or Hansen about his plans for a coup; they had no idea what sort of revolt was going on.

As a result the armoured cars and the troops of 2 Battalion, based at Burma Camp, were paralysed, without clear orders, and it was left to one depleted company of Kotoka's Tamale battalion to take control of Flagstaff House, while nothing prevented all the might of the President's Own Guard Regiment from stopping them in their tracks.

Why, then, did the coup succeed?

Simply because Nkrumah's universal popularity with the general public had declined almost to zero. A simple and unconfirmed announcement on the morning radio was enough to convince the commanders of the President's Own Guard Regiment at Shai Hills to allow the coup to go ahead without interfering; the same announcement convinced the deputy secretary to the Cabinet, Mr Impraim, District Commissioners and CPP functionaries around the country, the staff and faculty of the Ideological Institute at Winneba, even the foreign secretary, Quaison-Sackey on his way to the OAU meeting at Addis Ababa, that the era of Nkrumah's rule had come to a decisive end.

*   *   *

From the time that the coup plotters informed US agents that they were planning to overthrow the government there has been speculation that they were not merely onlookers but that they actively supported the action. The author found no evidence or hint of such assumptions.

The Americans were aware of the subversive intentions of a handful of soldiers and police. They were not consulted, nor did they know when or even whether such an event might occur. Talk of the coup being master-minded from outside, or even "engineered" by the Americans, was fanciful and misleading. The coup was emphatically "made in here" and it bore all the marks of its truly Ghanaian origin. Any suspicion of foreign interference would have been deeply unpopular with the Ghanaian public.

BIOGRAPHICAL NOTES

Kwame Nkrumah
born at Nkroful, Nzema, 1909 (suggested date 21 September 1909)
Roman Catholic elementary schools
Government Training College, Accra and Achimota 1927-29
taught at Catholic schools in Elmina, Axim, and Amisano
Lincoln University, Pennsylvania, USA, 1936, Bachelor of Theology 1942
University of Pennsylvania, M Sc 1942, MA 1943
political activity in London 1945-47
secretary of UGCC, Ghana, 1947-48
founded CPP 1948
CPP won general elections of 1951, 1954, and 1956, and local council elections of 1952
Ghana Independence 1957
Trades Union Act made strikes illegal
Preventive Detention Act 1958 allowed detention without trial
referendum of 1960 approved republican constitution and extended life of 1954 parliament till 1965
general election without voting 1965
Akosombo Dam opened January 1966
military coup overthrew Nkrumah February 1966
Nkrumah in exile in Guinea 1966-71
medical treatment in Romania 1971-72
died of skin cancer in Romania 27 April 1972

Emmanuel Kwasi Kotoka
born at Alakple, Keta District, 26 October 1926
Alakple Roman Catholic Primary School, Alakple

Anloga Senior School

apprenticed to a goldsmith after leaving school

enlisted as a private in the Infantry School of the Gold Coast Regiment at Teshie, 1947; sergeant 1948, sergeant-major 1951

trained as an officer at Eaton Hall Officer cadet School, England, 1952

commissioned as 1st lieutenant and seconded to British Army on the Rhine, Germany, 1954

captain and platoon commander, Second Gold Coast Regiment of Infantry, 1959

trained as company commander at School of Infantry, Warminster, 1960

company commander in 2nd battalion of Ghana army serving in the United Nations contingent in Leopoldville (now Kinshasa, Democratic Republic of the Congo), 1960

awarded Ghana Service Order for exceptional bravery in the Congo, 1963

commander, 2 Brigade, 1965

leading conspirator in 1966 coup which overthrew Nkrumah

abortive military coup "Operation Guitar Boy", led by junior officers of Reconnaissance Regiment squadron based at Ho, Volta Region, killed Kotoka on the spot at Accra international airport where his statue now stands; the airport was subsequently named after him.

John Willie Kofi Harlley

born 1919

head of Special Branch, Ghana Police, 1960

Commissioner of Police, 1964

first Inspector-General of Ghana Police, 1965

leading conspirator in 1966 coup

Minister for Interior 1966

Minister for Foreign Affairs, 1967-69

Joseph Arthur Ankrah

born 18 August 1915, Accra

Wesleyan Methodist school, Accra. 1921

Accra Academy 1932
school certificate, joined Ghana Civil Service, 1937
mobilized into Royal West African Frontier Force 1940, and served as second-in-command, Record Office, Accra, being promoted sergeant-major
trained as an officer at Marshfield Officer Cadets Training Unit in England, 1946
commissioned as 1st lieutenant, 1947, and served as headquarters Camp Commandant, and Chief Instructor of Education Unit
promoted major in command of a company of 1 Battalion, Tamale, 1956
lieut-col in command of 1 Battalion, 1960
brigade commander of Ghana army force serving in the United Nations contingent at Luluaburg, Congo
awarded Military Cross for acts of unsurpassed gallantry, 1961
promoted brigadier, and major-general
first Ghanaian Commander of Ghana Army, 1961, then Deputy Chief of Defence Staff
retired from Ghana Army by Nkrumah, 1965, following rumours of a plot to overthrow him
chairman of National Liberation Council and Head of State following coup, 1966
promoted Lieut-General
mediated between Nigerian and Biafran leaders during Nigerian civil war
forced to resign as Head of State following a bribery allegation involving a Nigerian businessman, 1969

Akwasi Afrifa
born 24 April 1936, Mampong Ashanti
Presbyterian Boys' Boarding School, Mampong
Adisadel College, Cape Coast 1952, expelled 1957
entered Ghana Army 1958
trained as an officer at Mons Officer Cadet School, Aldershot, then at Royal Military Academy, Sandhurst, England

commissioned 2nd lieutenant in Ghana Army
attended Defence College, Teshie, Accra
served with Ghana contingent in the UN operation in the
Congo
promoted major 1965

NOTES

1   Dennis Austin, *Politics in Ghana, 1946-60* (OUP)
2   *Ibid*, page 22
3   *Secret Service Chief* by U E Baughman (Heinemann, 1961)
4   The chief's stool is a symbol of authority in southern Ghana. A new chief is said to be "enstooled"; "destoolment" is the term for removing a ruler from office.
5   *Dr J B Danquah—Detention and Death in Nsawam Prison* (Ministry of Information, Accra, 1967) page 158
6   *Ibid*, page 113
7   *Ibid*, pages 116-117
8   *Ibid*, page 28
9   *Ibid*, pages 142-145
10   *Ibid*, page 170
11   *Ibid*, page 171
12   *Ibid*, page 176
13   Mabel Dove had made a mistake: Dr. Danquah was 69 in December 1964.
14   This correspondence is reprinted from the Accra *Evening News* of 11 March 1966, by kind permission.
15   Report of Commission of Enquiry into alleged Irregularities and Malpractices in connection with the issue of Import Licences (Ministry of Information, Accra, 1964)
16   Report of Commission of Enquiry into Irregularities and Malpractices in the grant of Import Licences (Ministry of Information, Accra 1967)
17   Dr J B Danquah—Detention and Death in Nsawam Prison (Ministry of Information, Accra, 1967), pages 192, 195
18   This account of Mabel Dove's interview with Nkrumah is based on her article in the Accra *Evening News* of 11 March 1966, by kind permission.

19   London *Daily Express*, 27 September, 1962, despatch from Walter Partington

20   What Cato actually said, and what Mr Quaison-Sackey actually quoted him as saying, was "Carthage must be destroyed" (*Delenda est Carthago*). Cato was speaking in the context of the third Punic War.

21   *The Spectator*, London, March 1966.

22   Nzegwu, an Ibo, was killed in action fighting in the Biafran Army against Federal Nigeria troops in 1967.

23   President Nasser was referring to the huge 12-storey office-and-residential block and the two nearby halls, which Nkrumah had built for the 1965 Summit meeting of the Organization for African Unity. Nkrumah had hoped the OAU would vote to set up their permanent headquarters in Accra, using these specially designed facilities. In the event it was decided to keep the OAU headquarters in Addis Ababa, and "Job 600" (as the conference centre was popularly called) looked like a vastly expensive mistake.

24   Officer Cadets' Training Unit

INDEX

A

Abban, director of Ghana Prisons, 40

Abraham, Professor Kojo, University of Ghana, Legon, 89

Achampong, Superintendent, Ghana Police, 194

Acquah, Col, Director of Military Intelligence, Burma Camp, and his wife Mrs Acquah, 158

Adamafio, Tawia, minister of Information and broadcasting, 12, 21, 22, 37, 53

Addy, Lt-Col John, commander, 3 Battalion (2 Brigade), Tamale, 108, 109, 115, 118, 134, 135, 136, 174, 175, 176

Adjei, Ako, minister of foreign affairs, 6, 21, 22, 34, 37, 43

Aferi, Brigadier N A, from 1965 Major-General and chief of defence staff, 82, 161

Afrifa, Major Akwasi, brigade major (2 Brigade), Tamale, vii, 105, 106, 107, 108, 109, 110, 111, 112, 113, 114, 115, 118, 131, 132, 133, 138, 141, 143, 144, 145, 146, 147, 167, 172, 207, 211

Agbale, Mr, senior officer at Nsawam Prison in 1964, 44

Agbledzo, Lt, 2 Battalion (2 Brigade, Tamale), 192

Akainyah, Mr Justice, appointed to lead enquiry into irregularities in issue of import licences, 56

Akwei, Kweku, secretary of the CPP's education and information bureau, 60, 72, 211

Ametewee, Seth Nicholas Kwame, the man who shot Superintendent Salifu Dagarti on 2 January 1964, 29, 31, 32

Amihere, John, one of the guard on duty on the day of the January 1964 shooting, 31

Amoako-Atta, Kwasi, minister in Kwame Nkrumah's government, 195

Amponsah, Reggie R, United Party member, viii, 36, 37, 196, 197, 198

Ankrah, Brigadier Joseph Arthur, later Major-Gen, deputy chief of Defence Staff; from February 1966 Lt-General and chairman, National Liberation Council, vi, xi, xii, xiv, 71, 72, 73, 74, 75, 82, 83, 108, 131, 188, 210

Apaloo , M K, United Party MP, viii, 36, 37, 150, 196

Arkhurst, a senior civil servant in Nkrumah's entourage, 202

Arnold, Mrs, East German lecturer at Winneba Ideological Institute in early 1960s, 103

Asare, Col, commander 2 Battalion (2 Brigade), Accra, 46, 109, 140, 148, 149, 150, 164, 165, 167, 179, 180, 181, 182

B

Baako, Kofi, minister of defence, 20, 56, 67, 88, 120, 158, 159, 160, 169, 170, 171, 172, 195

Badoe, Mr, Nkrumah's assistant secretary, 21, 27, 193

Baiden, Mr, officer temporarily in charge of Nsawam Prison around June 1964, 46

Banes, Howard T, political officer at US embassy in Accra, and CIA chief in Ghana, ix

Barwah, Brigadier Charles Mohamed, from 1965 Major-General, army chief of staff, 5, 88, 92, 93, 118, 138, 155, 160, 161, 164, 165, 168, 170, 171, 175, 181, 203, 204

Batsa, Kofi, editor *Spark*, the weekly journal of political comment, 90

Bentil, head of a department under the Office of the President, for Organisation and Methods 59

Bentum, B A, chairman of Trades Union Congress executive board, viii, 93, 94

Bing, Geoffrey, former British MP; former attorney-general under Nkrumah, 13, 23, 76,

Boahene, Yaw, Kofi Baako's father-in-law, 56

Bossman, Dr, Ghana's ambassador to France, and ambassador-designate to the UK, 77, 193

Botsio, Kojo, minister of foreign affairs till June 1965, 7, 12, 13, 77, 78

Bowers, Rt Rev, bishop of Accra, Ghana Catholic Church, 183

C

Cantey, Lawrence Otu, student of law at University of Ghana, Legon, viii, 25, 66, 67, 68, 69, 195, 196

Crabbe, Cofie, executive secretary of the CPP, 21, 22, 37, 53, 54

Coker-Appiah, Major, commander, Field Regiment of Engineers (1 Brigade), Teshie, vii, 109, 111, 112, 113, 114, 115, 116, 117, 130, 131, 134, 135, 139, 140, 145, 146, 148, 152, 153, 154, 159, 162, 164, 165, 181, 207

D

Dagarti, Salifu, Nkrumah's ADC and head of the security force, 15, 27, 28, 29

Daniels, Dr Ekow, lecturer in family law at University of Ghana, Legon, 196, 198

Danquah, Dr J B, lawyer and politician, detained under PDA from January 1964 to his death on 4 February 1965, ii, 4, 6, 9, 13, 34, 35, 37, 41, 43, 44, 45, 46, 47, 48, 49, 50, 61, 63, 64, 65, 66, 67, 68, 70, 195, 213

Darkoh, Captain, Reconnaissance Regiment, (1 Brigade), Burma Camp, viii, 185, 186

Davies, Harold, British MP and personal acquaintance of Nkrumah, 125

Dedjoe, Major, officer of 2 Brigade based in Kumasi 149, 152, 154

de Graft Johnson, J W, lawyer and fighter for an independent Gold Coast, a founding member of UGCC, 4

Dei-Anang, Michael, senior civil servant viii, 202, 204

Deku, Tony, deputy head of Special Branch, Ghana Police; head from 1965, viii, 16, 18, 19, 31, 47, 56, 72, 79, 83, 108

Dontoh, Major, commander, Reconnaissance Regiment, (1 Brigade), Burma Camp, vii, 109, 140, 148, 149, 164, 165, 167, 179, 180, 181, 183, 184, 185, 186, 207

Dove, Mabel, former wife of Dr J B Danquah, 48, 49, 64, 65, 213

Dowuona-Hammond, minister in Kwame Nkrumah's government, overseas at time of the coup, 198

E

Otoo Eric, secretary on security matters, viii, 22, 65, 66, 153

F

Fathia, Madam, Nkrumah's wife and First Lady of Ghana 139, 193, 194, 195, 196, 201, 204

Fordjoe, Ben, head of Ghana Police Special Branch 1964-65, 47, 56, 57, 58, 59, 60, 61

Fraiku, Kwaw, chairman of Presidential Commission, in absence of Kwame Nkrumh who was out of the country, 160

G

Graham, Billy, American Baptist preacher, 169

H

Harlley, J W K, head of Special Branch, Ghana Police; from 1964 Commissioner of Police, viii, xii, xiv, 14, 16, 18, 19, 31, 32, 33, 34, 47, 56, 57, 71, 72, 73, 74, 75, 79, 82, 83, 108, 114, 115, 116, 118, 131, 156, 157, 158, 162, 172, 183, 188, 207, 210

Hassan, Brigadier, director of military intgelligence, 81, 82, 84, 86, 87, 88, 111, 135, 138, 144, 145,152, 154, 155, 160, 162, 170, 177, 180

Ho Chi Minh, President of North Korea in 1966, 131, 132

Howarth, Rev Arthur, chaplain of the Ridge Church, 51

I

Ikoku, Nigerian lecturer at Winneba Ideological Institute in early 1960s, 102

Impraim, T K, deputy secretary to the cabinet, viii, 57

Indira Gandhi, Mrs, prime minister of India, 142

Inkumsah, A E, minister of the interior in 1964, 44, 123, 160, 171, 172

K

Korsah, Sir Arku, chief justice of Ghana, 21, 22, 23, 24, 27, 34, 67, 74

Kosi, Superintendent, Ghana Police, Nkrumah's bodyguard and ADC until the grenade attack in 1962, 1, 2, 190

Kotoka, Lt-Col Emmanuel Kwasi (commander, 2 Brigade), Kumasi, vi, vii, ix, xi, xiv, 72, 73, 82, 83, 85, 86, 87, 103, 105, 106, 107, 108, 110, 111, 112, 114, 115, 116, 117, 118, 119, 120, 130, 132, 133, 134, 135, 138, 139, 141, 143, 144, 145, 147, 155, 156, 158, 159, 161, 162, 163, 164, 165, 167, 172, 173, 174, 178, 180, 181, 183, 188, 189, 199, 201, 203, 206, 207, 209, 210

Kuti, Musa, head of the Ghana Workers' Brigade, a paramilitary force devoted to agricultural work, 153, 154

Kwaku Boateng, minister of the interior, 14, 22, 208

Kwashie, Capt, Secretary, 37 Military Hospital, Accra, viii, 19, 72, 73, 83, 105, 115, 116, 117, 118, 130, 138, 159, 161, 162, 167

L

Lamptey, Obetsibi, lawyer and politician, member of UGCC, 6, 21, 34, 35, 36, 175

M

Madjitey, E R T, Commissioner of Police till January 1964, 18, 20, 21, 33, 37

Mahoney, Wiliam P, US ambassador to Ghana, xii, xiii

Makonnen, T R, West Indian politician in London in the 1950s, 3

"Mensah, Mr", name used for Young Pioneers officer on staff at Kibi Women's Training College, 97, 98, 99, 100, 101, 102, 126, 127, 129, 150, 202, 203

N

Nasser, President of Egypt, 139, 227

N A D E C O (National Development Company) – an apparently legitimate commercial company which Nkrumah established to channel bribes of 10% into a fund which he could use as he wished, 16, 17

Ne Win, General, military ruler of Burma, 142

Nkrumah, birth and education; at Lincoln University, Pennsylvania, USA; degrees; in London; general secretary of UGCC, 1948; detained after 1948 disturbances; formed CPP 1948; imprisoned; elections 1951, 1954, 1956, 1960 (presidential election with referendum on republican constitution), 1965 (without voting); visit to Soviet Union; Kulungugu grenade attack August 1962; dismissed Korsah December 1963; (referendum on one-party state January 1964; shooting in Flagstaff House January 1964); at Commonwealth prime ministerss' conference in London; member of Vietnam peace mission; speech on Southern Rhodesia; in Peking February

219

R

Risberg, clerk in Ghana National Construction Corporation, and his sister Emily, members of CPP, Ward 16, Accra, 55

Robert Otchere, convicted of involvement in 1962 grenade attack, 24

S

Sagoe, Mr, officer at Nsawam Prison in 1964, 44

Seshie, Capt, a company commander in 2 Battalion (2 Brigade), Tamale, viii, 138, 167, 168, 173, 174, 176, 177, 179, 180, 181

Seddoh, P E, leader of NLC's delegation to represent Ghana at OAU, Addis Ababa, 194

Selassie, Haile, Emperor of Ethiopia, 194

Sissala, Corporal, in charge of the section of men from the President's Own Guard Regiment who were on guard duty at Flagstaff House on the day of the January 1964 shooting, 28, 29

Sloan, Pat, British lecturer at Winneba Ideological Institute in early 1960s, 96

Sweskov, Russian securitye expert, 15, 16, 17, 18

Swanzy, Kwaw, attorney-general, 24, 25, 26, 64, 96

Szamuely, Tibor, Hungarian lecturer at Winneba Ideological Institute in early 1960s, 96

T

Tandoh, S K, secretary of the CPP Organisation Bureau, 55

Telli, Diallo, OAU secretary-general at February 1966 meeting in Addis Ababa, 194

Touré, Sekou, President of Guinea, 94

Twum, J K, MP for Asankrangwa, 90

V

VC 10, name of a British-made jet passenger aircraft widely used by international airlines, including Ghana Airways, 103, 135

W

Welbeck, N A, executive secretary of the CPP, later minister of party propaganda. 54, 55, 67, 160, 171

Y

Yankey, Ambrose, head of counter-intelligence unit, 14, 15, 16, 56, 57, 58, 59, 60, 61, 124, 145, 165, 190

Yankey, Ambrose, junior, 58, 59, 60

Yaw Manu, convicted of involvement in 1962 grenade attack, 24

Yeboah, Samuel Kennedy, contributor of poem to Accra *Evening News*, March 1966

Z

Zanlerigu, Capt David, commander, President's Own Guard Company; from Stockwell John, US diplomat stationed in Côte d'Ivoire in 1960s, 151, 153, 154, 162, 173, 175, 177, 183, 184, 191

Zwart, David, editor serving with Ghana Publishing Corporation in 1967, 40, 41